LEARNING FOR LIFE

How Continuous Education
Will Keep Us Competitive in
the Global Knowledge Economy

Jason Wingard and Michelle LaPointe

American Management Association
New York • Atlanta • Brussels • Chicago • Mexico City
San Francisco • Shanghai • Tokyo • Toronto • Washington, D.C.

Bulk discounts available. For details visit:
www.amacombooks.org/go/specialsales
Or contact special sales:
Phone: 800-250-5308
Email: specialsls@amanet.org
View all the AMACOM titles at: www.amacombooks.org
American Management Association: www.amanet.org

This publication is designed to provide accurate and authoritative information in regard to the subject matter covered. It is sold with the understanding that the publisher is not engaged in rendering legal, accounting, or other professional service. If legal advice or other expert assistance is required, the services of a competent professional person should be sought.

Library of Congress Cataloging-in-Publication Data

Wingard, Jason.
    Learning for life : how continuous education will keep us competitive in the global knowledge economy / Jason Wingard and Michelle LaPointe. — First Edition.
        pages cm
    Includes bibliographical references and index.
    ISBN 978-0-8144-3363-8 (hardcover) — ISBN 978-0-8144-3364-5 (ebook) 1. Labor supply—Effect of education on. I. LaPointe, Michelle. II. Title.
    HD5706.W56 2016
    331.11—dc23   2015010330

About AMA
American Management Association (www.amanet.org) is a world leader in talent development, advancing the skills of individuals to drive business success. Our mission is to support the goals of individuals and organizations through a complete range of products and services, including classroom and virtual seminars, webcasts, webinars, podcasts, conferences, corporate and government solutions, business books, and research. AMA's approach to improving performance combines experiential learning—learning through doing—with opportunities for ongoing professional growth at every step of one's career journey.

Printing number

10 9 8 7 6 5 4 3 2 1

CONTENTS

Section III   Employers

Section IV   Coordinating Agencies

FOREWORD

I believe that the key ingredient to corporate success is human capital. Global companies, across sectors and across industries, depend on the quality and preparedness of their people to produce leading-edge products and services that result in competitive advantage in an ever-changing marketplace. In recent years, the American labor market has failed to source an adequately skilled workforce to satisfy these changing needs. Our collective education-to-work system in this country is in transition, and there is an urgent need for change.

Throughout my career, I have recognized and appreciated the benefit of human capital and consistently invested in a wide range of development initiatives. At Pearson, I have continued our long-standing tradition of supporting workforce development initiatives. Through a number of programs, our executive team is strategically committed to partnering with community and educational organizations to equip our employees with the requisite skills and competencies to do their jobs at an optimum level. In addition to developing the skills of our employees, we want to contribute to the development of a local, regional, and national system that leverages multiple partners in pursuit of a structure that is better equipped to prepare the workers for tomorrow. For example, in 2012, Pearson partnered with the Kentucky Community and Technical College System (KCTCS) to change the way adult learners in Kentucky access educational resources and invest in their academic futures. The goal was to revolutionize KCTCS's already successful Learn on Demand (LOD) program, using Pearson's technology (in particular our *MyLab* platform) to facilitate increased competency-based learning opportunities. Through this adaptable and customizable curriculum, students now have an opportunity to obtain workforce skills and earn their academic credentials more quickly while remaining focused on genuine learning—and all at a lower cost. Through this program, we are pioneering a new precedent for the responsibility and role of a public company in collaboration with a broader system of partners committed to helping people successfully "skill-up" and transition in today's economic realities.

This handbook clearly and proactively articulates the changing environment and market context facing today's businesses and related workforce. It highlights the imminent challenges that dictate success or failure and establishes an aggressive call-to-action for organizations to work together to create a lifelong learning system that is responsive and sustainable. The profiles of successful models provide insights into best practice approaches that can be leveraged for replication and further enhancement.

Jason Wingard and Michelle LaPointe are leading scholars in the areas of professional education, lifelong learning, and policy development. Their collective research and practical experiences have enabled them to develop a book that sounds the alarm on the universal problem, demonstrates key components of potential success, and offers a guiding framework as a solution for change. *Learning for Life* is a handbook for lifelong learning that will help employees and employers alike bridge the gap between relevant education needs and contemporary skills demands.

John Fallon
CEO, Pearson

PREFACE

Shift to a Knowledge Economy

The economy has changed quickly and significantly in recent decades. However, our understanding and response to the shifting economic context is still rooted in the mid–20th century. In the 1950s and 1960s, it was possible to sustain a career and support a family with semi-skilled factory work. But today, even if that factory worker has specialized skills to troubleshoot an automated assembly line, there are fewer and fewer well-paying manufacturing jobs available.

In the past 50 years, the United States economy has dramatically decreased dependence on manufacturing. In 1960, manufacturing was responsible for roughly one-quarter of the gross domestic product (GDP). Today, manufacturing has decreased to 10% of GDP (Exhibits P-1 and P-2). During the same time period, professional services increased from 6% of GDP to nearly 20%. Professional services include the legal field, business consulting, and scientific and technical consulting—all fields that require considerable education. The shift from an industrial economy to a knowledge economy has implications for workforce availability and readiness.

In the contemporary knowledge economy, individuals and companies alike are constantly adjusting to new tools, new strategies, and new norms. Regardless of the field, one can no longer escape the need to adapt and apply new skills at an ever-increasing rate of change. Today, even assembly lines are complex, high-tech operations and essential employees continuously train to keep up with computer-driven systems.

Despite the labor shift in the economy over the last decades, nearly half of the current workforce has no education beyond high school (Exhibits P-3 and P-4). Even with years of schooling beyond high school and preparatory training for entry into a field, workers in all occupations are now expected to take on increasingly more skilled positions throughout the trajectory of their careers. So, whether to maintain a job or reenter the workforce, continuous retraining for new skills is critical for occupational readiness and success. Lifelong learning is an essential component of the new economy.

Exhibit P-1. Value-added to GDP by sector, 1960.

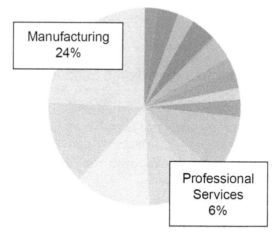

Source: U.S. Department of Commerce, Bureau of Economic Analysis.

Exhibit P-2. Value-added to GDP by sector, 2010.

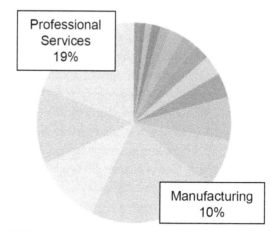

Source: U.S. Department of Commerce, Bureau of Economic Analysis.

Exhibit P-3. 1960 Educational Attainment, U.S. citizens 25 and older.

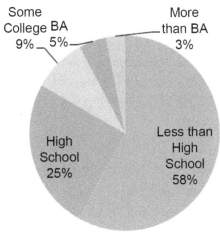

Source: U.S. Census data, 1960.

Exhibit P-4. 2010 Educational Attainment, U.S. Citizens 25 and older.

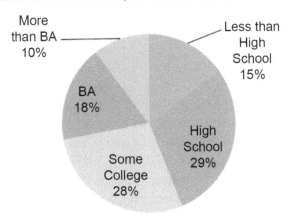

Source: U.S. Census data, 2010.

New Skills for a New Economy

The global economic crisis that began in 2008 hit hardest among workers with the least education.[1] As the country recovers from the downturn in the economy, there are too many workers sitting on the sidelines looking for a suitable job in the new economy. This is no longer a problem for just the individual; it has become a problem for the entire nation. Society can no longer afford a labor market where roughly half of the workforce has only basic skills. As a society, we are not providing the support to improve competence and provide mastery.

The economic crisis underscores a decades-old discussion of the so-called skills gap.[2] The skills gap is an issue not only for youths entering the workforce, but also for workers dislocated by the recession. The recession provided stark reminders that the current education and job-training programs in the United States do not foster the skills required for work and citizenship in the 21st century.

In the past, the 3 R's (reading, writing, and arithmetic)—combined with on-the-job training—were adequate for a stable, lifelong career. Today, the knowledge economy requires the 4 C's: communication, collaboration, critical thinking, and creativity (Exhibit P-5). In fact, a recent survey of employers indicated that a lack of technical skills is not the biggest problem when they recruit younger workers. The skills gap is not primarily about traditional technical and academic skills, but rather about productive and responsible habits and dispositions toward work.[3] Younger workers, in particular, have not been prepared for the collaborative and dynamic nature of work in the knowledge economy, and the 4 C's are the foundation of success.*

Unlike earlier economic eras, basic literacy and numeracy are no longer even a minimum foundation for success at work. Content knowledge is less important because it can be accessed so easily through digital environments. In the new economy, workers need to be able to think critically about available information, apply it in new and creative ways, collaborate with a team of coworkers to bring each person's skills to bear on the challenges at hand, and, finally, communicate what the team has accomplished and why it is important. A system of lifelong learning not only facilitates learning the 4 C's but also fosters the ability to adapt to fluid situations. It cultivates the habits of self-motivated learners—eager to expand their understanding of their world to better participate in society and the economy.

---

*Younger workers may be caught in a vicious cycle: Because of the downturn in the economy, they were not able to find part-time employment when they were in high school or college. Youth employment appears to be a good predictor of future earnings and employment. Individuals who gain work experience while in high school and college tend to earn more as adults and are less likely to be unemployed. This may be because any kind of job experience is likely to develop the "soft" job skills that employers report are in short supply among new graduates.[4]

Exhibit P-5. Four C's.

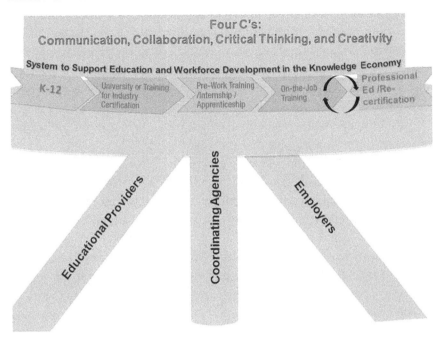

The second decade of the 21st century provides daunting challenges as the world economy recovers from the recession that began in 2008. We are not recovering to the economy that made the United States a world power in the 20th century. Although the world and the economic system have irrevocably changed, our workforce is primarily ready for the semi-skilled work of the mid–20th century. Now that the global economy is based on technology and the ability to adapt quickly, too many individuals in the United States cannot find work that supports the high quality of life at the center of the American Dream.

Although education and training provide strong benefits directly to individual workers, the benefits to employers and society are equally important. Hiring talent is expensive. The cost includes not only the resources devoted to the job search, such as paying the human resources staff or a recruiting firm and buying advertisements in appropriate places read by qualified applications, but also the productivity lost as a position remains vacant.[5] Replacing talent is estimated to cost between 30% and 45% of the base salary of the position.[6]

Employers pay dearly to hire talent, but the cost of training is generally recouped in higher productivity from new employees. For instance, multiyear employer-sponsored apprenticeship programs begin to cover the cost of investment in the last year of a 3-year program when the apprentices earn a training wage but are able to function as productive employees. When they are converted to regular employees, they are much more productive than people hired directly into the positions.[7]

Not only do employers and individuals pay a high price for limited investments in lifelong learning and training, but the U.S. economy and our society stagnate in a world where geographic borders are increasingly meaningless. Companies easily relocate to countries with lower wages or to countries that make solid investments in lifelong learning. Reliance on old models of education and training is dangerous for an economy struggling to expand. Public policy must better integrate education and workforce development in order to maintain a strong pathway from school to training to successful employment and full participation in society. Across sectors and types of organizations, we must work together to prepare every citizen for life and work in the knowledge economy.

Partnerships for Systemic Change

Research indicates that organizational partnerships are essential to developing and maintaining successful programs and initiatives that support lifelong learning. Effective systems of lifelong learning engage three distinct types of organizations: education providers, employers, and agencies to coordinate the initiative. It may not matter which type of organization takes the lead in creating supports for lifelong learning, but each has a part in a successful system of lifelong learning.

School systems, postsecondary institutions, community organizations, and employers all have a strong role to play in providing systematic supports so that individuals can continue developing skills and knowledge to stay abreast of changes in society and the economy. The foundation of such a system remains prekindergarten to grade 12 (PK-12) of schooling, but it must become a system that fosters the engagement and life skills necessary for children to develop into adults who are motivated to continue learning throughout their lives. In order to develop active, self-motivated learners, schools must embed learning in authentic tasks or projects that simulate real-world experience.

In high school and college, work-based placements enable students to apply classroom knowledge while gaining an awareness of different careers. At the same time, employers become familiar with potential employees, and can groom them for future positions. In turn, adult learners need support from their employers to maintain the skills and credentials to further their own careers and also benefit the organization's mission. Employers need to know that the education system ensures that employees have the proper certification in a trade or profession and that they can stay current with ever-changing technical skills.

Education institutions and employers provide crucial learning opportunities but, with a tight focus on their organizational missions, they may have little time for the logistics of partnering. Research indicates that successful systems of lifelong learning include a coordinating agency[8] to facilitate the partnerships between education providers and employers. Employers and educators who already have jobs may not have time to develop and sustain the business–education partnership. Rather than draining resources of educational institutions or employers, a coordinating agency can take the lead in developing standards for education and training, resolving logistical issues in placing learners in workplace settings, and providing incentives for partnering.

In addition to highlighting shifts in the U.S. economy and the skills gap, this book provides an overview of the evolution of the formal system of education, identifies supports for workforce development in the United States, and documents the slow pace of change that resulted in the skills gap. The skills gap is further illustrated by current data about adult skills from global competitors. The core of the book is composed of examples of programs and policies that demonstrate how to best support lifelong learning. One section illustrates each of the types of organizations. The sections begin with the executive perspective—an interview with the leader of an exemplary program. (See Exhibit 6 for a summary of each interview.) The sections include case studies that detail programs and initiatives that support lifelong learning. The conclusion offers recommendations for creating and sustaining an effective system of lifelong learning.

The programs and initiatives discussed in this book represent a variety of organizations involved with education and workforce development, including educational institutions, employers, and agencies that coordinate partnerships between them. They include private companies, nonprofit organizations, and public agencies. They operate on different scales: regional, state, national, and global (Exhibit P-7). These cases represent a range of programs and initiatives

Exhibit P-6. Executive perspectives.

Executive/Organization	Mission
Edward Verrier, Joint Council on Thoracic Surgery Education	Medical education has a particularly urgent responsibility to incorporate the best current science to save life. Technology can help keep pace with new research and latest techniques. This professional association is piloting technology solutions to enhance the residency of aspiring surgeons.
Elizabeth Amato, United Technologies Corporation (UTC)	UTC is committed to the lifelong learning of all employees. The prime example of this commitment is a generous, comprehensive tuition benefit program available to full-time and part-time workers at all levels of the company.
Scott Ralls, North Carolina Community College System	North Carolina created its community college system in the 1950s as part of an economic development strategy to provide the workforce with the skills necessary to diversify the economy. The community college system works closely with employers to provide customized training at no cost to the company.

Exhibit P-7. Case studies.
Education Providers

Organization	Mission
JPMorgan Chase Foundation	The Fellowship Initiative was created to develop untapped talent by providing mentoring and academic support for African-American boys in New York City. The program targets boys with average academic experiences and provides support and enrichment to help them reach their potential.
World Economic Forum (WEF)	Most famous for the annual conference in Davos, WEF has developed a program to enhance ongoing learning for leaders from all sectors and around the world. Includes a selective fellowship resulting in an executive master's degree in global leadership.
Middlesex Community College (MCC)	MCC offers programs for students of every age: summer programs for children, dual enrollment for high school students to earn both high school and college credit for the same course, as well as associate's degree programs that seamlessly lead into bachelor's degree programs at partner universities. To maintain an effective education and training program, MCC works very closely with local employers.

Organization	Mission
University of Liverpool	The University of Liverpool is a pioneer not just in online education but also in using the technology to reach students across the globe. Specifically, they offer an online global MBA program with students from dozens of countries.

Employers

Organization	Mission
National Football League (NFL)	The NFL works with football players at different levels to support them on and off the field. This includes supports for college athletes, to help transition into the life of a professional athlete and mentoring and support as former professional players decide which second career to pursue.
Aramark	The Aramark Building Community (ABC) program provides awards/grants to community organizations to support workforce readiness. Since the program began, it has provided solid training in the food service industry and Aramark has hired many program alumni.
Boeing	Boeing is committed to lifelong learning and continuous career development. It established the Business Career Foundation Program (BCFP) that hires recent college graduates and rotates them through all the business functions in order to develop their leadership skills and cultivate a holistic understanding of the company.
JP Morgan Chase	JP Morgan Chase is continually working to expand its pool of qualified workers. In response to an inability to recruit candidates with strong skills in both technology and finance, it partnered with Syracuse University and the University of Delaware.

Coordinating Agencies

Organization	Mission
National Urban League (NUL)	The NUL's Urban Youth Empowerment Program delivers career exploration and personal development services to adjudicated young adults and high school dropouts 18 to 24 years old.
Carnegie Center for the Advancement of Teaching	The Carnegie Center for the Advancement of Teaching is working with a national network of community colleges and leveraging dramatic improvements in teaching and learning.

(continues)

Exhibit P-7. *(continued)*

Organization	Mission
Africa-America Institute	This leadership development program works in conjunction with major universities in Africa to target leaders and potential leaders in African communities. After completing leadership training, participants are expected to work in their communities to provide employment and training to strengthen the capacity of more than just the one individual who was able to return to school.
Northern Tier Industry and Educational Consortium	This consortium of large and small businesses, schools, and community organizations was created to develop the skills of the potential workforce in this very rural area. Their signature program is a Youth Apprenticeship Program for 11th and 12th graders.
Jobs for the Future (JFF)	JFF researches best practices in education-to-career initiatives and works with practitioners to implement these practices. The Pathways to Prosperity State Network is adapting and implementing vocational educational and training programs commonly available to youth in the European Union.
Switzerland's Federal Vocational Education and Training System	Switzerland has maintained a strong system of workforce development within the Swiss context that emphasized local control, federalism, and capitalism. This program supports individuals completing advanced career training and credentialing.

and can offer lessons to all types of organizations interested in improving education and workforce development in the United States.*

In addition to the case studies of exemplary programs, the interviews highlight best practice approaches and recommendations from executives who have provided oversight of world-class programs. The executive perspectives are featured at the beginning of each of the three sections that profile the cases (educational providers, employers, and coordinating agencies).

---

*In order to develop the case studies, we first interviewed officials leading the programs or agencies, or implementing the policies discussed in the book. Cases were drafted by program leaders themselves to best reflect the perspective of the field. As such, the cases are presented in different formats reflecting the diversity of the programs.

Lessons Learned

This book's exemplars of lifelong learning programs promote reflection on the support and the policy changes that might help the United States leverage existing resources into a new, more effective system. After presenting the cases, this book discusses how the United States might align and coordinate existing policies and programs in the PK-12 education system, in higher education, in workforce development, and in corporate training. It also analyzes gaps in the four components of an effective system of support for lifelong learning, and examines how to promote partnerships to support ongoing learning.

The following research questions (as well as others) are addressed:

- How has the workforce readiness and development model evolved throughout this country's history? What have been the key historical drivers of influence?
- Why is the current relationship between workforce skill needs and education/training largely ineffective for contemporary labor demands?
- What are the components of an effective system of lifelong learning in support of continual workforce readiness?
- What are some exemplars of successful local, regional, and national lifelong learning and development systems?
  - What are the implications (opportunities for and barriers to lifelong learning) influencing shifts in educational policy and practice?
- How can we incubate more relevant coordinated support from community and workforce development agencies to generate more effective initiatives that can be expanded or replicated to serve a wider population?
- How can organizations and employers better inform, support, and leverage (1) educational providers that are formally preparing the next generation of workers, and (2) coordinating agencies that have the capacity to provide further training needs and to maintain skill relevance and placement demands in the workforce in the new economy.

Reflecting on lessons learned from these exemplars, we offer suggestions for leaders who work for or with educational institutions, coordinating agencies, and employers. These lessons emphasize the importance of working across sectors.

We invite you to reach beyond your specific field to create a system that can support schooling for youth and ongoing learning opportunities for adult workers. Perhaps this book will prompt reflection on the general disconnect between education, work, and the lack of lifelong supports for learning. At a minimum, we hope to ignite a conversation about how organizations can partner to develop the infrastructure of an effective system of lifelong learning.

Notes

1. Mitchell, J. (2013). *Government Job Losses Hit the Young, the Less Educated, and Women the Hardest.* Washington, DC: Urban Institute. http://www.urban.org/UploadedPDF/412756 -Government-Job-Losses-Hit-the-Young-the-Less-Educated-and-Women-the-Hardest.pdf.

2. Secretary's Commission on Achieving Necessary Skills. (1991). *What Work Requires of Schools: A SCANS Report for America 2000.* Washington, DC: U.S. Department of Labor; Grubb, N. & Lazerson, M. (2004). *The Education Gospel: The Economic Power of Schooling,* Cambridge, MA: Harvard University Press.

3. Capelli, P. (2012). *Why Good People Can't Get Jobs: The Skills Gap and What Companies Can Do About It.* Philadelphia: Wharton Digital Press.

4. Ruhm, C. (1997). "Is High School Employment Consumption or Investment?" *Journal of Labor Economics,* 15 (October): 735–776; Mroz, T. & Savage, T. (2006). "The Long-Term Effects of Youth Unemployment." *Journal of Human Resources,* 41 (Spring): 259–293.

5. Capelli, *Why Good People Can't Get Jobs*; Destiny Solutions. (2012). *Lifelong Education and the Labor Market.* Toronto, Canada: EvoLLLution http://www.evolllution.com/research/

6. Destiny Solutions, *Lifelong Education and Labor Market Needs.*

7. Lerman, R. (2014) "The Role of Apprenticeship Systems in Rebuilding the Middle Class," paper presented at the International Conference of the Association of Policy Analysis and Management (APPAM): "The Decline of the Middle Classes Around the World?" Segovia, Spain: APPAM.

8. Hoffman, N. & Litow, S. (2011). *Schooling in the Workplace: How Six of the World's Best Vocational Education Systems Prepare Young People for Jobs and Life.* Cambridge, MA: Harvard University Press; Mourshed, M., Farrell, D., & Barton, D. (2012). *Education to Employment: Designing Systems that Work.* London: McKinsey Center for Government, McKinsey & Company.

ACKNOWLEDGMENTS

With sincere appreciation, we wish to thank the following individuals for their contributions to this book: Elizabeth Amato, Tony Bryk, Leah Backhus, Pete Butler, Elizabeth Chmielewski, Bernard Choi, Gay Clyburn, Carol Cowan, Curt Cox, Murray Dazliel, Corey Donahue, Bev Dribin, John Fallon, Saroya Friedman-Gonzalez, Courney Smith, Goodrich Rick Gross, Calvin Hadley, William Helms, Melanie Henniger, Megen Hoenk, Nancy Hoffman, Melissa Howell, Lela Wingard Hughes, Eun Joo Hur, Myria Jacobs, Amini Kajunju, Carolyn Kelley, Diane LaPointe, Mark LaPointe, Amy Liedke, Jennifer Mc-Dermott, Vera Moore, Twinkle Morgan, Rob Morrissey, Devon Nolt, Brendan O'Grady, Al Phelps, Gilbert Probst, Ursula Renold, Mark Ridgon, Eric Roland, Mary Rucci, Jeffrey Saltz, Andreas Schleicher, Gillian Seely, Hal Smith, Bianca Swift, Rebecca Tessier, Edward Verrier, Troy Vincent, John Willig, Gingi Wingard, Levi Wingard, and Marcy Wingard.

We would also like to recognize the support of the following organizations: Academy for Educational Development, Africa-America Institute, Aramark, Boeing, Carnegie Foundation for the Advancement of Teaching, Jobs for the Future, Joint Council on Thoracic Surgery Education, JPMorgan Chase, Middlesex Community College, National Football League, National Urban League, North Carolina Community College System, Northern Tier Industrial Tier Consortium, Organization for Economic Cooperation and Development, Pearson, Public Consulting Group, Swiss Economic Institute, Swiss Federal Institute of Technology, United Technologies Corporation, University of Liverpool, University of Washington Medical School, University of Wisconsin, Wharton School of the University of Pennsylvania, and World Economic Forum.

THE CONTEXT

The slow job growth in the recovery from the Great Recession of 2008 underscores the disarray of the education and training system in the United States. This section explores how we arrived at this point—and how global economic competitors compare. As you read, please consider the following:

- How has the workforce readiness and development model evolved throughout the history of the United States?
- How do the education and skills of the workforce in the United States compare with the workforce in other developed nations?

CHAPTER 1

How Did We Get Here? A History of Education and Training in the United States

Michelle LaPointe and Jason Wingard

For millennia, skills learned as a novice were honed over decades to increase mastery but were essentially the same skills. Early in the 19th century, the majority of American workers were still employed on farms or self-employed as tradesmen or artisans. The industrial revolution changed the nature of work (see Exhibit P-2 in the Preface). By the end of the 19th century, most people were employed in low-skilled manufacturing work.[1] The pace of change in the economy only increased in the 20th century, when all types of jobs were transformed by technology. Now, in the new knowledge economy of the 21th century, change is constant, and we must continuously improve our professional skills to keep up.

The Economy Recovers to a New State

Although industrialization was introduced almost a century earlier, we can trace the dramatic shift in work and education to the Long Depression of 1873, when a dramatic decline in global demand for silver resulted in a series of bank failures and widespread unemployment (see Exhibit 1-1). As the United States recovered from that depression, the economy was dramatically restructured and became more industrialized. This restructuring opened up categories of work that barely existed earlier in the century—and certainly not on the scale required to industrialize the economy. Eager for work after the Long Depression, workers moved to the new centers of manufacturing from

Exhibit 1-1. Gap Between Job Skills and Education.

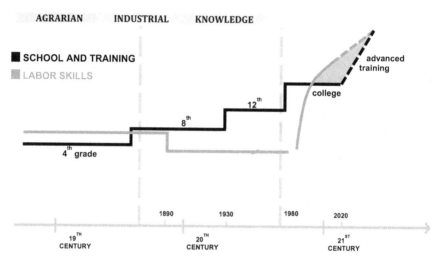

across the United States and Europe. Initially, these new jobs were primarily semi-skilled.[2] Although immigration produced an almost unlimited number of workers, few trained artisans or laborers sought employment in these new types of jobs. Given a limited supply of skilled workers, factory owners further reorganized the work. Semi-skilled positions were specialized into specific routine tasks to allow for the hiring of less skilled workers.

In contrast to the earlier agrarian economy, when youths learned trades and crafts through apprenticeships that lasted years, in the beginning of the industrialized age training was performed almost entirely on the job. Given the low-skilled nature of the work, there was little promotion potential and very flat compensation. Nationally, in the decades immediately following the Long Depression, annual worker turnover exceeded 100%, and 75% of the turnover appeared to be due to employees quitting.[3] Despite the constant flux of workers, employers paid little attention to developing the capacity of their workforce or retaining workers in their factories.

This changed during World War I, when immigration into the United States halted. Without a steady stream of workers, employers had to develop their local job markets, enhance the capacity of existing labor, and retain the workers in their factories.[4] Companies had to compete with one another to hire and retain competent employees. The value of labor and the power of workers increased. Strong unions and increased labor protections further strengthened the position of employees. Employers began investing in their workforce by providing pensions, better working conditions, and training for specialized roles within the factory.

National Policies to Support Workforce Development

The employers' investments in developing their workforce set a precedent for labor policy in the United States. We have a history of very limited public involvement or investment in improving the quality of work. Formal evidence for this dates to the Cardinal Principles of Secondary Education of 1917, issued by the national Commission on the Reorganization of Secondary Education during the period when secondary education became common in the United States. This period was marked by a debate about the role of education and about whether the focus should be on developing academic skills or work-related skills. The cardinal principles explicitly laid the burden for developing work-related skills on individuals with little if any support from the school*:

> The student gets to know him- or herself and a variety of careers
> so that the student can choose the most suitable career. The student
> should then develop an understanding of the relationship between
> the vocation and the community in which one lives and works. Those
> who are successful in a vocation should be the ones to teach the
> students in either the school or workplace.[5]

In keeping with those principles, in the United States job training, professional development, and adult education have typically been either offered by employers to increase organizational capacity or paid for by employees themselves to increase their knowledge and skills. The emphasis on private individuals and private companies has impeded the creation of a system for lifelong learning. Employer-sponsored programs have tended to be very job-specific, rather than providing portable skills and credentials or expanding an employee's career path within the organization. Outside of employer-sponsored training, individuals have primarily relied on trade schools and community colleges. Despite an intention to allow the market to provide training for needed skills,

---

*The commission outlined seven cardinal principles: health; command of fundamental processes (reading, writing, oral expression, and math); worthy home membership (art, music, social studies); vocation; civic education; worthy use of leisure; and ethical character. The full text of the report is available at http://tmh.floonet.net/articles/cardprin.html.

the reality is that, given a lack of information for consumers and loose credentialing of institutions, the market for job training, professional development, and adult education in the United States is inefficient and does not meet the needs of workers.

However limited, public investment in training and education for adults dates to President Franklin D. Roosevelt's New Deal and was embedded in the Works Progress Administration, the Civic Conservation Corps, and the National Youth Agency. These programs were run through community organizations rather than connected with existing education institutions. These programs touted "a new technique in education—that is, education through work."[6] New Deal investments in job training ended when World War II began.

Job Training for the Disadvantaged

In the 1960s, the federal government created new job training programs with the primary goal of getting the unemployed into jobs—any jobs. These included the Manpower Development Training Act of 1962, which only funded short-term (10- to 15-week) programs and offered job-specific training. In 1973, the Comprehensive Employment and Training Act (CETA) consolidated existing job training programs and gave a greater role to states in designing and implementing programs. In 1982, the Job Training Partnership Act (JTPA) encouraged public–private partnerships to assist employers with worker training. In the 1980s, the federal government created numerous education and training programs, mostly targeted to provide second chances to the unemployed or those who failed to develop basic literacy and numeracy in high school. By 1995, the General Accounting Office reported that the federal government was spending $20.4 billion on 163 training programs, spread across nearly every federal agency. There was no effort to coordinate these programs into a coherent system. The Workforce Investment Act (WIA) of 1998 provided additional funding for training for those who were unemployed and had limited job skills, but the services were mostly informational. Allowable education programs included the general equivalency diploma (GED), adult remedial education, and English as a second language (ESL) classes.* WIA

---

* Although these services are typically provided by community colleges, and although community colleges are considered the linchpin of the workforce development and adult education system, few community colleges participate in WIA programs. The mismatched goals and incentives and the bureaucratic nature of WIA programs are disincentives to participate.

also created and funded One-Stop Centers and Individual Training Accounts. During this time, the federal government implemented Work First and the Personal Responsibility and Work Opportunity Reconciliation Action, which undermined previous efforts for workforce development by emphasizing the need to take any job, rather than building skills for a more stable career.[6]

Formal Education in the United States

In addition to job-based training and development, formal education became more relevant to career readiness in the early 20th century. A recurring debate raged (and still rages) among policymakers: *What is the purpose of public education?* Many called for increased vocational education in the developing concept of high schools. In 1917, Congress passed the Smith-Hughes Act, which devoted the first federal dollars to vocational education. It was also during this time that secondary education became more common.

In the 1920s, as comprehensive high schools were built across the United States, it became expected that young people would earn a high school diploma. Although secondary education was not mandatory during the Great Depression, it was strongly encouraged, largely to limit the entry of young workers into the already tight job market.[7]

After World War II, U.S. policy encouraged college as a way to expand the middle class, and high schools began to focus on preparing students for higher education. The GI Bill is a famous example of a public policy to support college education. During the 1950s and 1960s, attitudes shifted in support of secondary education programs that emphasized college readiness over job readiness.[8] This emphasis on college remains the prevailing attitude in the United States, despite the fact that, on the one hand, many professions require additional education beyond a 4-year college degree, and that, on the other hand, an even larger number of jobs require technical skills but not a college degree.

Changes in the Economy, Lags in the Educational System

Although college was increasingly seen as a direct path to a secure middle-class lifestyle, during the 1950s and 1960s it was possible for a factory worker to support a family. Manufacturing dominated the U.S. economy. Jobs were plentiful, and semi-skilled labor was highly valued. By the 1970s, however, manufacturing jobs were disappearing, due in part to mechanization[9] and in part to competition from the reinvigorated economies of Japan and Germany.

In the new economies of Japan and Germany the role of the worker was quite different from that in the United States. Even on an automated assembly line, manufacturers in those two countries used experienced workers to monitor and control quality on the line.[10] Workers were empowered to stop the assembly line to adjust quality. Accordingly, labor and education policy in those countries invested in developing workers with critical thinking skills and refined technical skills. This autonomy did not exist in the American factory. Factory work in the United States remained semi-skilled.

The last decades of the 20th century marked another transition in the economy with parallel shifts in essential skills. The explosion of the computer and technology industry created many skilled jobs, although not necessarily jobs that require a 4-year college education, especially since higher education has not caught up to the rapid changes in technology. Today, the U.S. economy is characterized by innovation. Perhaps more than a college degree, work in the 21st century requires good skills in communication, collaboration, critical thinking, and creativity (the 4 C's[11]). These skills appear to be strong predictors of success in the technology industry and more generally in the knowledge economy.

Despite the new skills required to compete in the knowledge economy, the U.S. system of education and job training is still preparing a majority of youths for semi-skilled work that has not been available since the early 1970s. Adults in this country who are already on the job have few supports to retool their skills for the new economy. Like Japan and Germany, other developed countries have invested in their education and training systems to better provide youths with 21st-century skills when they enter the workforce. As noted before, Germany and Japan have long trained factory workers in problem solving and leadership skills so that they can monitor assembly lines and ensure the quality of the products manufactured. The misalignment of education and work in the United States, combined with lower labor costs in developing countries and better primary and secondary education systems in other developed countries,[12] has driven jobs out of the U.S. economy.

In addition, the financial crash of 2008 reduced demand worldwide, further limiting the need for semi-skilled manufacturing work. But the recession that began in 2008, like the Long Depression of the late 19th century, can serve as a catalyst to better align our systems of education and workforce development with the realities of life and work in the new knowledge economy. Education providers, driven initially by lean budgets, are collaborating with employers to strengthen their programs and connect students with authentic experiences relevant to opportunities in this economy. Employers are realizing that there is so much undeveloped talent, and support for innovative education, focused on the 4 C's, will provide companies with employees who can adapt to the constant change in the global economy. Public and community agencies have focused reduced resources on combining and aligning investments by employers and education providers. As it did in the late 1890s, the United States is again recovering from an economic downturn to face a new era. Continued prosperity depends on seizing the opportunity to collaborate in the global knowledge economy.

Notes

1. Rosenbloom, J. (2002). *Looking for Work, Searching for Workers: American Labor Markets During Industrialization*. New York: Cambridge University Press.
2. Ibid.
3. Brissenden, P. & Frankel, E. (1920). "Mobility of Labor in American Industry." *Monthly Labor Review*, 10 (June): 1342–1362.
4. Rosenbloom, *Looking for Work*.
5. Grubb, N. & Lazerson, M. (2004). *The Education Gospel: The Economic Power of Schooling*, Cambridge, MA: Harvard University Press, p. 109.
6. *Ibid*.
7. Walters, P. (1984) "Occupational and Labor Market Effects on Secondary and Postsecondary Educational Expansion in the United States: 1922 to 1979." *American Sociological Review*, 49(5): 659–671.
8. Daggett, B. (2006). *Jobs and the Skills Gap*. Washington, DC: International Center for Leadership in Education.
9. Walters, "Occupational and Labor Market Effects."
10. Helms, M. (2006). "History of Continuous Improvement," in Encyclopedia of Management. Available at http://hamidfarid.com/wordpress/wp-content/uploads/2013/05/Encyclopedia-Of-Management-5th-edition_4.pdf#page=158.
11. More information available at www.p21.org.
12. U.S. Department of Education. (2006). "Comparative Indicators of Education in the United States and Other G-8 Countries." Available at nces.ed.gov/pubsearch/pubsinfo.asp?pubid=2007006; Organization of Economic Cooperation and Development. "Strong Performers and Successful Reformers in Education: Lessons from PISA for the United States." Available at http://dx.doi.org/10.1787/9789264096660-en.

CHAPTER 2

Better Skills, Better Jobs, Better Lives

Andreas Schleicher

Skills transform lives, generate prosperity, and promote social inclusion everywhere. And if there is one lesson the global economy has taught us over the last few years, it is that we cannot simply bail ourselves out of a crisis, that we cannot solely stimulate ourselves out of a crisis, and that we cannot just print money to get out of a crisis. A much stronger bet for countries to grow themselves over the long term is to equip more people with better skills to collaborate, to compete, and to connect in ways that drive our economies forward.

If there is one central message emerging from the Organization for Economic Cooperation and Development's new Survey of Adult Skills, it is that what people know and what they do with what they know has a major impact on their life chances (Exhibit 2-1). For example, across countries, the median hourly wage of workers scoring at level 4 or 5 in literacy—who can make complex inferences and evaluate subtle truth claims or arguments in written texts, is more than 60% higher than for workers scoring at level 1 or below, that is, workers who can, at best, read relatively short texts to locate a single piece of information that is identical to the information given in the question or directive or who can understand basic vocabulary. Those with low literacy skills are also more than twice as likely to be unemployed. The survey also shows that this impact goes far beyond earnings and employment. In all 23 countries surveyed, individuals with poorer foundation skills are far more likely than those with advanced literacy skills to report poor health, to believe that they have little impact on political processes, and not to participate in associative or volunteer activities. The United States is a case in point: Almost

Exhibit 2-1. Likelihood of positive social and economic outcomes among highly literate adults (2012).
Increased likelihood (odds ratio) of adults scoring at Level 4/5 in literacy on the OECD Survey of Adult Skills reporting high earnings, high levels of trust and political efficacy, good health, participating in volunteer activities and being employed, compared with adults scoring at or below Level 1 in literacy (adjusted)

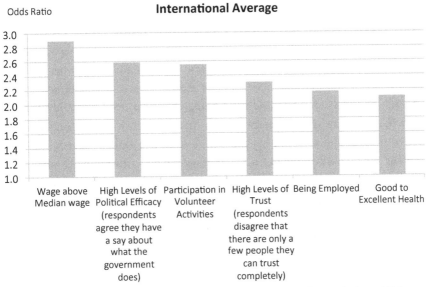

Notes: Odds ratios are adjusted for age, gender, educational attainment and immigrant and language background. High wages are defined as workers' hourly earnings that are above the country's median.

Source: Based on data from the Survey of Adult Skills (PIAAC) 2012.

a third of low-skilled adults in the United States report having poor or fair health, and the odds of having low levels of health are four times higher for low-skilled adults than for those with the highest skills. That ratio is higher than that for nearly any other surveyed country, and double the across-country average. At the aggregate level, too, the distribution of skills relates closely to how the benefits of economic growth are shared among individuals and social groups.

So in one way, skills have become the global currency of 21st-century economies. But this "currency" can depreciate as the requirements of labor markets evolve and individuals lose the skills they do not use. For skills to retain their value, they must be continually developed throughout life.

Furthermore, the toxic coexistence of unemployed graduates and of employers who say that they cannot find the people with the skills they need underlines that more education does not automatically translate into better economic and social outcomes. To succeed with converting education into better jobs and lives, we need to better understand what those skills are that drive outcomes, ensure that the right skill mix is being learned, and help economies to make good use of those skills.

The essential starting point is anticipating and responding to the evolution of skill demands. Government and business need to work together to gather evidence about skill demands, present and future, which can then be used to develop up-to-date instructional systems and to improve education and training systems. During the past few decades there have been major shifts in the economic underpinnings of industrialized countries and, more recently, of many emerging and developing countries, too. In countries such as the United States, the steepest decline in skill demands is no longer in the area of manual skills, but rather in routine cognitive skills. When we can access the world's knowledge on the Internet, when routine skills are being digitized or outsourced, and when jobs are changing rapidly, accumulating knowledge matters less, and success becomes increasingly about ways of thinking (creativity, critical thinking, problem solving, and judgment), about ways of working (collaboration and teamwork), and about the sociocultural tools that enable us to interact with the world.

The OECD's Programme for International Student Assessment (PISA) is an attempt to measure schooling outcomes in these terms. It looks at the capacity of 15-year-old students not just to reproduce what they have learned, but to extrapolate from what they know and apply their knowledge in novel situations. The results show that a comparatively large proportion of 15-year-olds in the United States do not acquire even a minimum level of skills in key domains such as mathematics, reading, and science.

Early deficiencies in initial education and training will not go away by themselves. Indeed, the OECD Survey of Adult Skills shows that the performance of the initial schooling system is closely linked to adult skills. Between 2000 and 2009, 15-year-old students in the United States tended to score below the across-country average in the PISA assessment of both literacy and numeracy. Consistent with this finding young adults (now in their late teens or twenties) scored below average in the Survey of Adult Skills. Weak basic skills (literacy and numeracy) are now more common in the United States than in many other countries. One in six U.S. adults (about 36 million) have weak literacy skills; in Japan, the comparable figure is one in 20 (Exhibit 2-2).

Exhibit 2-2. Literacy proficiency among adults.

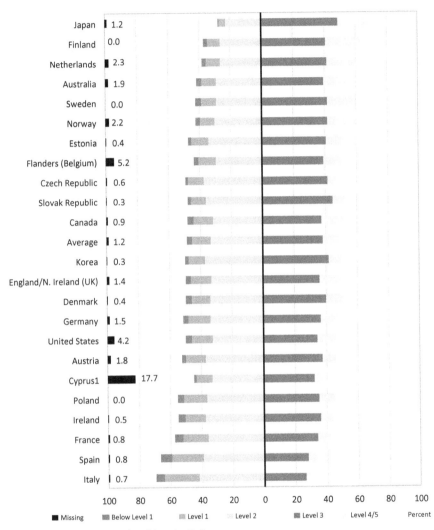

Percentage of adults scoring at each proficiency level in literacy.

Countries are ranked in descending order of the mean score in literacy.

Notes: Adults in the missing category were not able to provide enough background information to impute proficiency scores because of language difficulties, or learning or mental disabilities (referred to as literacy-related non-response).

Source: Survey of Adult Skills (PIAAC) (2012), Tables A2.1 and A2.2a.

Nearly one third of U.S. adults have weak numeracy skills as compared with an across-country average of 19%. Looking at stronger performers, while one in nine U.S. adults score at the highest level in literacy, similar to the across-country average, only one in 12 score at the highest numeracy level, well below the average. Even in problem-solving skills in technology-rich environments, which are central to the success of the U.S. economy, adults in the United States do not outperform the across-country average.

What is troubling, too, is that there have been few signs of improvement in basic skills in the United States. Today in the United States, adults demonstrate similar or weaker literacy skills on the Survey of Adult Skills than did adults in the mid-1990s, and the average basic skills of young adults are not hugely different from those of older persons. This contrasts with some other countries such as Finland, South Korea, and Japan, where younger adults score well above their older compatriots—and well above young adults in the United States.

What is also noteworthy is how much information literacy and numeracy skills vary for individuals with similar qualifications, both within the United States and when comparing the United States with other countries. Although the Survey of Adult Skills assesses only some components of the knowledge and skills certified by educational qualifications, proficiency in literacy, numeracy, and problem solving represent outcomes that are expected to be developed through formal education. Irrespective of any other outcomes, the differences in the extent to which graduates of similar qualifications differ in their proficiency in information processing skills between countries are striking. In the United States, as in a number of other countries, the Survey of Adult Skills shows that actual skill levels differ markedly from what data on formal qualifications suggest. For example, the United States ranks much higher internationally in the proportion of 25- to 34-year-olds with college degrees than in the literacy or numeracy skills of the same age group. Even more striking is that a large share of Japanese 25- to 34-year-olds who have completed only high school do as well as a large share of U.S. college graduates (Exhibit 2-3).

There are many reasons why the skills people currently have may differ from the formal qualifications they once attained. People may have moved on and acquired new skills since they completed their formal education or lost some skills developed in their formal education that they did not use. Indeed, the longer the time since a person completed his or her education, the weaker

Exhibit 2-3. Distribution of literacy proficiency scores and education
Mean literacy proficiency and distribution of literacy scores, by educational attainment

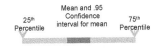

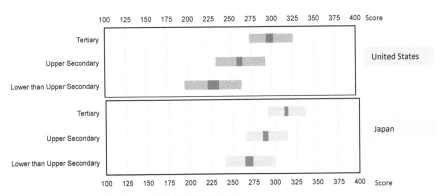

Source: Based on data from the Survey of Adult Skills (PIAAC) 2012.

the direct relationship between his or her formal education and proficiency, and the greater the role of other factors that may affect proficiency, such as the work or social environment. In other words, a 55-year-old's experience in formal education is likely to have less of a direct influence on his or her proficiency than that of a 26-year-old. Furthermore, the quality of education may also have changed considerable over the decades, even within the same country, so that individuals with ostensibly the same qualifications or level of attainment may have had very different educational experiences. And again, educational qualifications typically encompass a much wider range of competencies than literacy or numeracy skills.

Finally, social background matters more in the United States than in other countries. Socioeconomic background, parental education level, and literacy skills are more strongly linked in the United States than in any other country with comparable data. Race and ethnicity are also important: 35% of black adults and 43% of Hispanic adults have low literacy skills, compared with only 10% of white adults. For Hispanics, recency of migration makes a difference; U.S.-born Hispanics score on average higher than black adults, whereas foreign-born Hispanics score lower. Racial differences in skills remain even among adults with similar levels of education. More positively, however, the link between socioeconomic background and skills is weaker among young adults in the United States.

All of these considerations are important, because individuals who have low levels of skills due to a lack of access to good-quality education, a lack of success in education, or a lack of opportunity to improve their skills later on are much more likely to have poor employment and social outcomes, and more so in the United States than in other countries.

Although many of these findings are worrying, another finding, more positively, suggests some pathways of opportunity: 63% of low-skilled adults in the United States are employed, more than in other countries. This means that strong workforce development measures could reach many of the low skilled. Stronger basic skills also tend to be rewarded with better chances of employment and higher wages, even when taking educational attainment into account. The wage reward for basic skills is higher in the United States than in almost any other surveyed country, so the incentives to strengthen basic skills are strongly present.

One area where the United States could learn from countries such as Denmark, Germany, and Switzerland is in education, and specifically shifting more of the premium in education from qualifications-focused education up-front to skills-oriented learning throughout life. OECD's Learning for Jobs analysis shows that skill development is far more effective if the world of learning and the world of work are linked. Compared with purely government-designed curricula taught exclusively in schools, learning in the workplace enables people to develop "hard" skills on modern equipment, and "soft" skills, such as teamwork, communication, and negotiation, through real-world experience. The experience of these countries also suggests that hands-on workplace training is an effective way to motivate disengaged youths to re-engage with education and smooth the transition to work. They succeed in preventing youths from dropping out of school by offering more relevant education and second-chance opportunities, and by offering work experience to young people *before* they leave school. Employers have an important role in training their own staff, even if some small and medium-sized enterprises get public assistance to provide such training. Trade unions in these countries also help to shape education and training, protect the interests of existing workers, ensure that those in work use their skills adequately, and see that investments in training are reflected in better-quality jobs and higher salaries.

Preparing young people for entry into the labor market with up-front education and training is only one facet of skills development; working-age adults also need to develop their skills so that they can progress in their careers, meet the changing demands of the labor market, and maintain the skills they have already acquired. A wide spectrum of full- or part-time adult-learning activities needs to be available, such as work-related employee training, formal education for adults, second-chance courses to obtain a minimum qualification or basic literacy and numeracy skills, language training for immigrants, labor-market training programs for job seekers, and learning activities for self-improvement or leisure.

According to the Survey of Adult Skills, participation rates in adult education and training are higher in the United States than in most other countries at all skill levels, which is encouraging. However, there is more that can be done to dismantle barriers to participation in continued education and training. First, making the returns on adult education and training more transparent can help to increase the motivation of users to invest in adult education and training. Governments can provide better information about the economic benefits (including wages, employment, and productivity) and other benefits (including self-esteem and increased social interaction) of adult learning.

Second, less educated individuals tend to be less aware of education and training opportunities or may find the available information confusing. A combination of easily searchable, up-to-date online information and personal guidance and counseling services to help individuals define their own training needs and identify the appropriate programs is needed, as is information about possible funding sources.

Third, clear certification of learning outcomes and recognition of non-formal learning (outside of formal education programs) are also incentives for training. Transparent standards, embedded in a framework of national qualifications, should be developed alongside reliable assessment procedures. Recognition of prior learning (especially on the job or from other informal learning settings) can also reduce the time needed to obtain a certain qualification and thus the cost of forgone earnings.

Fourth, it is important to ensure that programs are relevant to users and are sufficiently flexible, both in content and in how they are delivered to adapt to adults' needs. A number of countries have recently introduced one-stop-shop arrangements, with different services offered in the same institution. This approach is particularly cost-effective as it consolidates infrastructure and teaching personnel and makes continuing education and training more convenient. Distance learning and the open educational resources approach have significantly improved users' ability to adapt their learning to their lives.

Cross-border skills policies are important too. Countries may not have an adequate supply of skills because they have booming emerging sectors and not enough people trained in those fields, because their societies are aging and there are too few young people to replace retiring workers, or because they want to move major parts of the economy to higher value-added production, which requires a well-trained workforce. Similarly, while skills policies are typically designed nationally, an increasing number of employers operate internationally. Some countries have begun to invest in the skills of people abroad. This has the double advantage of providing well-trained workers to branches of firms located abroad and reducing the incentives to emigrate, especially among highly skilled individuals.

International student mobility has increased dramatically over the past years but it is a much more diverse market than a decade ago, and no country in the industrialized world has seen a more rapid decline in the market share of international graduates than the United States. The advantage of international students for host-country employers is that they have a qualification that can be easily evaluated. Many of them also work part-time during their studies, allowing them to develop ties with the host-country society and labor market, which in turn facilitates their transition from learning to work. To make better use of this source of skills, several OECD countries have eased their immigration policies to encourage international students to remain after their studies for employment. The overall stay rate varies, averaging 25% in 2008–2009 among international students who did not renew their student permits in OECD countries.

Also, while skills policies are typically designed nationally, an increasing number of employers operate internationally and must derive their skills from both local sources and the global talent pool. Some countries, therefore, have started to consider skills policies beyond their national borders and have begun to invest in the skills of people in other countries. This has the double advantage of providing well-trained workers to branches of firms located abroad and reducing the incentives to emigrate, especially among highly skilled individuals. Another way to encourage skills development globally is to design policies that encourage cross-border post-secondary or tertiary education.

This can help a country to expand its stock of skills more rapidly than if it had to rely on domestic resources alone.

And yet, building skills is still the easier part; far tougher is providing opportunities for young people to use their skills. Employers may need to offer greater flexibility in the workplace. Labor unions may need to reconsider their stance on rebalancing employment protection for permanent and temporary workers. Enterprises need reasonably long trial periods to enable employers to give those youths who lack work experience a chance to prove themselves and to facilitate a transition to regular employment. The bottom line is that unused human capital represents a waste of skills and of initial investment in those skills. As the demand for skills changes, unused skills can become obsolete, and skills that are unused during inactivity are bound to atrophy over time. Conversely, the more individuals use their skills and engage in complex and demanding tasks, both at work and elsewhere, the more likely it is that those skills will not decline due to aging.

But even developing skills and making them available to the labor market will not have the desired impact on the economy and society if those skills are not used effectively. The OECD Skills Survey shows that, in some countries, skills mismatch is a serious challenge that is mirrored in people's earnings prospects and in their productivity. Knowing which skills are needed in the labor market and which educational pathways will get young people to where they want to be is essential. Skills mismatch on the job can be a temporary phenomenon; for example, the demand for skills takes time to adjust to the fact that there is a larger pool of highly skilled workers available. Thus, not all types of skills mismatch are bad for the economy. Skills surpluses, which can result from an underuse of skills in specific occupations, can serve as a skills reserve that may be used in other, more advanced jobs and for building knowledge economies over the long term. However, the mismatch between workers' skills and their tasks at work can adversely affect economic and social outcomes. The underutilization of skills, in specific jobs in the short- to medium-term, can be a problem because it may lead to skills loss. Workers whose skills are underused in their current jobs earn less than workers who are well matched to their jobs and tend to be less satisfied at work. This situation tends to generate more employee turnover, which is likely to affect a firm's productivity. Under-skilling is also likely to affect productivity and, as with skills shortages, slow the rate at which more efficient technologies and approaches to work are adopted.

Successful entry into the labor market at the beginning of a professional career has a profound influence on later working life. The scarring effects of a poor start can make it difficult to catch up later. Strong basic education, in conjunction with vocational education and training programs that are relevant to the needs of the labor market, tend to smooth the transition from school to work; so do hiring and firing rules that do not penalize young people compared with other groups, and financial incentives that make it viable for employers to hire young people who require on-the-job training. Such policies can help prevent skills mismatch and unemployment later on.

High-quality career guidance services, complemented with up-to-date information about labor-market prospects, can help young people make sound career choices. Some countries also have effective active labor-market measures, such as counseling, job-search assistance, and temporary hiring subsidies for low-skilled youths, and they link income support for young people to their active search for work and their engagement in measures to improve their employability.

None of this will work unless skills become everyone's business: governments, which can design financial incentives and favorable tax policies; education systems, which can foster entrepreneurship as well as offer vocational training; employers, who can invest in learning; labor unions, which can ensure that investments in training are reflected in better-quality jobs and higher salaries; and individuals, who can take better advantage of learning opportunities. Countries also need to take a hard look at the financing of education and job training. Governments need to design financial incentives and tax policies that encourage individuals and employers to invest in continuing education and training. In countries where tertiary education is financed entirely through public funds, some individuals may shoulder more financial burden for their own tertiary education. Conversely, in countries where high levels of tuition fees pose barriers for access to tertiary education, income-contingent loans and means-tested grants can help to improve access and progression.

It is worth getting this right. If the industrialized world would raise its learning outcomes by 25 PISA points, to the level of improvement that we have seen in a country like Brazil or Poland over the last decade, its economies could be richer by over 40 trillion euros over the lifetime of today's students. Many countries still have a recession to fight, but the opportunity cost of low educational performance is the equivalent of a permanent economic recession.

SECTION II

EDUCATION PROVIDERS

This section describes the role of education providers in promoting life-long learning. Education providers are not just schools; they are a wide range of organizations that offer direct instruction for learners seeking job preparation and enhancement training.

We begin the section with a discussion with Dr. Edward Verrier, the director of a medical residency program that leverages technology to ensure that doctors receive training in the most current science. The exchange highlights the following issues, which all types of education providers discussed in this section confront:

- How these institutions adapt to the changing demographics of their target populations and the shifting demands of the economy for new skills
- The need to work closely with employers and other stakeholders to ensure that content is relevant and current
- How current program delivery combines technology, hands-on practical experiences, and classroom activities to foster effective learning environments

Executive Perspective

Joint Council on Thoracic Surgery Education: e-Learning and Surgical Residency

Edward Verrier

During the 2013–2014 school year, the Joint Council on Thoracic Surgery Education piloted an online course for residents in thoracic surgery at the University of Washington School of Medicine. Like an increasing number of education providers, the surgical residency program has "flipped" the classroom. Rather than attending traditional lecture-based courses, students access content information online, and class time is used to for discussion to deepen and apply knowledge.

This new model is relevant for the knowledge economy and vital to the medical field. Highly skilled physicians must apply cutting-edge scientific knowledge in real-time situations with immediate impact on patients. An online environment facilitates the digital transfer of the latest information, saving the time traditionally required to print medical journals or textbooks.

The following questions and answers are drawn from conversations with Edward Verrier, M.D., professor of surgery at the University of Washington Medical School and a member of the board of the Joint Council on Thoracic Surgical Education.

Why an online program? Why is the old model no longer adequate?

There is a sense among surgeons that if the traditional residency was good enough for them, it's good enough for the next generation. But the whole world has changed. We no longer allow residents to teach. We have more safety standards. There's more transparency and more accountability.

The whole environment is different, so we had to change. Resident education is no longer the model of "see one, do one, teach one." We are flipping the classroom with this online course: content is available online; residents can move at their own learning pace, when they have time to focus on the material. During weekly conferences, rather than a power-point lecture, the faculty can lead an interactive session. They can focus on what the residents don't know and what they need to understand and how to apply knowledge to cases.

Education is evolving at all levels: from kindergarten to high school, as well as college and medical school. It's much more learner-centric. It has to be internally driven by the learner, not just externally defined by the faculty. Online courses acknowledge the fact that everybody learns at his or her own rate.

What is a basic description of the online program? What are the goals for the program?

Our intention was to create a meaningful online approach to thoracic surgery resident education. We've created 88 weekly units, to match the number of weeks in the 2-year residency. Each unit includes learning objects, learning points, and teaching pearls.

For each unit there are required readings and clinical case scenarios, which are in-depth cases, of about six or seven pages, with extensive references. There are vivid images, each of which is linked to learning objectives, discussion points, learning points, and teaching pearls. At the end of the unit there is an online test. The content and assessments are aligned with the milestones laid out by the residency review committee, and residents meet some of those milestones by completing those online tests.

Ultimately, the resident's goal is to pass the medical boards. The materials in the online course are aligned with the board exams. Half of the board exam is examining cases, and one third of residents struggle with that section of the exam. So, to address this issue, the online course was designed to teach them to apply information rather than just memorize it.

What was the design process? How did you develop the curriculum?

To start, we conducted a robust needs assessment. We went to the American Board for Thoracic Surgery and to the residency review committee. We gave presentations at national meetings about what competency-based medical education really means. We talked to faculty members in other surgical disciplines and learned from what they are doing to improve both resident education programs and continuing education. We used this information to better define the requirements to be a heart or lung surgeon in the United States. This process resulted in a 60-page detailed document, separated into the four categories associated with a cardiothoracic surgery: heart, lungs, esophagus, and other organs in the chest.

Next, we needed to find a good navigation system, one that was readily available and that could work on a variety of platforms (PC, tablet, smartphone). It needed to be very fast in bringing up pertinent information. When you click open an article, the PDF comes up immediately. It's seamless. The system also needed to be able to handle a lot of traffic. Even in the pilot program there were 1,400 users (including residents, program staff, and faculty).

Then, we negotiated with publishers to acquire the rights to the course content. In addition to journal article, we were able to get permission to use electronic versions of 11 textbooks.

We also realized we needed a content management system (CMS). We reviewed different systems and chose PersonalBrain (Softonic International, Barcelona, Spain). It's a mind-map system, which we organized by each of the four categories of thoracic surgery, and residents can drill down by topic. The system provides access to appropriate chapters of the texts, journal articles, videos of procedures, and audios of lectures. In addition, each student has an electronic portfolio to document his or her progress through the course. Finally, all the content on the site was reviewed by a professional advisory board, similar to a journal's peer review process.

The content management system functions as a database so we also needed a learning management system (LMS) to provide guidance to learners. The LMS allows us to organize the curriculum into weekly units. Initially, we used an open-source system, but we are now moving to a platform with an enhanced CMS and LMS. We needed better reporting mechanisms and multi-tendency capabilities that the open-source system could not provide. We needed better coordination between the CMS and LMS with fewer clicks to proceed through the content and to the LMS. We are partnering with Astute Technologies (Fairfax, VA) to enhance the platform.

What were the barriers to implementation?

Copyright issues. Creating good assessments. Oh, and getting people to accept an online program.

These were some of the issues we faced:

- We needed to be familiar with the copyright issues for course materials. In our field, most journal articles are open source after a few years, but some journals never make their materials publicly available. We are hoping to negotiate longer-term agreements so we don't have to worry about copyright issues every few years. Or about developing our own materials.

- We found that the toughest part is writing the assessment questions to help student prepare for their boards. We have used some old board questions, but with all the tests embedded in the course, we have had to write a lot of new questions. It's taking longer than anticipated to get good questions.
- Finally, we need to get the users to accept it. The faculty and the residents are still embedded in an antiquated system of learning, focused on memorization and lectures. But once we have results for our residents, I think they will begin to change their minds.

How was the work coordinated? Who supported this work?

Initially, the four thoracic surgery societies sponsored this work, but two had to pull out for financial reasons. Now most of our funding comes from the Society of Thoracic Surgeons and the American Board of Thoracic Surgery. We also raised some money from industry.

The Joint Council on Thoracic Surgery has a board with two members from each of the societies, and the board advises us. There are some subcommittees to focus on specific topics. I also have a kitchen cabinet of four surgeons at other medical schools. They each focus on a different area: working with PersonalBrain, general issues related to medical education, developing simulations, and outreach to medical school faculties.

How do you measure success?

The program is just finishing its inaugural year. Although the course was designed before the year started, we are rolling it out one feature at a time, one per month. We won't have outcome data until the end of the school year, but the content management system was designed to track usage. Anytime users sign in, the system tracks what they access and how much time they spend in the system. We review usage data every week. In addition, the system allows access to the residents' portfolios. Information can also be aggregated to the program level, to assess program effectiveness. Faculty not only can look at their residents' progress but also can compare outcomes with the other programs around the country.

We have a lot of data to gauge how the program is working, but the big test will be how residents do on their medical boards.

What are the next steps? What changes do you anticipate?

We believe that this online course module has appeal way beyond the thoracic surgery residency. We showed it to colleagues in the cardiothoracic anesthesia community and to associates who develop cardiac devices, and they want to be part of this. They would love access to this kind of content and this type of CMS. When we presented at the Europe Society for Thoracic Surgery, we noted a lot of interest, but I expect this program will be more popular in countries that are developing their medical education system. It may take longer to catch on in the United States and Europe.

There is also potential to use online courses for continuing medical education (CME). Currently, physicians earn CME credits by attending conference. These conferences often present research studies and information about registries, but they have little to do with competency-based education. There is currently no accountability for professional learning, but ultimately, society is going to ask, "Did you learn anything? How do we know if you learned anything?" Without assessment, there is no way to know if the professional even attended the lecture, let alone learned anything. How do you make a curriculum accountable, how do you make developing technical skills accountable?

Online education is emerging as the way forward in medical education, particularly in a specialty like cardiothoracic surgery, in which new technology is introduced every week. We see this as a first step toward an accountable curriculum.

CHAPTER 3

JPMorgan Chase Foundation
Fellowship to Improve Educational Outcomes for Young Men of Color

Twinkle Morgan, Calvin Hadley, and Mark Rigdon

An increasing number of business leaders and corporations understand how the crisis facing young men of color impacts their ability to attract and retain the diverse talent they need to compete in the global economy. To address this issue and help build a prepared, diverse talent pool, JPMorgan Chase & Co. (JPMC) created The Fellowship Initiative (TFI), an innovative program designed to equip young men of color with the knowledge, skills, and experiences needed to succeed in life.

Program Description

The Fellowship Initiative pursues its mission by providing program participants with the academic, social, and emotional supports they need to complete high school, earn a college degree, and launch successful professional careers. JPMC's commitment to TFI reflects its belief that corporations have an obligation to actively engage in efforts to address critical social issues and its recognition that while money is important, it's not enough. Firms like JPMC can bring multiple resources to bear, including, money, talent, and ideas, on the most pressing social issues of our time in ways that drive beneficial outcomes for deserving individuals and communities.

To ensure TFI's success, the firm leveraged current best practices by recruiting experienced partners and integrating their diverse approaches into a cohesive program. As new, often unanticipated program needs emerged,

TFI adapted its framework to address those needs and discontinued areas that were found to be less critical. This approach ensured that the program could be scaled easily and modified in appropriate ways that were responsive to participants' needs. The firm's decision to cover all of the costs associated with TFI for all students also ensured that the students were able to participate fully in all program activities regardless of their financial circumstances.

Target Audience

The first cohort of TFI Fellows was recruited from 25 public (non-charter) schools. Leaders from each school were asked to nominate up to five young men of color in 9th grade who showed academic potential but were not yet living up to that potential. Applications for the program were recruited from this pool of 125 nominated students.

The Fellowship Initiative's admission process was rigorous and demanding. The 12-page application included three student essays; a detailed school/teacher evaluation; two short parent statements; academic records; and general household, financial, and demographic information. The selected students were then invited to participate in two one-on-one evaluations and a group interview with TFI's selection committee. The information collected from all of these stages in the admission process provided multiple opportunities for the admissions committee to look into the hearts and minds of the candidates and better understand their families, school experiences, and social backgrounds.

While academic achievement and intelligence were factored into the selection process, the core mandate was to identify the least-served students with average grades who exhibited the following characteristics:

✓ A strong interest in attending and graduating from college
✓ Determination and perseverance in the face of challenges
✓ Leadership potential and a commitment to public service
✓ Financial need

After candidates were recommended by the selection committee, TFI's program staff narrowed the final pool down to the 32 Fellows who were admitted to the program. The most challenging aspect of this task was deter-

Exhibit 3-1. Recruiting Highlights and Demographics of the Fellows Selected (Class 2017).

Recruiting Highlights		Demographics	
Target schools invited:	25	Average grade point average (GPA):	84%
Students nominated:	125	Ethnicity: 69% Black/African	
Students interviewed:	48	22% Latino	
Schools participating:	18	9% Asian	
Fellows recommended:	32	Parents' education: 3% grade school	
Schools represented in		38% high school	
final selection:	15	31% some college/no degree	
		25% college/professional degree	
		3% information not provided	
		Income: 7% low income (below $30K)	
		41% moderate income ($30K–$60K)	
		13% high income (>$60K)	
		Free reduced-priced lunch: 75% eligible	
		25% not eligible	

mining the proper balance of candidates across the higher, middle, and lower segments of the midlevel student population to ensure that the program could properly address the students' individual and collective needs.

Of the 32 students admitted to the program, 16 (50%) fit squarely in the academic middle (grade point averages [GPAs] of 80 to 85); eight (25%) were higher performing students, with GPAs in the 85 to 90+ range; and eight (25%) were lower performing students, with GPAs under 80. The decision to admit these students was ultimately driven by applicants' demonstrated desire to succeed, family, recommendations of school leaders, and their ability to navigate difficult circumstances (Exhibit 3-1).

From the moment the candidates started the program in July 2010, the TFI Fellows were held to high standards, and their families were expected to reinforce these expectations at home. To ensure that everyone understood what was expected, TFI required the Fellows and their parents/guardians to sign a code of conduct agreement that affirmed their commitment to the program and their willingness to comply with all of the demands associated with preparing the young men for college and successful professional careers.

Partners

Implementing TFI necessitated partnering with a number of proven youth development organizations. The initial partners included the following:

- LEAD Global: a national partnership of top multinational corporations and graduate business schools that encourages students to pursue careers in business
- Sponsors for Educational Opportunities (SEO): an academic enrichment and career development program that prepares high school students to gain admission and succeed at competitive colleges and universities nationwide
- Youth About Business (YAB): an entrepreneurial training program that delivers an innovative curriculum designed to prepare youths for workplace success

Shortly after starting the program, TFI staff recognized that the TFI Fellows were going to need more than the services and supports offered by the initial set of program partners. As a result, the following additional partners were recruited:

- Academic: Princeton Review for SAT and ACT preparation
- Global: African Leadership Academy
- Experiential learning: Alpine Endeavors, US Navy SEAL Consultant, Outward Bound
- Infrastructure: iMentor
- College access/success: College Summit, Venture Forth Consulting (scholarships/college selection), Essay Intensive (college admissions essay writing and coaching), Write for the Future (college admissions essay writing), JPMorgan Chase Volunteers
- Social/emotional support: Mary Pender Greene Group

Once assembled, this powerful group of partners was able to address virtually all of the Fellows' needs. It's worth noting that the Fellows' enthusiasm about working with the partners inspired a sustained level of commitment to the program by these organizations and their staff. They came to feel a strong sense of ownership over the welfare and successful development of the students.

Program Model

The Fellowship Initiative's design emphasized (1) academic development, (2) access to resources and opportunities that disadvantaged students often lack, (3) exposure to people and places that were able to broaden the Fellows' personal and global awareness, and (4) strong social and emotional supports that encouraged personal growth and accomplishment. Specifically, the core elements included the following:

- Academic preparation through summer and Saturday academies
- Entrepreneurial training and professional development
- Global exposure: South Africa immersion
- One-to-one mentorship via JPMorgan Chase executives
- Social and emotional supports
- Leadership training via classroom and experiential learning opportunities
- College visits
- SAT/ACT preparation
- College access support
- Cultural exposure and networking
- College and scholarship essay coaching via JPMorgan Chase executives
- Speakers series/super-mentors
- College success skills training

To help ensure the success of comparable programs replicating TFI's model, its core elements are detailed in the following subsections.

Year 1: From the Summer After Freshman Year to the End of Sophomore Year

Once admitted, each student attended a 1-week business camp designed to enhance analytical, leadership, and teamwork skills. This launching point, hosted on Columbia University's campus, was also selected to provide students with residential college experience and the opportunities associated with higher education. Two days of intense instruction in the basics of corporate finance were followed by a 3-day mergers-and-acquisitions exercise during which the Fellows assumed the roles of company chief executive officers (CEOs), chief financial officers (CFOs), and chief operating officers (COOs) who were responsible for trying to negotiate a merger deal. The experience provided an opportunity for the Fellows to apply what they learned earlier in the week, and exposed Fellows to the broad world of the financial services sector. The Fellows reported that the experience motivated them to excel in school so that they could qualify for the kinds of careers they learned about during the week.

Immediately following the business camp, the Fellows participated in a rigorous 3-week summer academy and a 9-month Saturday academy curriculum. The curriculum was adopted from the SEO Scholars Program, which used the New York State learning standards and core curriculum in English and mathematics as the foundation for advanced lessons. The supplemental academic instruction focused on critical thinking, reading comprehension, vocabulary acquisition, writing, grammar, and math. The Saturday academies were held three Saturdays per month, during the school year and the curriculum introduced each week was modified repeatedly to ensure that it responded to the unique needs of the Fellows as their academic strengths and weaknesses became more apparent.

In the third month of the program, Fellows were paired with mentors from the firm. The mentors were tasked with helping to identify developmental needs among the Fellows and counseling them about what was required to succeed in college and the corporate world. All mentors were JPMC professionals who committed to working with their mentees for at least 1 year and ideally for the length of the high school program. Mentors were also asked to maintain weekly email contact with their mentees and to participate in four to six TFI group events annually.

Beginning in the second semester starting in January, mandatory tutoring was added 1 day per week for those Fellows who struggled most in math and English. Students' performance during the previous week's Saturday academy was used to drive the content that tutors worked on with the Fellows.

Year 2: From the Summer After Sophomore Year to the End of Junior Year

Recognizing that personal growth is accelerated when individuals are taken out of their comfort zones, TFI selected an outdoor leadership experience that was designed to expose Fellows to a variety of stressors intended to help them understand that they were capable of much more than their current perceptions of their personal limits permitted.

In consultation with qualified wilderness experts, TFI designed a 10-day outdoor leadership experience that included a 6- to 10-mile daily hike through high mountains, rock climbing, and rappelling up and down 100+-foot elevations, and a series of challenges that required teamwork, as facilitated by strong leaders. The first half of the expedition focused on teaching outdoors skills—cooking, equipment usage, camping, use of map and compass, and so on. The second half put these skills into practice and culminated with a task that required quick decision making under adverse conditions and forced the Fellows to think out of the box to solve vexing wilderness survival challenges.

The experience was extremely demanding physically, mentally, and emotionally, but a majority of the Fellows reported that it had a profound impact on them. They noted that the trip strengthened their capacity to make sound decisions under extreme pressure with limited information. It also helped them develop strategies for managing stress, controlling impulses, and persevering in the face of obstacles. Finally, it broke down the remaining barriers that separated the Fellows and facilitated a bonding among them that proved critical to the program's long-term success. However humbling it was for the Fellows to live out in the wilderness for close to 2 weeks, their collective experience helped build the Fellows' resiliency and self-confidence.

Following this experience, TFI hosted a 3-week summer academy that focused on English and mathematics (see curriculum above). Students continued these lessons through the fall of their junior year at Saturday academy sessions, again held 3 weekends per month.

January to May of junior year was dedicated to a 12-week Saturday SAT preparation course taught by the Princeton Review for June SATs. TFI also hosted a 3-day college trip to five colleges in the northeast to help determine the best match for each Fellow's needs. The schools visited included a large state school, a small liberal arts school, a private college/university, and other colleges with distinguished programs. Fellows later visited a historically black college and completed a brief ACT preparation course as well.

Exposing the Fellows to current trends in culture, business, and politics was a fixed element of TFI's programming each year. Examples included the Fellows' participation in the Steve Harvey Mentoring Weekend, attending an off-Broadway show about the Tuskegee airmen, and visiting the White House and the U.S. Capitol.

These experiences allowed the Fellows to engage in discussions with some of the country's most well-known icons, who served as super-mentors and shared their life stories, pointing out the similarities they shared with the Fellows. This experience helped the Fellows understand that their distant dreams were achievable if they remained focused and worked relentlessly to achieve success.

Year 3: From the Summer After Junior Year to the End of Senior Year

In the summer after the Fellows' junior year, TFI partnered with the African Leadership Academy (ALA) in Johannesburg, South Africa, to offer the Fellows a global immersion learning experience. The ALA is notable as a school that trains future generations of African leaders. The Fellows were paired with these remarkable students for a 2-week civic leadership development program that also included related cultural visits to the Apartheid Museum, Soweto, other historical sites, and the Pilanesberg Game Reserve. Having an opportunity to live with the African students, many of whom came from backgrounds of extreme hardship and poverty, provided the Fellows with a sense of perspective that helped them view their own circumstances in new ways that further inspired them to achieve their own transformative dreams and become more active in the civic life of their communities.

College Access

Following the trip to South Africa, the remainder of the Fellows' summer was devoted to kick-starting college applications and writing their personal essays. This process helped the Fellows explore their personal histories and take stock of their strengths and weaknesses. It also convinced the staff that the group needed more intense college access support to ensure that the Fellows were successful in positioning themselves for admission to a range of schools that offered the quality academic programs and support systems the students needed to thrive.

Recognizing this need, TFI partnered with a number of college access specialists to ensure that the Fellows positioned themselves in the best possible light. The first of these partnerships was with College Summit, a nonprofit organization working to increase college enrollment rates among low-income students. Fellows and TFI staff attended College Summit's 4-day summer program, where they spent hours mining their personal histories to discover critical details that could help explain why they would be an asset to any college or university program. TFI's in-house writing teacher then coordinated a 5-month extended effort to recruit and engage a team of JPMC volunteers as one-on-one writing coaches who helped the Fellows further develop their essays through December of their senior year. Concurrently, TFI engaged experienced and well-respected consultants in the admissions and scholarship community to assist with school selection decisions and help identify suitable scholarships for which the students would be compete for.

The Fellowship Initiative also engaged psychosocial counselors to deliver programming designed to help the Fellows learn how to seek the critical social supports needed to transition successfully from high school to college. This meant explicitly addressing the challenges of transition from high school to college and proactively working with the Fellows to develop their self-awareness and coping skills.

There are a lot of reasons why students of color, particularly young men, fail to finish college. They include financial, academic, and social stressors that negatively impact students' ability to be successful in college. TFI's college success programming focused on helping them develop success strategies— everything from navigating roommate issues, to identifying on-campus resources, planning for effective time management, and obtaining internships during the spring of their senior year.

Following their enrollment in college, the Fellows have continued to receive support from SEO's college counselors who interact with the Fellows regularly to make sure they are applying the strategies that they learned prior to their graduation from high school. In addition, during holiday breaks, the Fellows are given opportunities to participate in workshops on GPA management and effective study strategies. Other key collegiate skills will be provided throughout their college career.

Program Impact

The Fellowship Initiative was designed to change the life trajectories of young men of color. Measuring that change is difficult in the best of circumstances, because the causal link between TFI and the Fellows' development is not always direct or linear. Because program evaluation models prioritize quantitative data so heavily, they can become blind to—or easily discount—great, even life-changing, progress that occurs imperceptibly over time. Recognizing this issue, TFI attempted to capture appropriate qualitative and quantitative data that could help tell a more integrated story about the impact that the program had on the life outcomes of its participants.

Retention

The Fellowship Initiative recruited 32 students in 2010. After the 3-year high school pilot, 24 students (75%) completed the program. Eight students did not complete the program for the following reasons:

- Six left due to poor mission and culture fit, including discipline problems. TFI encouraged these Fellows to leave the program.
- One left because he did not like the program design and the focus and scope of offerings.
- One left because he and his family relocated elsewhere.

Employee Engagement

More than 100 JPMorgan Chase professionals worked with Fellows as mentors, coaches, role models, speakers, or volunteers in various capacities. These business leaders and professionals were instrumental in reinforcing TFI's culture of excellence and its aligned values.

High School Graduation

All the Fellows graduated from high school on time.

College Entrance Exams

The Fellowship Initiative's Fellows outperformed national test-takers on both SAT and ACT composite scores, with a score of 1536 for TFI versus 1500 for the SAT national average, and 21.7 for TFI versus 21.1 for the ACT national average. On the SAT, TFI Fellows scored 21% higher than African American males and 11% higher than Latino males. On the ACT, TFI Fellows scored

28% higher than African American students and 15% higher than Latino students.

College Acceptance

All participating Fellows were accepted into 4-year colleges, with an average of nine acceptances per students; 70% of Fellows enrolled in colleges rated as very competitive to most competitive in *Barron's 2011 Profile of American Colleges;* 58% of Fellows are first-generation college students.

Scholarships

Students in the program were awarded a total of $8.4 million in institutional awards and private scholarships in 2013.

College Financing

Over half of the Fellows (54%) have 90% or more of their college costs covered by institutional or public grants and scholarships.

Psychosocial Development

One of the program's greatest outcomes was the influence it exerted on the healthy psychosocial development of the Fellows. Their experience in the program will fundamentally alter the Fellows' life opportunities and their viability in the upper echelons of the workforce. The best proxy indicator of this comes from the voices of the Fellows themselves, who acknowledged the role the program played in elevating their academic goals and career aspirations, in addition to, facilitating life-changing personal growth. These voices were captured as part of a documentary about TFI produced in 2013 and in survey data collected from the Fellows. Notable insights gleaned from this information include the fact that 90% of the Fellows are committed to pursuing a master's degree or other graduate degree following college. The Fellows made the following observations:

- "I am able to see potential in myself that was always there; now I strive for excellence."

- "I set higher goals."
- "I am more mature; I push myself harder."
- "In the years when I could not find the light within the darkness, TFI helped me find my own way to create my own light."
- "I am much more confident."
- "The way I carry myself professionally, personally, and socially has improved."
- "I have been able to unlock my inner drive."
- "TFI has helped my professional development and has pushed me to always think critically about my self-image."
- "I learned to take advantage of all of the opportunities before me."
- "I have become aware of my actions and I have homed in on and refined my raw talent."
- "The way I carry myself has people thinking I am older than I am. I am more organized."
- "I actually care about academics and my future."
- "I think of how my actions will affect me in the long run."
- "I don't talk as much; I listen more."
- "I've learned that I have to take responsibility for things I do."
- "My attitude, work ethic, skills, and professionalism are better."
- "I've become more responsible and mature."
- "I understand ambition and what it takes to be successful."

Conclusion

Our experience with TFI generated many lessons about how best to expand the horizons of young men of color and assist them in achieving their potential. Specifically, we learned the following:

- **The cause and effect of success is not always precise or linear.**
  - The Fellowship Initiative's original paradigm for "success" was focused on achieving linear gains in academic performance that correlated with the amount of time spent in the program. In reality, TFI staff observed that Fellows lives were changing so much as they acclimated to the program during its early phases that merely sustaining academic performance levels became a benchmark of success. Only when the initial social/emotional work required by TFI had taken root

among the Fellows were they able to see themselves as successful students and to improve their performance. Ultimately, this transformation in the Fellows perceptions of themselves as academically capable students was deemed as important an indicator of success as the actual gains in the Fellows' GPAs.

- **Address social and emotional needs first to set the stage for academic development.**
  - Within the first 12 months, TFI lost seven Fellows from the program. This attrition prompted TFI staff to examine more closely how the structure of the program impacted its participants. Through this process, staff learned that the program offered limited opportunity during the Saturday academies for open discussions that could help students process and manage the complicated issues they were facing in their lives. From 9 a.m. to 5 p.m. each Saturday, the Fellows took six rigorous academic classes, with only 1 hour for lunch/social time. This regimented schedule meant that there simply wasn't enough informal time to facilitate proper relationship building among the Fellows and with the staff. As staff worked to correct these problems, they restricted the Saturday academies to permit more time for interaction and discussion. This proved critical to helping Fellows improve their social and emotional management skills that were interfering with their ability to focus on improving their academics.

- **Increase programming/direct contact hours/psychosocial partnerships.**
  - When TFI shifted its model to accommodate more informal interaction between the Fellows and staff, it became clear that their emotions and their relationships with their family and peers had significant impact on what they learned and how constructively they were able to apply it. As a result, during the second and third years of the program, TFI worked closely with partners to develop programming and workshops that bolstered the Fellows' ability to manage stress effectively and become more resilient in the face of adversity. This proved to be a critically important driver of the program's success.

- **Designing an effective method to build trusting relationships is as valuable as designing a curriculum.**
  - As TFI staff built stronger relational trust with the Fellows, they began to seek help more often, allowing the staff to provide proper, timely guidance. Consistency in staffing was important in sustaining

deep trust with the Fellows. It allowed the staff to become extended family members for the Fellows. Finally, it was important to establish a culture in which the Fellows never felt judged by staff early on in the life of the program. This allowed students the freedom to express themselves and share their innermost thoughts, which helped them resolve issues more quickly and proactively.

- A key finding was that relationship building could have been accelerated by engaging with the Fellows in activities similar to those of the outdoor leadership experience at the beginning of the program. These experiences forged bonds and provided staff with stronger insights about and understandings of the Fellows.

- **Not shirking from the challenging profiles of students proved inspiring to everyone involved.**
  - The Fellowship Initiative sought to achieve the best possible outcomes for the Fellows. To facilitate this, the program leveraged each Fellow's individual strengths to motivate and inspire the group as a whole. Those Fellows who marshaled the strength to overcome significant life challenges became models of perseverance and emotional fortitude, while those who faced academic challenges head-on became role models of scholastic resiliency. Once everyone realized that together they were stronger than the sum of their parts and that it was okay to lean on one another for support, the Fellows were able to deal with their individual and collective challenges more productively.

- **JPMorgan Chase was able to lend its institutional "blue chip" excellence to individual lives.**
  - Hosting the TFI program on JPMC premises proved to be important because it communicated to the Fellows that they were important to the firm and the broader world. The stability of coming to the Saturday academies also proved to be an important constant in the unstable lives of many of the Fellows. For these students, JPMC's classrooms became not only a symbolic home, but a place where people expected excellence from them, despite their circumstances. This helped them to feel proud of who they were and where they were going.

- **Academic enrichment must be multifaceted and flexible.**
  - The Fellowship Initiative's reliance on *whole* group instruction was not always optimal given the diverse academic needs of the Fellows.

A more effective instructional approach would likely have included the following:

- Differentiated instruction that permitted more personalized academic support.
- More activity-based learning that provided outlets for releasing Fellows' stored-up energy.
- Better control of the diversity of school course content and rigor. As an example, TFI could have used diagnostic tests as part of the recruitment process to better understand the range of academic abilities represented among the applicants and assess their suitability for the program's level of rigor.
- Capacity to offer direct-service to students whose school GPA suffered as a result of social-emotional challenges.

- **The people are the key to leadership, creativity, program design, and implementation.**
  - The original TFI model called for a full-time executive director charged with designing the program, identifying program partners, and overseeing program implementation. During the recruitment process, the team recognized that a day-to-day program manager was also needed to provide continuity across program staff; to build relationships with students, families, schools, and partners; and to be a role model and disciplinarian. Together, the executive director and the program manager were also responsible for developing a culture that was accepting of all the Fellows, supportive of their efforts to grow, and rigorous in demanding that that they do their best.
  - The Fellowship Initiative recognized that, beyond a job description, one of the most important roles for the staff—full-time or part-time—was to serve as living, empathic role models for the Fellows. This necessitated the recruitment of people who not only were expert in their content areas but also understood adolescent development and the myriad issues that the Fellows experienced in their daily lives. All staff also needed to maintain a high level of cultural sensitivity to how family traditions/religion/community expectations impacted Fellows' identity, views, and career aspirations. Finally, TFI staff had to possess the ability to offer ongoing constructive feedback when Fellows made poor decisions and to use these decisions to create teaching

moments that reinforced the skills and strategies that the program sought to instill in its participants.

- **Stability of operating infrastructure (facilities) and funding resources extended staff capacity.**
  - ○ The Fellowship Initiative's guaranteed funding freed staff from the pressures of fund-raising and enabled them to support the holistic development of the Fellows. This might not have been possible if they constantly had to demonstrate the program's effectiveness in improving student GPAs.

- **Teaching the family is as important as teaching the Fellows.**
  - ○ It is critical to establish strong partnership with families, especially when they have other children to care for and work long hours to support their families. To do this, it is critical to communicate early and often with families to ensure that they are supportive of the program's goals.

- **Many times you have to "break down" before you can "build up."**
  - ○ There is a growing body of psychology research focused on essential traits that contribute to human development and success, such as persevering despite obstacles, building stamina, and developing "grit." These traits are notoriously difficult to teach. Key to the development of these traits was the Fellows' 10-day outdoor expedition. The challenges posed by caring for themselves in variable and unpredictable outdoor conditions, hiking steep terrain, or climbing rock walls involved real risks. These risks, both physical and emotional, helped to educate the Fellows about their true character and their ability to cope in adverse conditions.
  - ○ The time spent outdoors also promoted more authentic communication among the Fellows and created a safe space where they could express themselves freely, expose their innermost fears, and discover new strengths. This helped them acquire an increased self-awareness and the ability not only to recognize their emotional states but also to self-regulate their emotions and behaviors, new skills that were critical to their overall development.

- **Enhance mentoring relationships: create opportunities to build natural bonds and maximize get-to-know-you time.**
  - ○ There is inevitable variation in the strength of mentoring relationships across any mentoring program. When TFI began recruiting and

training mentors, program leaders were mindful of the research that indicates that poor mentoring relations, particularly those ending within 3 months, have a greater negative impact on a young mentee than having not engaged in the mentoring relationship at all. With this understanding, TFI took great care to make the best possible matching decisions, and aimed to provide mentor–mentee pairs with guidance and support that would facilitate high-quality mentoring relationships. That said, 45% of Fellows reported their 3-year mentoring experience with TFI was very positive, 40% reported it being somewhat positive, and 15% reported it being somewhat negative.

○ Fellows and mentors were matched in September 2010, approximately 10 weeks after the Fellows began TFI and 14 weeks after the mentor recruiting and training process was launched. The TFI team ultimately learned that the compatibility of the mentor–Fellow matches would have been stronger had staff waited longer to create pairs. As an example, the level of knowledge gained about the Fellows after the outdoor experience or from repeated Saturday programming would have been valuable in understanding what type of adult might work best with each one. Mentor–Fellow matches also would have benefited from an informal period beyond the mentor training to get to know one another through shared activities. Then more organic bonds would have grown, and mentors would have had sufficient time and gained sufficient trust to develop a high caliber of communication with Fellows.

Program Update

In the fall of 2013, the firm reviewed the results from TFI and concluded that they merited recruiting a second student cohort in New York and expanding the program to Chicago and Los Angeles. To facilitate this expansion, additional program staff was hired in early 2014. Then the new staff began recruiting new students. Between April and early May, the staff collected applications from more than 300 students across all three cities. Qualifying students and their parents/guardians were then invited to interview for admission, and, by mid-June, 120 students (40 in each city) were admitted into the program. In late July/early August, the new Fellows attended week-long residential orientation sessions at local universities in each of the three cities to prepare them for the program and to begin the process of building TFI's distinctive culture. In early October, the Saturday academies began meeting and will continue to do so three Saturdays a month during the next three school years. We are fortunate to have an opportunity to apply the lessons learned from the first TFI cohort and will strive to innovate our model as we adapt it to meet the needs of the 120 talented young men with whom we are currently working.

CHAPTER 4

The World Economic Forum
Global Leadership Fellows Program

Gilbert J.B. Probst and Eric S. Roland

he modern global arena features a set of unprecedented challenges that are transnational, transcultural, and even transcendental in nature. Finding viable solutions to worldwide environmental degradation, bridging the global divide in access to health care and education, and stabilizing ever-changing geopolitical tensions all require thinking that stretches the boundaries of individual imagination and creativity. These and other intractable issues exceed the capacity of an individual actor or, as history has demonstrated, a single sector. Global issues require multi-stakeholder collaboration, with private, public, and civil society leaders working in conjunction with one another. Indeed, such concerted and collaborative effort offers the greatest promise of enacting transformative, global change.

This cross-sectoral and multi-actor approach to international affairs resides at the core of the World Economic Forum and has served as a strategic signpost for the organization throughout its four decades of existence. In 1971, Klaus Schwab, who founded and continues to lead the Forum, theorized that business enterprises are responsible not only to customers and shareholders but also to governmental and societal institutions, among others.[1] That notion has come to define the World Economic Forum's purpose. Today, the Forum convenes gatherings, both in-person and virtual, of emerging and experienced leaders from all industries and from every level of political and social arenas, including outstanding academics, artists, religious representatives, philanthropists, and other notable stakeholders, to tackle the important issues of the day.

Since the inaugural World Economic Forum event in Davos, Switzerland, in 1971, multi-stakeholder activity has expanded and accelerated throughout the world. The 21st century has already offered various examples of collaborative efforts between business and civil society, which promise benefits to the economy, to citizen-consumers, and to overall corporate identity.* Institutions worldwide have demonstrated their willingness to shift from unilateral approaches to multi-stakeholder initiatives. Recent decades have proven that leveraging the resources and insight of dissimilar entities can generate powerful input into what is needed most: diverse, original thinking and innovative action. As this idea continues to take hold, the argument that the world finds itself in a "multi-stakeholder era" gains credence. Future global activity will only be more multi-sectoral in nature. As this aligned landscape approaches reality, leaders are needed in every sector who can collaborate in this transnational, multi-sector context.

The World Economic Forum and Lifelong Learning

Lifelong learning is inherent in the mission of the World Economic Forum. The Forum itself is a platform for converting information and data into applicable knowledge and higher-order wisdom to guide a multi-sectoral exchange of ideas and insight related to the global agenda. Through regional and transnational events, gatherings of Global Agenda Council thoughts leaders, internationally relevant projects, and other Forum channels, opportunities are offered to delve into the participants' particular fields while also gaining vital, cross-sectoral knowledge.

Viewed through another lens, the World Economic Forum represents an *education system*, gathering experts and generating knowledge, culled through a robust set of convergent and divergent viewpoints, and inviting and encouraging participants to act. By providing opportunities for young leaders, current leaders, and veterans of industry in the public sphere and in civil society, the Forum aims at developing a network of responsible global citizens who

---

*One such example of an effort made possible through the collaboration of the private sector, government, and civil society is the creation of the Global Fund to Fight AIDS, Tuberculosis, and Malaria, an organization whose aim is to utilize "partnership, transparency, constant learning, and results-based funding." (For more information, go to http://www.theglobalfund.org/en/about/.)

act as catalysts of societal change. The World Economic Forum actively involves multi-stakeholder perspectives on global issues to produce a rich learning environment. Ultimately, the organization aims to create an environment that enables leaders from all walks of life to creatively address challenges and realize change on a global scale.

To achieve these academic and education goals, the Forum offers a comprehensive catalog of learning opportunities. This includes creating communities of young global leaders and global shapers and, within the Forum itself, Global Leadership Fellows, all of whom represent the future generation of global leadership. Each community is encouraged to be more than the sum of its component parts. By first understanding the motivations of global business, the engagement of governments, and the interests represented by civil society, and how to leverage them for positive change, these communities, with the support and interaction of the Forum, can develop solutions to key challenges.

Global Leadership Fellows Program

Recognizing the need for collaborative, creative multi-stakeholder and multi-sectoral leadership, the World Economic Forum created the Global Leadership Fellows Program (GLFP) in 2005. The GLFP helps emerging leaders work across different sectors and acquire professional tools that can be applied in virtually any setting or context. The GLFP is situated in the Forum's Geneva headquarters. Switzerland's neutrality serves as a symbol for exploring and questioning from an objective standpoint. Geneva's geography provides an ideal and idyllic setting in which Fellows can embrace the life lessons that enable them to become outstanding leaders themselves. Further, the approach of the World Economic Forum as an organization directed toward a global constituency—and guided by a mission to improve the state of the world—provides an ideal environment through which Global Leadership Fellows come to embody the practice of agile, servant leadership by putting the needs of others first (Exhibit 4-1). Responding to the evident need for purpose-driven leaders who espouse humility and adaptability, the GLFP emphasizes the elements of self-awareness, interpersonal skills, effective communication, contextual intelligence, change agility, and a results-driven orientation throughout the entirety of the program.[2]

Exhibit 4-1. The Global Leadership Fellows Program: educational, coaching, and mentoring elements.

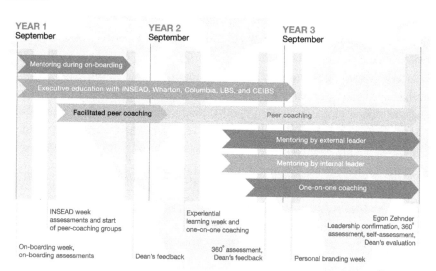

YEAR 1
September

YEAR 2
September

YEAR 3
September

Mentoring during on-boarding

Executive education with INSEAD, Wharton, Columbia, LBS, and CEIBS

Facilitated peer coaching

Peer coaching

Mentoring by external leader

Mentoring by internal leader

One-on-one coaching

INSEAD week assessments and start of peer-coaching groups

Experiential learning week and one-on-one coaching

Egon Zehnder Leadership confirmation, 360° assessment, self-assessment, Dean's evaluation

On-boarding week, on-boarding assessments

Dean's feedback

360° assessment, Dean's feedback

Personal branding week

Abbreviations: CEIBS, China Europe International Business School; LBS, London Business School; INSEAD, formerly known as the Institut Européen d'Administration des Affaires.

Fellowship Selection Process

Fellows are selectively chosen from applicants in their mid-career phase who demonstrate their desire to use their leadership potential to serve society. Each year, approximately Global Leadership Fellows are ultimately offered positions from a candidate pool of more than 6,000 applicants. Applicants have at least 6 years of professional work experience, including a record of interdisciplinary and multidisciplinary work within and across government, business, and civil society. Through the submission of a curriculum vitae and a written motivation statement, candidates must initially provide evidence of compliance with the requirements of specific World Economic Forum positions while also exhibiting leadership potential as well as a broad intellectual background reflected, at minimum, through the possession of a master's degree or equivalent from a major university. Following this initial screening, a narrowed list of candidates participates in a virtual interview process, from which a handful of applicants are offered the opportunity for in-person screening. Prior to those office-based interviews, candidates complete the Hogan High-Potential Report, which identifies those most aligned with the future leadership needs of the Forum. Utilizing baseline business competencies, the report provides insight into the potential of a candidate as a World Economic Forum employee. Onsite, candidates write an essay elucidating a current, global issue; take part in an emotional intelligence test; and interview with an array of Forum staff, including a human resources staff member, representatives of the position's team, current Fellows, the GLFP dean, and the senior Forum directorate.

Program Design

The fellowship is a 3-year commitment, during which time Fellows assume full-time, community, or initiative management positions within the World Economic Forum, earn postgraduate credits in leadership studies, and are mentored by leaders from various sectors.

Working at the Forum

The core of GLFP is a full-time position at the World Economic Forum. Fellows leave their current employment to work in Geneva, New York, Beijing, or Tokyo, and are integrated into all Forum activities by taking positions with the organization. Here are comments from Fellows about their work experiences:

"As a Knowledge Manager, I work with groups of experts from around the world to curate content that aims to provide new perspectives and solutions on pressing global issues. In addition, I collaborate in-house to connect experts' ideas with agendas driven by businesses and regional partners."—Isabel de Sola, Global Agenda Councils

"As a Senior Manager of the Global Shapers community, I lead a community of exceptional young shapers in the age group of 20 to 29 to drive local impact leveraging global insights. I design strategies and execute in clinical fashion to help my team achieve their mission in South Asia and help the Global Shapers Community achieve their global vision. At the same time I co-create processes that will help all the internal and external stakeholders."—Vijay Raju, Global Shapers Community, South Asia

"Contributing to the Technology Pioneer and Global Growth company programs, I am in charge of identifying and integrating some of the most innovative, entrepreneurial and thought-provocative business leaders. Representing emerging technologies and new markets, they bring diversity, opportunities, and drive to the global Forum community." —Marjorie Buchser, Knowledge Integration New Champion Communities

"As part of the Membership Team, I am responsible for building the African membership community while improving the regional value proposition. It is imperative that the Forum's African membership base is representative of the African business community and that they are engaged to design Africa's role in the new global economy." —Marius Hugo, Middle East and Africa Membership

Postgraduate Education

The program has a second component. The Fellows participate in a "2 + 1" year professional program designed to develop the next generation of global leaders committed to improving the state of the world. Academic credits are earned through modules conducted in partnership with leading academic institutions during the first 2 years, including the Wharton School of the University of Pennsylvania, Columbia University, London Business School, the French graduate school INSEAD, and the China Europe International Business School (CEIBS). During the third year, Fellows participate in coaching mentoring activities while also developing and leading a series of Forum-relevant taskforces. These modules result in a master's degree in advanced studies in global leadership.

During the 3-year experience, Fellows dedicate 2 weeks to a classroom-experiential social impact module that explicitly provides both design- and systems-oriented learning opportunities. In conjunction with the Wharton School, Columbia University's Mailman School of Public Health, and the design consultancy firm IDEO, Fellows engage with a variety of thought leaders around issues of poverty, unemployment, homelessness, disaster relief, healthy living, obesity, and others. These discussions provide an opportunity to delve into the complex intricacies of each topic while also mapping the interconnectedness of the broader system. Thus, Fellows develop insight into the root causes and challenges involved in resolving such issues. Discussions are complemented with visits to and collaborations with various organizations, meeting with leaders and clients, and providing assistance through targeted projects and in an applied manner, further underscoring the learning process. The intrinsic flexibility of the program curriculum enables Fellows to tackle the most pressing, current concerns affecting major metropolitan areas while also exploring the structural elements that explain the reality for such locales. By the conclusion of the social impact modules, Fellows have journeyed from "egosystem" to "ecosystem," exploring their individual effect vis-à-vis their local and global context.

Interactions with Leaders

The program has a third component. Through interactions with the most important leaders from around the world and across all sectors, the Fellows observe global leadership in action. The GLFP provides the Fellows with current and past examples of lived, experienced leadership and facilitates "face-to-face" conversations with notable leaders from all sectors and geographies. It is not unusual for a Fellow to have more than a dozen encounters offered on an annual basis—from leading corporate executives to civil society visionaries to the highest ranking political officials worldwide. These interactions offer a unique insight into the trials and tribulations of the leadership journey. Such regular discussions, coupled with personal, introspective reflection that is a hallmark of the program, set Fellows on the path toward discerning, lifelong learning. They are afforded the many vantage points by which to judge a successful leadership life and then provided the space to practice it on a daily basis.

A key aspect of the GLFP is coaching and peer mentoring. Fellows benefit from conversations with professional coaches as well as a cadre of cohort Fellows. The dual-stream process allows for individual transparency and objective assessment, seeding the opportunity for individual behavior change and developing the habit of lifelong learning. Through peer mentorship, the Fellows learn to coach and guide one another through the complex, transnational issues in which they are immersed through their professional attachment. Such guidance resonates as particularly significant in light of the aforementioned, outsized, global information database. Peers gain the skills to serve as vital arbiters between individuals and ambiguous information, encouraging veritable growth over the long-term. Such professional companionship can pay serious dividends. In the entrepreneurship arena, such mentors, or "personal enablers,"[3] can mean the difference between an idea getting off the ground and resting in peace. As the lifelong learning concept establishes itself with some permanence, the need for reliable, objective mentors increases. The need for others to journey with individuals who can strengthen competence and confidence—and make sense of seemingly intractable issues and challenges—intensifies. Further, the mentor model serves as a nontraditional version of workforce development, equipping individuals to channel effort in order to become thriving employees and, as demanded by the global marketplace, informed information entrepreneurs. Over time, the Fellows assume responsibility for one another's ongoing professional and personal development.[4]

Experiential Lessons

In addition to the three major program components, the 3-year tour includes a "crucible" week in the mountains, complete with an intensive negotiation practicum and sessions dedicated to the subtleties of pursing a collective mission. These experiential lessons serve as readily usable ones, as GLFP graduates identify the insight from that week as particularly meaningful. Together, the program components help the Fellows develop into well-rounded leaders who can interact with people from multiple sectors, regions, and cultures. Furthermore, the Forum provides the Fellows with the capacity to maintain a sense of agency amidst complexity, a conviction that they can effect change in the most multidimensional of situations by identifying and focusing their energies, and their teams' energies, on the area where they can have a genuine impact.

Program Impact

Various assessments are regularly conducted with the Fellows to monitor progress and development impact. Measurements take place on two levels and are supported by various measurement tools (Exhibit 4-2):

- *Individual level:* Assessments and the dean's evaluations are based on observations and feedback collected throughout the organization. These assessments provide regular, individual feedback to Fellows on a personal level, providing insight into areas of ongoing development. Some feedback elements are provided by external consultants and are solely available to the individual Fellows, whereas other data are provided through the GLFP office.

- *Institutional level:* Data are gathered through the aggregated related to all Fellows, providing trend observations and assessments related to the overall success of the GLFP.

Exhibit 4-2. Global Leadership Fellows Program measurement tools.

Measurement Tool	Description	Timing
Meaning-making systems, measured through subject/object interviews	An approach by Robert Kegan's team from Harvard Education, based on Adult Development theory; it measures the development of an individual in terms of his or her mental complexity; this assessment reflects changes in each Fellow's meaning system as a result of the program	Beginning of year 1 and end of year 3
360-degree competency-based development assessment	Fellows are regularly evaluated by their peers, supervisors, and subordinates on their performance and on their leadership qualities	Annually
Egon Zehnder International Assessment of Leadership Potential	Assessing Fellows' potential and performance in the current role, benchmarking against external top-performer data and internal expectations for future directors at the Forum	End of year 3
MSCEIT Emotional Intelligence Test	The Mayer-Salovey-Caruso Emotional Intelligence Test (MSCEIT) is an ability-based test designed to measure the four branches of the emotional intelligence (EI) model of Mayer and Salovey: 1, perceive emotions; 2, facilitate thought; 3, understand emotions; 4, manage emotions	Part of hiring process; used for development at Wharton after year 1; planned for end of year 3
Self-assessment	Qualitative measurement: Fellows introspectively evaluate their own development and growth	End of year 3

(continues)

Exhibit 4-2. *(continued)*

Measurement Tool	Description	Timing
HoganLead Suite	The Hogan Leadership Forecast Series includes four development-focused reports. Based on Hogan's trademark assessments, the Hogan Personality Inventory, Hogan Development Survey, and the Motives, Values, Preferences Inventory, each report offers information regarding the characteristics, competencies, and values that underlie how a leader approaches work, leadership, and interaction with others in the workplace; for more information, go to http://www.hoganassessments.com/?q=content/hoganlead	Part of hiring process; used for development during the program; planned for end of year 3
Dean's assessment	Qualitative measurement: the dean provides regular feedback to each Fellow with respect to his or her development on all three desired outcomes	Every 6 months
Satisfaction with the program	Various statistics based on alumni surveys and available data	Annually
Alumni stories	Qualitative measurement: collecting success stories of alumni and tracking the development of their career after the program	Continually

The insight and experience garnered through the GLFP reveals that the training serves as a readily applicable, academic-experiential bridge for Fellows. Close monitoring at all stages of the program indicates that fellows consistently progress on several measures of collaboration, adult development, and leadership.

Following their 3-year participation and through the aforementioned assessments, an exhaustive, 360-degree review, which incorporates feedback from peers as well as mentors,, and a concluding self-analysis,* Global Leadership Fellows report having availed themselves of designing and executing activity in a true multi-stakeholder environment, gaining "a multi-sector, multi-discipline, and multi-regional perspective," acting with a more systemic viewpoint and breaking away from a more traditional, "siloed" mindset.[5] In addition to sharpening their understanding around these concepts, the Fellows live the experience of stakeholder management and leadership by virtue of their professional posts as community managers or equivalent within the World Economic Forum and thus practicing the cooperative mantra exercised by the organization. Reflective of the world stage, they note their increased comfort with the collaborative nature of work, citing their work as "builders of networks or communities."[6] The Fellows pinpointed the complexity and ambiguity facing their own work as critical challenges, in parallel with the environment of external actors engaged with Forum activity, not unlike the global environment.[7] Further, the GLFP assessment serves as a proxy for discerning the learning experience of *external* Forum participants, most of whom take advantage of the Forum's educational resources, including sessions at events, Forum Academy, Global Agenda Councils, and Forum projects.

Close attention is paid also to the evolution of the Fellows in line with the adult development stages of maturity or the "minds at work" adult development methodology. Created by developmental psychologist Robert Kegan, the framework provides a means by which to evaluate the progress of individuals with respect to their growth in self-awareness and systemic awareness. Close monitoring at all stages of the program, with extensive surveys at its outset and conclusion, reveals that more than half of the Fellows move from stage 3 (socializing mind) to stage 4 (self-authoring mind) over the course of the GLFP journey** (Exhibit 4-3). Such progress reflects the success of the

---

* At the conclusion of the GLFP, the Fellows complete an introspective self-assessment, describing various aspects of their individual journey, including responsibilities; achievements; lessons learned; skills, attributes, and behaviors; and development needs. The final report is reviewed with the Fellows' coaches as well as the dean.

** Literature on the methodology indicates that fewer than 10% of all leaders evaluated reach stage 5 (self-transforming mind), which is exemplified by leaders who enable themselves, their organizations, and their surrounding systems to realize success. Those who do evolve into this stage usually do not do so before midlife, in contrast to the average GLF cohort age (early 30s). The challenges associated with reaching the self-transforming phase underscore the serious need for continual, lifelong learning that can enable leaders to reach stage 5.

Exhibit 4-3. The "minds at work" methodology of Robert Kegan's adult development theory (stages 3, 4, and 5).

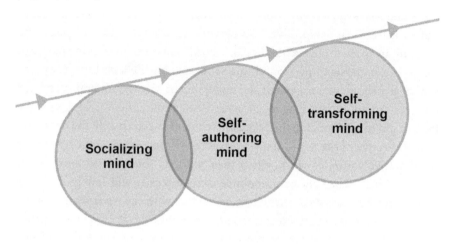

program in facilitating the movement of Fellows through stages at an accelerated rate.[8] Additionally, participants in the program demonstrate increased capacity with respect to three key dimensions of leadership development: leadership of self, leadership within organizations and collaborative systems, and leadership within a global context. Through rigorous qualitative and quantitative reporting, the Fellows demonstrate that because of their professional-academic arrangement, they are equipped to navigate—and excel in—each aspect.

On a biennial basis, and in collaboration with a Harvard University–based research team, assessments are conducted on the capacity of Fellows for "meaning making" as well as their ability to handle complexity. Developmental interviews are conducted with the Fellows right after joining and at the end of the program. The Fellows are given feedback on their individual results, which is followed up by the dean and by their coaches. In the end, an overall comparison is made with the conclusions about the development of the Fellows.

Each set of interviews is analyzed by Robert Kegan's research team based on the constructive developmental theory to determine whether or not the way that the Fellows make sense of their personal and professional experiences become more complex over the years. The Fellows are ranked based on where they stand regarding three key development stages of the increasing complexity in adult meaning-making: socializing mind, self-authoring mind, and self-transforming mind.

Results of the Report: Excerpt from the 2009 Summary of the Results of the 2006 Cohort

Developmental growth among the Fellows was remarkable in two ways. First, the fact that nearly every Fellow demonstrated transformational change suggests that their experiences over the 3 years were richly rewarding. Second, the rate of growth was very positive, with at least three Fellows making fairly large gains of almost half (.04) a stage or more.. While only one of these 11 Fellows constructed experience as complexly at the self-authoring mind at the outset of the program, five of the 11 did so at its end. While only four of 11 constructed experience at the beginning of the program in a fashion closer to self-authoring than socializing, by the end of the program nine of 11 were doing so.

These gains are somewhat exceptional within our research data, where trends have showed a longer time span for similar gains in developmental capacity. Specifically, the scores represented in Exhibit 4-4 indicate the following:

- Eighty-two percent of the Fellows' meaning-making became more complex over the 3 years at the World Economic Forum.
- None of the Fellows demonstrated meaning-making that was less complex than the third stage or more complex than the fourth stage of adult development in 2006 or 2009.
- Fifty percent of the Fellows whose meaning-making was dominated by the underlying principles of the third stage in 2006 evolved to be dominated by underlying principles of the fourth stage in 2009

Conclusion

Today's most pressing international issues transcend simple binary decision making and instead tap into the deepest reserves of both individual energy and collective commitment. Amidst a global backdrop that features both intricacy and uncertainty and that limits the capacity of individual actors, collaborative action serves as a compelling strategy. Through deliberately arranged partnerships, those in the public, private, and nonprofit spheres stand to mutually

Exhibit 4-4. Developmental scores from interviews.

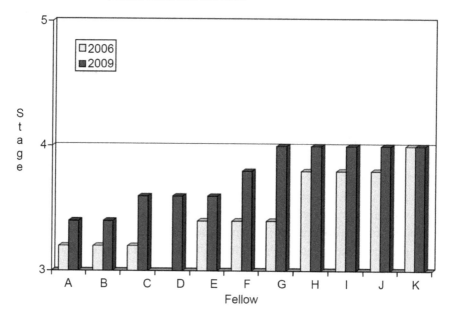

benefit while also positively shaping the global agenda. By accumulating unique experience and perspectives, collaboration represents the most viable means of generating critical solutions to the world's concerns.

Delivering such cooperative efforts requires leadership that can see beyond one sector.. Heads of organizations, corporate or otherwise, alongside societal leaders must demonstrate the willingness to engage the dissimilar insight of altogether different sectors and discern what is most valuable. In addition to executing multi-sectoral practices, leaders must guide others through a decidedly systemic lens: challenges are best addressed as part of a system rather than piecemeal. The profound nature of economic, political, and social challenges necessitates simultaneous understanding of the "micro" and the "macro." Inspiring innovative action emerges from leaders accounting for micro-decisions at individual institutions within their immediate sphere as well as the broader, macro-level, and then finding solutions that resonate across sectors and levels.

Indeed, the demands on today's leaders are numerous. The shifting dynamics and growing complexity of the international system serve as a clarion call for lifelong learning systems that make sense of the global reality and equip leaders to probe creative solutions. In the face of ambiguous information, such systems ought to provide space for reflection and introspection as well as provide a platform for creative application across sectors and geographies. In addition, lifelong learning itself should serve to encourage further learning and continual development. That is, learning systems should serve an inherently *perpetual* function. Doing so would provide leaders and citizens with an unquestionable advantage: an endless desire to fully question, explore, and develop.

Notes

1. World Economic Forum. (2009) *A Partner in Shaping History: The First 40 Years.* Geneva: World Economic Forum, p. 7.
2. Swisher, V. (2012). *Becoming an Agile Leader.* Minneapolis: Lominger International.
3. Booz & Company. (2011). "Accelerating Entrepreneurship in the Arab World.' Geneva: World Economic Forum. http://www3.weforum.org/docs/WEF_YGL_AcceleratingEntrepreneurshipArabWorld_Report_2011.pdf.
4. Millar, R. (2013). "Getting Personal: The World Economic Forum and the Power of Coaching," *Developing Leaders: Executive Education in Practice*, Issue 10: 42–48.
5. Khurana, R. and Baldwin, E. (2013). *The World Economic Forum's Global Leadership Fellows Program.* Boston: Harvard Business School Publishing, p. 6
6. Ibid.
7. Millar, "Getting Personal."
8. Millar, R. (2012). "Global Leaders for Tomorrow," *Developing Leaders: Executive Education in Practice*, Issue 6: 45–50; Khurana and Baldwin, *The World Economic Forum's Global Leadership Fellows Program.*

CHAPTER 5

Middlesex Community College
Evolving Programs to Meet Community Needs

Carole Cowan and Michelle LaPointe

iddlesex Community College (MCC), in Middlesex County, Massachusetts, was founded in the 1970s and originally designated as a health careers college. In support of that mission, the college was located in the Bedford, Massachusetts, Veterans Medical Center for two decades before moving to its own campus not far from the VA Medical Center. MCC expanded to Lowell, Massachusetts, in 1986 and now occupies a large, historic facility downtown and other facilities in the city, including the MCC's Health, Science, and Technology Center. MCC has continued to focus on careers in health, which gives the students an advantage in Massachusetts where the economy is booming in the areas of health care, medical research, and biotechnology research.

Lifelong Learning at Middlesex Community College

In the late 1950s, the Commonwealth of Massachusetts recognized a need for a greater diversity of programs and institutions in the higher education system. In the 1960s, the Commonwealth's first community college was founded in the Berkshire Mountains of Western Massachusetts. Within the Massachusetts higher education system, the community colleges were designed to be open pathways to bachelor's degree programs and to careers and career advancement. At their founding, each community college was created with a focus on a particular career area, but now all offer comprehensive programs. Each of the colleges has a distinctive program, though, because they adapt to local needs and partner with local organizations.

Middlesex Community College has adapted to economic and community changes to best serve the residents of Middlesex County. From the health-focused program in the VA hospital, it now offers courses off-site for a variety of employers and some public high schools. The college has formal articulations programs to facilitate transfer of credits between Middlesex and partnership schools, both to help high school students earn community college credit and to help Middlesex students transition to 4-year programs at other institutions. At the request of the local school district, the college created one of the first charter high schools in the Commonwealth to provide more applied experiences to students who were not succeeding in a traditional high school setting. Middlesex also has a contract with the Commonwealth to run career centers for the state Department of Labor. Throughout these changes, the faculty and staff of Middlesex Community College have relied on evidence of best practices, have collected data to ensure effective implementation, and have been willing to continually adapt as local needs change.

Programs for Every Stage of Life

Through a variety of programs, Middlesex serves students from ages 8 to 88. This includes summer programs for elementary students, a project with the local Girl Scouts to foster awareness of science, technology, engineering, and mathematics (STEM) careers, a charter high school, dual-enrollment programs for high school student (on campus and at a few local high schools), general equivalency diploma (GED) programs, college credits, professional certifications, training for workers (on campus and on their worksite), retraining for unemployed workers, and tuition discounts for retired residents of Massachusetts. Middlesex also participates in the federal Trio[1]* program, providing support to low-income students to succeed in high school and become first in their family to attend college. Students at the community college have great needs; 70% take developmental courses to prepare them for college-level work and half of the students receive financial aid.

---

*When the federal Trio programs were created as part of President Lyndon B. Johnson's Great Society initiative, there were indeed three programs: Upward Bound, Educational Talent Search, and Student Support Services. These services for low-income, first-in-their-family college students have expanded to seven programs, but the nickname persists. For more information, go to http://www2.ed.gov/about/offices/list/ope/trio/index.html.

Partners

Middlesex is able to adapt to local needs because of close relationship with local organizations. Not only do these relationships help Middlesex stay abreast of shifts in the economy and in the skills and education prized in the community, but they facilitate the implementation of programs at every stage of life. Although relationships may develop around short-term projects and initiatives, they often develop into enduring relationships to support formal education and professional training and certification. Partners foster both formal education and workforce training.

Partners to Support Continuing Formal Education. Middlesex has both articulation agreements with high schools (dual enrollment) and transfer agreements with other colleges. The Commonwealth of Massachusetts provides a strong framework to facilitate transfers within the public system of higher education, and Middlesex goes further to develop specific articulation agreements so that the students can seamlessly begin a program at Middlesex and complete it at a partner institution. In addition, MCC participates in joint admissions with four University of Massachusetts undergraduate programs with seven of the state universities and Suffolk University in Boston. These programs allow students to be admitted to both institutions simultaneously and, contingent on successful completion of courses, the students are guaranteed a place at the partner university.

Partnerships to Strengthen Workforce Development. Middlesex has a strong model for partnering with local employers to promote workforce development (Exhibit 5-1). The partnerships rest on three pillars: (1) relationships between faculty and employers, (2) faculty and administrators staying abreast of changes in the local economy, and (3) the strong reputation of alumni. This model is particularly successful due to the college's history of being responsive to local employers. For example, the Leahy Clinic approached Middlesex Community College to provide nursing certification for their employees. Leahy employees were having trouble getting certification given the long waiting lists for nursing programs. Leahy pays tuition for their employees to attend courses at Middlesex, and the clinic established a nursing lab at its own facility to support the training. In addition, the college and Lowell General Hospital have a grant so the college can adapt training programs to meet the

Exhibit 5-1. Organizational partners.

Other colleges and universities	• Boston University • Suffolk University • Other Massachusetts institutions of higher education
Local high schools	• Lowell High School • Billerica High School
Employers	• Bedford VA Hospital • TJX Companies • Smaller local employers (primarily hospitals and direct/in kind support for specific programs)

ongoing needs of the hospital. It is common for employers to repeatedly hire graduates of the college and, once they witness the success of individual employees, and to reach out to the college to provide ongoing training to all their employees.

Program Design

Middlesex Community College is a cost-effective option for learners at every stage, although the focus of this study is adult education and workforce development, such as adults who are seeking professional certifications to provide more career options, and unemployed workers who receive training and job search assistance. The college also offers special education and remedial education services to help students improve their academic readiness for the demands of college. Also, some MCC students are traditional college students who are taking introductory courses at Middlesex to save tuition money as they earn a 4-year degree. The following is a brief description of the types of programs offered at Middlesex.

Professional Certifications

Middlesex Community College offers 24 programs leading to professional certification. Many are targeted at the important sectors in the Massachusetts economy: biotech and research (biotechnology technician, clinical laboratory assistant), and health care (medical assistant, dental assistant, nursing assistant, phlebotomy medical office administration). Students in these programs accrue credits toward an associate's degree, and, in many cases, upon passing a certification exam, they receive a professional credential. Other programs document mastery of professional skills (computer-aided design, graphic design, hospitality management) and students accrue credits toward an associate's degree. There are also programs targeted at professionals who have completed a bachelor's degree and are seeking a professional credential or state certification.

One-Stop Centers

About 20 years ago, the Commonwealth of Massachusetts redesigned its workforce development system and created the one-stop centers as part of a new federal model of workforce investment boards, which primarily serve the unemployed. These centers connect people with retraining programs, sponsor job fairs, and generally helping place clients in jobs. Initially, MCC successfully competed for the one-stop center in its geographic district. In the most recent competition to manage the one-stop centers, MCC took over the management of a second one-stop center when the incumbent organization failed to meet the standards in the annual evaluation. Now MCC runs two centers in Middlesex County.

Developmental or Remedial Courses and Tutoring

These special services can be divided into three broad categories: (1) developmental or remedial courses and tutoring; (2) basic education (e.g., GED courses, English as a second language courses); and (3) special education and services for students with disabilities. These services are important at MCC because experience and outside research shows that community colleges with a strong support system for students who need remediation have improved course completion rates.[2] In addition, the more time students spend in development classes, the less likely they are to graduate.[3] Although there may not be immediate gains in pass rates, there appear to be gains when the support services have been in place longer.

Many MCC students received special education services in high school, but these programs are harder to secure at the college level. These students require services above and beyond the remediation that has been traditionally offered at community colleges. Although the Americans with Disabilities Act requires that any student who enrolls at a community college must receive support and accommodations, there is little funding to support these services.

For example, while the Commonwealth pays for special education in elementary school and high school, there are no supports for special education in the higher education system. MCC has invested considerable resources in supporting students with special needs despite the fact that, in some cases, these services cost much more than the students pay in tuition and fees. Middlesex does have a federal Trio grant, but MCC's service model is very labor intensive and may not be sustainable if that grant funding is cut.

Special education at MCC has a service model that combines classroom instruction and supplemental support (including one-on-one tutoring), case management, metacognitive supports, self-advocacy training, as well as helping students develop interpersonal skills. The college has worked diligently to accelerate developmental education to minimize the amount of time spent preparing to take for-credit courses. One strategy for acceleration is the newly developed math program called Ramp-Up Mathematics© (Pearson). Ramp-Up© includes 12 online modules (up through Algebra II). Passing the course requires finishing four modules, but students can finish all 12 and place out of developmental math in one semester. Although it is a self-paced, online program, students enroll in 3 hours of class and one lab period per week. Classes are facilitated by a teacher and a tutor.

College-Level Courses

In addition to helping students prepare for work and college, MCC also offers college-level credits. These credits also lead to an associate's degree from MCC or can be transferred to a 4-year degree program. About 20% of MCC students continue their formal education, transferring to a variety of competitive institutions.

In addition to supporting students who apply to transfer, Middlesex participates in articulation agreements with specific institutions. These include a joint admissions program, a bachelor's completion program, and transfer paths for specific MCC majors. In addition to helping student transition to the next stage in their lifelong learning, some of these agreements include scholarships or tuition discounts.

Middlesex Community College has a joint admissions program* with the four University of Massachusetts undergraduate campuses, seven state universities, and Suffolk University. Students apply to both schools at once and

---

* The Commonwealth of Massachusetts is phasing out this program.

complete their introductory courses at Middlesex. If they maintain a 2.5 grade point average, they can continue at the partner institution where they were jointly admitted. Students with at least a 3.0 average receive a 33% discount on in-state tuition at the public universities participating in the joint admissions program.

Additional programs facilitate completing a bachelor's degree. Middlesex has a bachelor's completion program with Salem State University, leading to a 4-year degree in either criminal justice or early childhood education. The biotechnology program also has articulation and transfer agreements with Boston University and the University of Massachusetts–Lowell. Other universities also accept the 66 credits of the MCC biotechnology program. Students have also transferred biotechnology credits to other University of Massachusetts campuses and Northeastern University. Students transferring to Boston University also receive a Boston University community scholarship, which pays for 50% of their tuition.

Impact

Middlesex Community College has worked diligently for over 40 years to meet the needs of its students and the local community. The impact of the college can be seen in many ways. Program statistics for MCC are impressive, with most students successfully completing a program or degree. This in turn improves career opportunities and outcomes for alumni. MCC has also had an impact on employers, building relationships that meet their workforce development needs. All of this translates into a strong return on investment.

Program Outcomes

Middlesex Community College has been in existence for 45 years. Beginning with space provided by the VA hospital, it has grown to be one of the largest community colleges in Massachusetts. Currently, the college serves 13,000 mostly part-time students (or the equivalent of 7,000 full-time enrollments).

Community colleges measure their success in both program completion and transfer rates to other institutions. Middlesex Community College is exemplary on both counts. Course completion rates average 75%. First-time pass rates on professional certifications exams are also high: dental hygiene, 100%; radiology technician, 86%; nursing education (National Council Licen-

Exhibit 5-2. Four-year colleges that commonly accept MCC transfer students.

• Amherst College	• Lesley University
• Babson College	• Mount Holyoke College
• Bentley College	• Northeastern University
• Boston University	• Regis College
• Brandeis University	• St. Joseph's College (ME)
• Johns Hopkins University	• Wellesley College

sure Examination in Nursing [NCLES-RN]), 83%. In 2012, MCC awarded degrees and certificates to 1,235 students, including 185 certificates and 1,050 associate's degrees. In addition, 20% of students are accepted into programs at another college or university.

As noted earlier, MCC has a variety of articulation agreements with 4-year degree programs. Of the 20% of MCC students who transfer to another college or university, most students transfer to a campus of the University of Massachusetts or Massachusetts State University system. Some of these students transferred to another community college. A significant number of students transfer to competitive private colleges and universities (Exhibit 5-2).

Middlesex Community College works hard to make every program and student successful. The organization partnerships provide students with hands-on experience to enhance mastery of professional skills and facilitate transfers to 4-year programs. Careful refection, awareness of best practices, and analysis of data are important for improving special education, remediation, and developmental education. The earlier description of the newly implementing RAMP Up is just one example of efforts to improve outcomes. In 2010–2011, fall-to-spring persistence rates for RAMP Up students were 60% compared with 51% for students enrolled in the traditional math sequence. The completion rate for the RAMP Up sequence is 68%, compared with 52% of students in the traditional math sequence in 2010. Middlesex constantly strives to improve programs and services.

Student Outcomes

These program outcomes have a direct impact on MCC alumni. All MCC students have jobs when they graduate, in part because they are likely to be already working part-time to pay for school, but also because many job placements and internships lead directly to jobs. Completing a program at a

Massachusetts community college is a big boost to a graduate's earning potential. A study commissioned by the Massachusetts Community College system[4] in 2002 found that completing a program at a Massachusetts community college more than doubles annual earnings—from $21,200 to $42,600. Over their working life, community college graduates earn $330,000 more than students who did not attend or failed to graduate.

Benefits to Employers

Local employers know that they can turn to MCC to recruit qualified, credentialed employees to fill staffing vacancies. In addition, when a business needs to provide credentials to an entire cohort of employees, the college will tailor a program to that employer's specific needs and often provide the courses on-site at the business. As noted earlier, this has led to many partnerships between the college and local employers. Employers who hire MCC graduates repeatedly return to recruit more employees. MCC has expanded the pool of qualified applicants in the region, which has improved the employment pipeline and made succession planning easier for local businesses. Businesses also report saving resources due to reductions in turnover, so less money is spent on recruiting.

Return on Investments

Nationally, return on federal investments in community colleges is almost $5 for each dollar spent.[5] The Commonwealth of Massachusetts estimates that completing a program at a Massachusetts community college more than doubles a worker's annual earnings, which, in turn, increases the Commonwealth's income tax revenue. Estimating that a career spans three decades, the Commonwealth can expect $25.2 million in additional tax revenues from the community college cohort that graduated in 2001. Given that 90% of community college graduates stay in the Commonwealth, this income tax revenue stays in Massachusetts.[6]

Conclusion

There are several factors that enable Middlesex Community College to sustain and improve its programs. Two of the most important are staying aware of best practices and weaving together myriad grants to support the diverse offering. Both of these factors have allowed MCC to continually meet the needs of lifelong learners in their community.

Best Practices

The faculty and staff of MCC are continually looking for ways to improve their programs and services. They use research and evidence to guide programmatic changes. College administrators also eagerly participate in state and pilot programs, not only to help refine what is known about best practices at community colleges but also to stay connected to other colleges. This knowledge of research and best practices allows Middlesex to innovate. One example of the innovation at MCC is the way the college embraced online learning as early as 1996, when it piloted one course with 77 enrollments. In the 2010–2011 school year, online enrollment was 8,283. Many of these are hybrid courses, and some target a specific area of concern, such as the RAMP Up developmental math program.

In addition, the college actively seeks out information about the local economy. Several years ago, the Donohue Institute of the University of Massachusetts released a report highlighting a lack of jobs for community college graduates in biotechnology. In reaction to the report, Middlesex approached employers and other community colleges to strengthen program requirements. This is typical of the college's evolution: curriculum is constantly adjusted based on the job market.

None of this is done in a vacuum. Every year MCC surveys students and reviews data on course completion, academic achievement, and the placements of graduates. The data it collects helps the school adapt best practices to best meet the needs of its students.

Leveraging Resources

Although community colleges are historically state-funded institution in Massachusetts, the Commonwealth provides less than 35% of MCC's operating budget. Continued success relies on actively seeking grants to support programing. During the 2010–2011 school year, MCC had about 50 different grants to support programming.[7]

Many of these grants came from federal and state education agencies, tied to innovative programming or targeted to specific populations. The college also received funding from other public agencies. At the federal level, MCC has grants from the Department of Labor, the Department of Energy, the Department of Housing and Urban Development, and the National Science Foundation. At the state level, additional grant funding comes from the Department of Labor, the Department of Mental Retardation, the Office of the Attorney General, the Executive Office of Health and Human Services, and the Massachusetts Campus Compact. Locally, the college receives grants from the Lowell Public School District, Lowell High School, and the Cultural Organization of Lowell. Finally, the college receives money from private foundations, national associations, and its own foundation. Leverage is key to MCC's success. These grants provide an opportunity to leverage services in a rich fabric that otherwise would not be possible.

Since its founding in 1970, Middlesex Community College has served increasing numbers of students by providing an increasingly diverse array of programs. Not only are the offerings diverse, but the options for where students earn credits continues to expand: two campuses, on-line courses, and on-site courses for employers. Middlesex Community College's dedication to change and improve is illustrated by the Ramp-Up program. Given the college's deep experience with online learning, this developmental program seemed a natural extension of existing development services. The passion is not just for innovation but also for providing high-quality services. Not only was RAMP Up a carefully designed program, but the college has monitored the implementation to be sure it is meeting the needs of students. This implementation reflects the priority Middlesex Community College puts on remaining adaptable so that it can meet the needs of students and employers in its community.

Notes

1. Gerlaugh, K., Thompson, L., Boylan, H. & Davis, H. (2007). "National Study of Developmental Education." Research in Developmental Education, 20, (4). Boone, NC: Appalachian State University. http://ncde.appstate.edu/sites/ncde.appstate.edu/files/RiDE%2020-4.pdf.
2. Burley, H., Cejda, B. & Butner, B. (2001). *Dropout and Stopout Patterns Among Developmental Education Students in Texas Community Colleges.Community College Journal of Research and Practice.* Volume 25, Issue 10, 2001, pp. 767–782. See also, the National Post-

secondary Education Cooperative (NPEC), http://nces.ed.gov/npec/papers.asp, and the reports from the National Symposium on Postsecondary Success.

3. Massachusetts Community Colleges Executive Office. (2002). A Smart Investment. Boston, MA. http://www.masscc.org/pdfs/economicimpactreport.pdf.

4. Eyster, L. (2010). "Cost-Benefit Analysis of the American Graduation Initiative." Paper presented at the APPAM Fall Conference, Boston, MA.

5. Ibid.

6. LaPointe, M. & Chmielewski, E. (2011). "Investing in Community Colleges of the Commonwealth: A Review of Funding Streams," *Mosakowski Institute for Public Enterprise*. Paper 7. http://commons.clarku.edu/mosakowskiinstitute/7.

CHAPTER 6

University of Liverpool
Online Degree Programs for Professionals

Murray M. Dalziel

C an you seriously learn in a completely asynchronous online environment? Over the past 10 years, the University of Liverpool has repeatedly answered this question: Yes, online learning allows working adults to deepen their professional knowledge as they apply their studies in their ongoing work experience. Until recently there has been a great deal of skepticism about nontraditional or non-classroom learning. While some suspicion of asynchronous, online education lingers, the debate has changed, and the University of Liverpool's management programs are now accredited by the Association to Advance Collegiate Schools of Business (AACSB). While we are in no way advocating our method of teaching online for every student and program, we believe that for the population we serve—the working professional—this is a viable alternative that provides quality education for many more people than can be reached by traditional methods.

Background

The University of Liverpool started to develop online programs in 2000. Why would a research-intensive, highly regarded university make this type of decision that bucked the tradition of attending courses in-person? The reasons are important because they shape the whole approach to the venture to date. Unlike some competitors in the United Kingdom, the University of Liverpool had never engaged in any type of "distance learning" (usually a blend of classroom and remote, self-paced instruction). From the start, there was a strong belief that the university would lead the wave of a new generation of methods for delivering graduate education. Accordingly, the university made a huge commitment to the online delivery method. At the time only the Open University, founded by British Royal Charter in 1969, was engaged in delivering "distance learning" at any level of scale, and most of its programs included a mix of online and face-to-face sessions. Given the novelty of online learning, the University of Liverpool partnered with Laureate International, an experienced provider of online education.*

The university committed to this method, and continues to work with a larger private sector provider, for the following reasons:

- The university felt it was too dependent on undergraduate teaching and the then Higher Education Funding Council grant. Revenue growth would come from graduate education. The Management School had just been established, and although there were considerable expectations about the growth in the number of master's degrees in business administration (MBA) that the school would award, undergraduates still dominated the revenue streams. Online provision that would be available globally and on a flexible basis would accelerate entry into the graduate market.

- Constraints of real estate expansion would be a barrier to growth. Online was an attractive alternative.

- There could be a different delivery method for a research-intensive university. On-campus academics would not have their research time constrained by rapid growth in numbers if the university developed materials that could be delivered under supervision through a network of other academics. Given the research objectives of the university, this was an equally compelling reason.

- These ventures and other ventures to expand higher education need more capital than either the United Kingdom Treasury was willing to underwrite or the university could sustain through regular cash flows. There was a belief, consequently, that more private sector providers would enter the market. The university believed that it was better to be on the leading wave of this movement rather than face competition from much better capitalized competitors later on.

The initial programs focused on business studies (MBA degree), public health (master's degree in public health), and information management

---

* Initially, the University of Liverpool worked with KIT E-learning, which is now part of Laureate International Universities (Laureate Education, Baltimore, MD).

(master's degree in information management). Subsequent programs have been added in law, and the portfolio within the original three areas expanded. Two professional doctorates have also been added. Today, more than 10,000 students are registered in degree programs.

Program Description

The University of Liverpool online degree programs are firmly focused on graduate education for working professionals and are based on the following pedagogical principles:

- Students are engaged in and responsible for their own learning, and they have some element of control over their learning environment. This is a principle that also applies to on-campus learning, but it is particularly relevant in an online environment and especially one that is targeted to professionals in the workplace.
- Relevance and authenticity: students learn better when the real test of their learning needs are the demands of their work. Therefore, students are encouraged to reflect on, test out, and apply their learning each week in their workplace setting.
- Co-constructed knowledge: there is group work and collaboration in learning. Classes are typically learning sets with an average of 14 students (and no more than 21), so that the work in the classroom is heavily interactive. In addition, students are geographically diverse, so they learn to collaborate on virtual, global teams.
- Learning is problem-focused and encourages reflection and application.
- Students follow a learning journey; learning tasks and assessments are appropriate to the stage of that journey. This affects program structure, and programs have a clear beginning, middle, and end.
- Students develop master's/doctoral level learning skills with a clear statement about what master's or doctoral level learning means. This is equivalent to what would be required on-campus.

Target Audience

Even though the mix of programs has expanded, the target audience is clearly defined as "professionals at work." The average age of students is 39. Most

Exhibit 6-1. Global participation in University of Liverpool programs.

Active Students by Region	2012
Africa	36.5%
The Americas	24.3%
Asia	10.4%
Europe	15.2%
Middle East	13.6%

students are looking to enhance their career (as opposed to changing industry or vocation). This drives the basic design of the curriculum (material has to be relevant to their working situations). The pedagogy has to respect the students' desire for flexibility, given the full-time demands of their roles. The faculty has to be able to work with mature adults engaged in solving problems at work.

The target audience of professionals at work is also geographically dispersed. Part of the mission is to make quality education accessible to a wide range of people who otherwise would not be able to take advantage of a purely campus-based experience. African and Middle Eastern countries send the most students because British institutions have already established brand reputations and the University of Liverpool has higher recognition there (Exhibit 6-1).

Recruiting Students

The Internet largely drives the marketing of these online programs worldwide, although there is more emphasis on those countries where the University of Liverpool has a brand presence and where online degrees are accepted by employers. Although many potential students in India or China tend to eschew online degrees, we do have students from these regions and we are actively recruiting in these large higher education markets.

Program Admissions

The entrance criteria are similar to those for campus programs. Students must have good academic preparation that will enable them to study at a master's level at a world-class, research-intensive university. Many applicants do not have traditional academic backgrounds, so their work preparation has to be significant, and they must demonstrate that they have both the discipline and the aptitude to take these courses. There is considerable room for innovation in serving nontraditional students. When we embarked on these programs, the academic community as a whole was quite skeptical of wholly online degrees, so to date our approach to recruiting and admissions has been very conservative.

Scale in this operation involves both geographic coverage and overall student numbers. Our belief is that the processes required to run an online operation differ in several respects from campus operations. The University of Liverpool does not have the core competencies to exploit large online operations. This is particularly true in marketing (to a large population of adults in several regions who want to study parttime) and in student administration (counseling large numbers of applicants, managing students in and out of small classes that are opening and closing each month, keeping track of part-time students, and having instructors available around-the-clock on a flexible basis). These functions are assigned to Laureate Education (Baltimore, MD).

In addition, to build online programs requires considerable capital. That is another reason that the University of Liverpool chose to partner with a for-profit company for this type of activity. Over the last 10 years Laureate Education has invested over $77 million in capital on these programs.

Program Design

Students work in small, interactive, virtual teams. We believe that this corresponds closely to the reality of working in global enterprises and global markets. Consequently, we embed key skills for the global marketplace and establish communities that are able to work across geographic boundaries. Students often report that this is one of the benefits of the program that they did not anticipate when they joined; working in small cross-cultural teams every day is challenging and sharpens their learning.

In addition to mirroring the work environment of the 21st century, the program is also driven by the following principles:

- *Co-construction of knowledge*: We use technology to create learning communities that collaborate in bringing their experiences to life. Discussion and sharing of information are equally important for these experienced professionals, as it helps them shape their own learning.

- *Learning not teaching*: We expect that instructors will facilitate learning rather than teaching from the "front of the classroom." We are gradually adding video and other segments as technology improves, but we see these as "add-ons." Traditionally, we have avoided "beaming in academics" from the classroom. While we have no difficulty seeing the potential benefits from MOOCS (massive open online courses), we take an approach in which the student is at the center, not the instructor.

- *Experience as a source of learning*: We do not believe that learning is achieved by accumulating experiences, but rather that these experiences are essential to the learning process. We help students to question traditional and commonly held beliefs. This is particularly important in subjects such as management, in which there is any number of popular fads that constitute part of the body of knowledge that our students must sift through.

- *Critical reflection*: This can take a number of forms. We encourage students to become much more self-aware. The nature of the basic pedagogy where students are in constant interaction with each other provides an important source for having them discover more about the relational aspects both with learning and with their actual work.

Another key competency that all the programs nourish is how to work interactively across cultures. Many visitors to our programs are skeptical that we can create the depth of discussion that they would expect to see in conventional classroom situations. However, both observers and students report that many times these discussions are as deep as and as intense as what happens in a classroom or indeed any work-based co-located team.

Finally, one of the fundamental competencies of the program is the discipline of self-directed, lifelong learning. Anecdotally, although most students are pleased to graduate, many report having developed a discipline that they wish to keep going. (This is one reason we introduced professional doctorates.)

Program Structure

To earn credits toward their degree, students enroll in a series of modules. Each module typically lasts 8 weeks (in the MBA program the introductory module, "Learning to Be a Leader," lasts 10 weeks). The modules are organized to provide one-to-one and one-to-many interactions. A range of learning devices are used, including the following:

- Group discussions: Each week the instructor poses a discussion question that requires students to elaborate on a problem. These discussion threads form the core of each week's seminars and are open for the whole of the module, so that students can use them as a basic referral resource and can see how learning is advancing.
- Group projects: Groups work together on a specific project. The work is largely asynchronous, although students can opt to conduct live conference calls as part of their preparation. Special spaces in the virtual classroom are designed for them to store discussions, and folders are available in which to post specific materials. Instructors are encouraged to enter this space and offer formative feedback.
- Individual assignments: These are completed independently and sent directly to the instructor.
- Informal discussions: There are spaces online for students to interact with each other and to contact their instructors "outside" of the formal classroom.

Throughout their program, students on average spend 15 to 20 hours a week in the classroom. Their time is divided equally among the following activities: reading and assimilating the week's content, readings, and lecture notes; participating in the weekly discussion; and completing and submitting assignments. The instructor gives continual formative feedback (summarized once a week), and submits grades at the end of each week for each assessed element. There is therefore a continual process of assimilation of theory (from the weekly content), creation of new knowledge through discussion, and the improvement of performance through formative and evaluative processes.

Every program ends with an independent piece of research or consultancy project. This occurs after students have successfully completed eight modules of instruction. To graduate they need to submit a dissertation or, for some programs (for example, MBA), a consultancy project. There is a dedicated online space to support this work, and students have access to their supervisor as well as to informal peer support groups as they progress in their work.

Neither part-time education nor online learning are a good fit for every student. Many students have difficulty with the self-discipline required to benefit from online learning. Inevitably, many students are unrealistic about their time commitments to work and to their personal lives, and they do not realize that they may have to change their priorities in order to accommodate the new program. In addition, our program is typically a student's first experience with online, asynchronous learning. There are variations by program, but generally about half of the students who enroll in an online course soon realize that an online degree program is not for them and they drop out. Therefore, the initial module is a key experience for students taking an online degree program, and students are not billed until the end of the second week; this is the case only for the first module. We also run "taster sessions" to encourage students to discover for themselves what is required. This is an area where there is considerable room for innovation, and over the next 5 years we will develop a program to test different approaches to preparing students for online learning.

Program Quality

All programs have defined learning goals and competency statements. The business programs have developed assessment of learning processes as required by the "assurance of learning" processes of the AACSB. Each program's learning goals are divided into observable traits that are measured in each of the core modules (Exhibit 6-2). These traits are assessed across a sample of students each time the module is taken. Modules that are not contributing to the learning goals are discussed at an annual program review and revised.

Academic Integrity

The maintenance of academic integrity is a central tenet of our online model, oriented primarily to educate, but ultimately to sanction unethical behavior. Students complete a number of assignments in their first module oriented to educating them about the principles and mechanics of academic integrity, and they sign an Academic Honesty Declaration at the beginning of every module. All online faculty members attend obligatory training in the detection and handling of plagiarism; all student assignments have to be submitted through matching software (Turnitin, iParadigms Inc., Oakland, CA). The university delegates the role of assessment officer to the senior Laureate academic, who recommends appropriate sanctions to the plagiarism subcommittee of the board of examiners (chaired by a University of Liverpool Management School faculty member). Additional protection is provided by the continual monitoring

Exhibit 6-2. Example of assurance of learning.

GOAL 4: Students will demonstrate that they are able to perform effectively within a team, selecting an appropriate leadership style for different situations

- Objective: Students will meaningfully contribute to a team demonstrating the ability to recognize and utilize individuals' contributions in group processes and to negotiate and persuade or influence others, leading to a decision on a management problem.

MAPPING:

Trait Number	Traits	Example Evidence of Learning
T4.1	Sustains a committed working relationship with colleagues	KMBA712 Finance and Accounting for Managers Wk 5 DQ2
T4.2	Contributes workable ideas, research, and analysis	KMBA712 Finance and Accounting for Managers Wk 5 DQ2
T4.3	Enhances the quality of the final deliverable	KMBA712 Finance and Accounting for Managers Wk 5 DQ2
T4.4	Operates effectively as part of a team with sensitivity to cultural diversity	KMBA712 Finance and Accounting for Managers Wk 5 DQ2
T4.5	Contributes to facilitation in teamwork	KMBA712 Finance and Accounting for Managers Wk 5 DQ2
T4.6	Recognizes and can evaluate the contribution and skills of self and others in teamwork	KMBA712 Finance and Accounting for Managers Wk 5 DQ2

DESCRIPTOR:

Traits	Does Not Meet Expectations	Meets Expectations	Exceeds Expectations
Sustains a committed working relationship with colleagues	Irregular attendance on group discussion board/ collaborative space (misses >30%)	Regularly interacts with group discussion board/ collaborative space but occasionally fails to interact or does not complete task	Engages fully with group discussions/collaborative space, punctual and flexible

Traits	Does Not Meet Expectations	Meets Expectations	Exceeds Expectations
Contributes workable ideas, research, and analysis	Rarely prepares for group discussions	Prepares adequately in advance but might not have read widely	Prepares thoroughly, reads widely, and carries out extensive research
Enhances the quality of the final deliverable	Rarely contributes ideas, research, or analysis	Suggests ideas and participates in research and analysis but is not proactive	Brings ideas and proactively engages in research and analysis
Operates effectively as part of a team with sensitivity to cultural diversity	Does not actively engage with alternative ideas or accept contributions from group members	Engages with others but might be weak in encouraging their contributions	Does not dominate, and encourages others to contribute
Contributes to facilitation in teamwork	Rarely facilitates the team	Is able to adequately facilitate the team but is not always forthcoming in such roles	Demonstrates the qualities of good facilitation in teamwork
Recognizes and can evaluate the contribution and skills of self and others in teamwork	Is unable to recognize and evaluate the contribution and skills of self and others in teamwork	Is able to recognize and evaluate the contribution and skills of self and others in teamwork but with some level of weakness	Demonstrates a good ability to recognize and evaluate the contribution and skills of self and others in teamwork

of the classes by University of Liverpool faculty, who identify and submit any suspicious assignments to the assessment officer for investigation.

Program Impact

Surveys of participants report the most satisfaction from work-related outcomes. For example, in an in-depth survey of 145 MBA students graduating in 2012, 76% reported career or job improvements that they attributed to the program. For many students there are multiple outcomes. According to the survey, one third of participants received salary increases. One year after completing the program, among those in the 2012 cohort who received a raise, the median salary increase was 20%. One third of respondents credit the program with helping them achieve a desired change in their professional career. Although most do this within their own organizations, about 20% switched organizations. Almost half of those were in a new organization that they had created themselves. One quarter of survey respondents believed that they are able to better contribute to societal issues.

Many employers value degrees from a university brand that they can trust. But for most employers the largest benefit of online learning is the flexibility it provides employees to continue working full-time. A wholly asynchronous online program provides even greater flexibility than other part-time options where students must be released for specific time periods. The University of Liverpool's online programs allow students to study at their own pace and in their time. But they continue working on job-related problems through the lens of their postgraduate studies.

Conclusion

Since 2000, over 7,000 students have graduated with degrees from the University of Liverpool's online programs. We have no doubt that online learning that is 100% asynchronous works. There are, of course, competencies that are harder to develop online as compared with in a classroom setting. For example, verbal presentation skills are quite hard to cultivate in an asynchronous, online program, although not impossible as advances in technology increases. On the other hand, the ability to work in global virtual teams, an increasingly common experience in today's corporate world, is very hard to foster in a classroom. As in any pedagogy, there will be trade-offs. We believe that for this group of students this trade-off is worth it.

Learning to be adaptable is highly correlated with effective work performance. Corporate training departments can foster some of this, but individuals globally have a great appetite to enhance their own learning. There is no reason to dream about one day visiting a campus and taking time off to do that. They can do that now—on planes, in hotels, in cafes, and in their own homes. Online programs at the University of Liverpool demonstrate that the quality of that experience can be high.

SECTION III

EMPLOYERS

This section reports on a range of employer-supported lifelong learning programs. Some employers focus on the professional development of their employees or on developing the skills of potential employees. Other employers focus on developing the untapped human potential in their communities. In each case, the organization recognizes that human capital is its most vital asset and invests in providing support for learning at different life stages.

We begin the section with an interview with the vice president of human resources and organization at United Technologies Corporation (UTC). UTC demonstrates its commitment to each employee's lifelong learning through a comprehensive tuition assistance program. The interview highlights the following issues, which are further developed by the featured employees:

- Remaining competitive requires direct participation to develop a competitive workforce pipeline.
- Workforce development and professional learning are complex endeavors that require coordination of multiple components and leveraging the resources of partner organizations.
- Investments in programs carry an expectation of realizing immediate impact, return, and results.

Executive Perspective

United Technologies Corporation: Employee Scholar Program

Elizabeth Amato

United Technologies Corporation's (UTC's) employer-sponsored education program has been touted as the best in the world.

Since 1996, UTC has encouraged employees to pursue the degree program of their choice. UTC pays tuition directly to the employee's school, ensuring accessibility for employees at all levels of the organization. The commitment is more than financial: employees are eligible for up to 3 hours of paid study time-off per week. Both full-time and part-time employees worldwide become eligible for the Employee Scholar Program after 1 year of service.

We interviewed Beth Amato, UTC's senior vice president of human resources and organization. She articulated how the Employee Scholar Program aligns with UTC's ACE (Achieving Competitive Excellence) operating model, which promotes a commitment to continuous improvement and best-in-class, innovative products and services.

United Technologies' employer-sponsored education program has been touted as the best in the world. From a historical context, what led UTC to decide to make this incredible investment in its people? In other words, why was it started and what was its original purpose?

We have benchmarked extensively and found UTC's Employee Scholar Program is, in fact, one of the best in the world. Our former chairman and chief executive officer, George David, created the program because he firmly believed that the ongoing education of employees played a significant role in ensuring their long-term success.

It is our philosophy that while private employers cannot guarantee lifelong employment, responsible companies can provide employees with lifelong learning opportunities. Evidence suggests that employees who utilize the program are twice as likely to be promoted and are less likely to leave the company than those who do not participate.

Can you describe how the program works, regarding such issues as eligibility, curricular options, and program partners? What differentiates it from other corporate models?

The UTC Employee Scholar Program is unique because it is designed to minimize the cost of higher education for our employees. UTC covers the cost of tuition, books, and fees for master's, bachelor's, and associate's degree programs. These costs are covered up front and paid directly by UTC to the college or university rather than reimbursed to employees after course completion. Employees may study any subject at any accredited UTC approved university, whether or not it relates to their current position with the company. UTC has more than 3,000 approved schools that employees can attend. Our methodology behind selecting these UTC-approved institutions is not based on cost, but rather on ensuring that employees are receiving a high-quality education. Ivy League schools, such as Yale and Harvard, are included on our approved list.

Additionally, employees are eligible for up to 3 hours of paid study time-off per week. Both full-time and part-time employees worldwide become eligible for the Employee Scholars Program when they have completed 1 year of service.

What are the current goals of the Employee Scholar Program? How do they align with and advance the priorities of the company?

United Technologies Corporation is committed to having the most educated workforce on the planet. Our highly skilled workforce helps us to constantly innovate and remain competitive in the aerospace and building systems industries. The program supports the company's goals of attracting and retaining talent in the highly competitive global market. The Employee Scholar Program reflects UTC's ACE (Achieving Competitive Excellence) operating model, which promotes a commitment to continuous improvement and best-in-class innovative products and services.

What other factors have you addressed or implemented to make the program a success: commitments/sponsorship of senior leadership, fostering an organizational culture that supports education and allows the necessary time for learning, or other factors?

Support for the UTC Employee Scholars Program begins from the top level of management and is embedded within our corporate culture. Since the program's inception in 1996, UTC has invested more than $1.1 billion in employee education, and UTC employees have earned over 36,000 degrees. Employees are encouraged to participate in the Employee Scholars Program, and all requests to participate are approved if basic eligibility requirements are met. Some UTC-approved educational institutions also offer unique teaching methods that may include web-based learning or on-site classes at UTC facilities, which makes it easier for UTC employees to complete courses. The program is designed to remove barriers for employees and make enrolling, studying, and completing a degree as seamless as possible.

What challenges/barriers have you had to overcome (or address regularly)? How do you manage the obstacles and maintain momentum?

One challenge we face is global participation. While the program was always global, participation outside of the United States continues to lag. The main reason for this is differences in the maturity of educational systems across the globe. Specifically, the availability and maturity of part-time education in the United States exceeds that of part-time education in other countries. Currently, 60% of UTC employees work outside of the United States, but they comprise only 30% of Employee Scholar Program participants.

How has success been measured on factors such as recruiting, retention, productivity, and innovation? Have you gotten a return on the investment?

More than 7,500 UTC employees worldwide are currently enrolled in UTC's Employee Scholar Program with more than 40% of current enrollees pursuing advanced degrees. Also, 52% of the program's graduates have earned advanced degrees. The majority of degrees earned through the program are in engineering and business-related fields.

The bottom line in measuring return on investment for UTC is that employees who participate in the program are nearly twice as likely to be promoted and less likely to leave the company than are those who do not complete the program. Our investment in education leads to greater workforce retention and attraction, which ultimately enhances the company's bottom line. Put simply, we believe lifelong learning benefits our employees and our business.

What lessons can other employers learn from your experience?

United Technologies Corporation remains one of the few corporations with no restrictions on the course of study an employee may pursue with no requirement that coursework pertain to an employee's current job. UTC covers the cost of tuition, books, and fees for employees seeking master's, bachelor's, and associate's degrees up front to minimize out-of-pocket costs to students.

Other companies may also realize this type of return on investing in talent and recognize that we have a shared responsibility to invest in an educated workforce. Between rising education costs and increasing student debt, corporate investment in education is critical to a talented workforce that can grow with the company.

United Technologies Corporation also partners with major universities to enhance and inform curriculum design. These partner schools provide highly technical and specialized science, technology, engineering, and mathematics (STEM) curricula to its students and prepare a workforce with UTC-ready skills.

Overall, the program is a great attraction and retention tool, delivering an engaged workforce, ready and able to take on the challenges we face.

CHAPTER 7

The National Football League
Player Engagement Program Prepares for Life After Football

Troy Vincent

The National Football League (NFL) is redefining the role of lifelong learning by using the pxlatform of sports to set new standards in education and training.

What began in the early 1990s as a former player's request for an off-field program has developed into the sports industry standard to support the players' transition to the next stage of their careers. The NFL Player Engagement (NFLPE) program facilitates this transition by promoting and providing education while players are still on the field. In just the past few decades, NFLPE's comprehensive number of educational offerings (ranging from boot camps to professional internships) have quadrupled. Even with the increased number of offerings, player interest in these programs has accelerated to where demand now exceeds supply. The interest reaches beyond the NFL, with other professional leagues soliciting advice about this program.

Program Description

Only 6.5% of high school football players go on to play in college, and only 1.6% of college athletes are drafted by the NFL. Athletes in the NFL play for an average of only 3 years (Exhibit 7-1). That is why the NFLPE has gone to the next level in becoming lifelong educators, starting early with high school programs, such as the PREP 100 Series, and continuing on by collaborating

Exhibit 7-1.   Number and percent of high school athletes who continue to play beyond high school.

Student Athletes	Men's Basketball	Women's Basketball	Football	Baseball
High school student athletes (number)	538,676	433,120	1,086,627	474,791
High school senior student athletes (number)	153,907	123,749	310,465	135,655
NCAA student athletes (number)	17,984	16,186	70,147	32,450
NCAA freshman roster positions (number)	5,138	4,625	20,042	9,271
NCAA senior student athletes (number)	3,996	3,597	15,588	7,211
NCAA student athletes drafted (number)	46	32	254	678
High school players who reach the NCAA (percent)	3.30%	3.70%	6.50%	6.80%
NCAA players who reach the professional leagues (percent)	1.20%	0.90%	1.60%	9.40%
High school players who reach the professional leagues (percent)	0.03%	0.03%	0.08%	0.50%

Source: National Collegiate Athletic Association (NCAA), 2013. http://www.ncaa.org/about/resources/research/probability-competing-beyond-high-school.

with the finest institutions of higher learning in the United States, with the goal of helping athletes develop a second career that last a lifetime.

NFLPE is available to competitive football players nationwide—not just NFL players. This player engagement (PE) model targets three main audiences:

1. Prep (high school and college student athletes)
2. Life (current NFL players)
3. Next (former NFL players)

The only requirement for entry into these programs is to play for a high school, university, or professional football team, and, at the Prep level, to meet academic eligibilities.

Clearly, no effort of this size and scope can operate in a vacuum on such a broad scale, and PE has partnered in this endeavor with a multitude of organizations, including venerable institutions such as the United States Army and the National Collegiate Athletic Association (NCAA). Teaching partners for various programs include business schools, such as Wharton (University of Pennsylvania), Kellogg (Northwestern), Stanford, and Notre Dame. Business partners, including companies such as Microsoft, Merrill Lynch, United Way, and Cisco, both underwrite programs and provide internship opportunities. To bolster this list of external expertise, PE utilizes internal sources as well through its Ambassadors Program, a cadre of past players who have been actively educated and involved with PE, who spread the word about the need for lifelong learning and to develop skills off the playing field. That message is rooted in PE's guiding principles of faith, family, and football that can lead to the desired outcome of total wellness, which is presented to players as "Q5" (the fifth quarter of their game) and features financial, emotional, personal, and physical services.

Ultimately, with so many services available, PE's goal is to teach the players at all levels to maximize the many off-field opportunities both during and after their playing days, starting in high school and progressing through life. The thinking behind this program is that players will best learn about their career options through the diverse combination of resources offered by the PE and its college, business, and agency partners. With these strong partners, NFLPE supports lifelong learning through a wide variety of offerings that are tailored to each stage of a player's career.

Prep

For student athletes, NFLPE offerings focus on academic excellence, financial literacy, character development, conflict resolution, communication, and health, safety, and wellness.* These topics are all important because, for the vast majority of Prep participants, their financial future is not in the NFL, but is in their education. These programs are divided into offerings for high school students and college students.

High School

Three strong examples of NFLPE programs for high school football players are NLF Prep 100 Series, Prep Leadership Program, and Prep Sports Career Expo.

NFL Prep 100 Series. Presented by Under Armour (New York, NY), this 2-day program has been specifically designed for high school athletes to further

---

* For more information, go to https://www.nflplayerengagement.com/prep/.

develop their leadership skills in academics and athletics. Of the hundreds of players who attend the regional sessions, the top performers are selected to attend a leadership forum during the week of the NFL rookie symposium. Highlights of this program include classroom sessions on player health and safety; on-field instructions highlighting technical drills and techniques; insight into the academic and athletic experiences of a professional athlete from current and former NFL players; officiating workshops offering an overview of potential career paths; and NCAA representatives leading classroom sessions for parents and student athletes on the most up-to-date information regarding eligibility, recruiting, and compliance information.

Prep Leadership Program. The Leadership Program, conducted at the University of Pennsylvania's Wharton School of Business, is for a select group of 36 top senior high-school student athletes. The program recognizes the success of the invitees and provides participants with a few days of specific leadership training and development programming. The rigorous coursework, breakout groups, and panels specifically designed by the Wharton School provide a formal foundation of leadership training for this next generation of leaders. The program curriculum includes basics of leadership (assessments, styles, motivating others); professional development (life skills, social media); career development (preparing for the future through résumé writing, mock interviews, public speaking, and networking); financial education (introduction to financial terms, tools, and the role of financial advisors); and basics of management.

NFL Prep Sports Career Expo. This expo, produced in conjunction with Why Not Sports, Inc. (Atlanta, GA), enlists professionals from all aspects of the sports industry to inform, educate, and enlighten student athletes on career opportunities within the professional sports arena. Students learn about the academic requirements to successfully transition from high school to college and a broad spectrum of career opportunities within the sports industry outside of being a professional athlete. Examples include the following:

- Sports journalism
- Officiating
- Player engagement
- Coaching
- Athletics administration

College Football

NFLPE provides supports for all NCAA football players, not just those drafted by professional teams. These include both direct programs for student athletes (for example, the Life Skills Roundtable for Student Athletes) and guidance for universities to help them support their students (the Life Skills Education and Professional Development Summit).

NFL-NCAA Life Skills Roundtable for Student Athletes. This event is designed to provide student athletes with a forum to discuss the resources and support that they need in order to meet their personal and professional goals. Through intimate discussions with a diverse group of student athletes (of both sexes, of various ethnicities, and of many sports), the NFL and the NCAA gain a better understanding of the personal and professional development needs and goals of student athletes. The student athletes have the opportunity to participate in professional development seminars as well as assessments to increase their self-awareness of skills and aptitudes.

NFL-NCAA Life Skills Education and Professional Development Summit. This summit is a partnership between the NFL and the NCAA focused on identifying and outlining the synergies that exist between NFL player engagement directors and intercollegiate athletics professionals. The summit is designed to provide relevant, effective, and practical training and professional development opportunities to enhance the ability of athletics professionals to serve student athletes in the areas of life skills and student athlete development. Attendees acquire a better understanding of how to enhance student athletes' personal growth based on their needs, and of how the NFL and NCAA can work collaboratively on student athlete programming and resources.

Program objectives are to create an environment where institutional and organizational best practices for development of student athletes can be shared and explored; to provide participants with education and training on methods and resources they can use to better support student athletes' personal development, and encourage their participation in programming; to collaborate on topical areas that have the potential to impact student athlete growth and success; and to educate participants about the structure of the NCAA and NFL and the resources and programs provided by both organizations.

Life

Becoming a professional athlete is a life-changing event. Accordingly, the NFL provides new professional players with the supports to manage their life and their new financial situation. These include, but are not limited to, the rookie symposium, the Rookie Success Program, a continuing education program, and professional development.*

NFL Rookie Symposium

This symposium is an orientation for all drafted rookies on the topics of NFL history, total wellness, experience, and professionalism. It includes presentations, videos, and workshops focused on these and other topics, including player health and safety, decision making, mental health, substance abuse and domestic violence prevention, nondiscrimination, and maintaining positive relationships. Rookies are provided with resources and best practices to assist them with their shared responsibility in successfully identifying off-the-field challenges and transitioning from college to the professional level.

Rookie Success Program

The Rookie Success Program is designed to reinforce the professional developmental activities addressed at the rookie symposium and further assist with the transition into the NFL. This 9-week, psychoeducational, classroom-based program is designed to teach players how to improve their decision-making skills, and to utilize the resources available to them and their families. It includes topics such as family safety, lifestyle management, impulse control, anger management, time management, stress management, domestic violence, and public safety.

NFL Continuing Education Program

The Continuing Education Program (CEP) helps players complete their undergraduate degrees or seek other higher educational opportunities to meet their career and life goals. In partnership with colleges and universities across

---

* For more information, go to https://www.nflplayerengagement.com/life/.

the country, the CEP staff help players to design detailed, individualized plans to reach their educational goals. Developed with the help of academic advisors, these individualized educational plans may include opportunities to pursue coursework in a player's franchise city, at his original institution, or through distance learning via Internet-based coursework.

Professional Development Program

The Professional Development Program is an interactive presentation designed to raise players' awareness of transitional opportunities in how to achieve success in their life after football. Topics addressed may include dealing with friends and family, managing finances, balancing work and family, and dealing with a high-profile environment.

Next

Recognizing that the average career of a player in the NFL is less than 3 years, NFLPE provides considerable support for players as they move onto their next career, including internships to facilitate learning about other sports-related careers (coaching, broadcasting) and other common second careers (restaurant management), and to foster the peer-to-peer support that helps with this major life transition. Programs in Next include, but are not limited to, the Transition Assistance Program, the Career Development Symposium, and Career Development Program internships.*

Transition Assistance Program

NFLPE recognizes that transition is a continual process, unique to each individual's situation. It encompasses all aspects of life, which is why the Transition Assistance Program (TAP) focuses on total wellness. TAP is a partnership between former players and Georgia Tech faculty to provide transitioning assistance for players and their significant others. The curriculum features sessions pertaining to fitness, nutrition, career development, financial success, and much more. Players and significant others receive peer-to-peer support from former NFL players who are trained as transition coaches.

---

* For more information, go to https://www.nflplayerengagement.com/next/.

Career Development Symposium

Program participants who are interested in coaching or management are nominated by their franchise. Participants develop necessary leadership skills and familiarize themselves with the hiring process through networking opportunities, interview preparation, and the chance to gain perspective from current owners, general managers, and head coaches. The program is designed to strengthen the pipeline of management and strengthen the pipeline for general manager and coaching positions.

Career Development Program Internships

The Career Development Program provides internships and job shadowing, that is, following another employee through the workday to learn the job, to help players learn about career options. As noted earlier, major corporations work with NFLPE to provide work placement for players evaluating their next career state. In addition to tose external business partners, players work as interns in NFL offices in China, Mexico, and Canada.

Program Impact

The NFLPE's arrival at this specific level of training has evolved over the past 20-plus years. It began from a simple request to the player development program and expanded into a full department focused on player engagement. Along the way thousands of players have participated in the program. Demand is high. One important milestone for the program in meeting players' needs is a quantum leap in the number of courses offered. After years of demand exceeding the number of offerings, now every one of the hundreds of annual applicants complete at least one player engagement course.

This "graduation rate" is a strong indicator that players are achieving success beyond their football career, which ultimately will prove to be an excellent return on investment for the NFL since fewer players may need assistance later. This is because the robust NFLPE staff serves players in pointing them to satisfying careers in a myriad of fields, from media and business to coaching and officiating. Countless players in every industry have climbed the corporate ladder or capitalized on their entrepreneurial skills to open successful businesses. In many instances, these new careers are extremely lucrative financially and can even create a brand beyond what the players established on the field, as is the case with NFLPE and broadcast boot camp veteran Tim Hasselbeck, who now may be known as much as a football expert on ESPN as he was as an NFL quarterback. This program is also beneficial for employers, who find a steady stream of still-young applicants who mostly come from college backgrounds and have already customized their career aspirations through NFLPE educational programs.

Conclusion

Today, players in the NFLPE program are offered four times as many programs and courses as were available just 3 years ago, and still more growth is planned for the future. The increased numbers of players involved in the program are the "best-of-the-best"—world-class overachievers who have made a lifelong commitment to reach the highest level the game has to offer. Their productivity is played out on the most public stage imaginable, and then they take those talents to the NFLPE programs to keep on learning in their lifelong quest for success.

The success of this program has drawn the attention of other professional sports leagues. This expanding interest is resulting in increased collaboration between the NFL and other sports leagues for advisory services and consultation to develop or replicate new initiatives.

CHAPTER 8

Aramark
Partnerships to Invest in the Community and Workforce

Bev Dribin

Philadelphia-based Aramark, a global professional services company, has for many years connected with the communities where employees live and work to offer a wide range of services to people in need, including job training and workforce-readiness programs.

In 2006, Aramark embarked on a process to create a company-wide community involvement strategy. Through the process, we learned that community centers, which provide a wide range of critical services to families in need, could benefit from Aramark's greatest strengths, not only in nutrition and wellness expertise and facilities enhancement, but also in workforce readiness and education. As a company with 270,000 employees, Aramark hires, trains, and develops hundreds of employees each year. This expertise has helped people in the communities in which Aramark operates develop the skills and opportunities for the local workforce.

Overview of Community Partnerships for Workforce Development

Aramark found an excellent partner in community centers, neighborhood gathering places where individuals and families go for the help and resources they need to succeed. Community centers help people feel empowered to improve their situation and their neighborhood. These local, independent centers often have their own buildings and provide comprehensive programs to address the needs of individuals and family members of all ages, such as day care and preschool, recreation facilities, charter schools, meal programs, after-school enrichment, senior services, career counseling, adult education, and much more.

Community centers address some of the nation's toughest challenges, especially during difficult economic times. In 2011, according to the U.S. Department of Labor, 9.5 million people remain unemployed or underemployed, and, according to the U.S. Census Bureau, poverty continues to grip over 46 million Americans.* These centers help families face the challenges of poverty, providing support services as they prepare for and find meaningful work to realize their potential and move out of poverty.

To help connect Aramark to the community centers most in need and help direct resources to the local level, the company works with existing non-profits in the communities, including those that are members of the Alliance for Strong Children and Families (Alliance). With a combined membership of more than 525 community-based organizations, Alliance members represent a significant force in the human services sector, serving more than 8,000 communities and millions of clients/customers annually. Aramark has been working with the Alliance for more than 7 years, providing grants, volunteers, and capacity building programs through the Aramark Building Community (ABC), the company's volunteer and philanthropic program that supports individuals and families working their way out of poverty. Today, Aramark partners with more than 52 community centers in the United States and abroad through ABC.

Working with these trusted, neighborhood-based organizations provides Aramark with an opportunity to enhance the workforce and training programs that are already in place at the centers, and to develop new programs that utilize Aramark employees' unique skills.

Program Description

Through the Aramark Building Community, Aramark develops long-term partnerships with local organizations and community centers to create workforce "opportunity zones" where people can access educational programs, learn skills, and explore new opportunities. Within these opportunity zones,

---

*For more information see: http://www.pbs.org/newshour/bb/business-july-dec11-poverty_09-13/.

Aramark volunteers enhance and upgrade classrooms, computer labs, and libraries to make them more inviting and efficient. Throughout the year, regional groups of Aramark employees, called "star teams," bring together Aramark's diverse workforce within designated geographic areas to support and respond to the needs of their local communities. These Aramark employees volunteer to help prepare youths and adults for careers and connect them to the workforce. Aramark also provides community centers with resources to implement a variety of workforce development and lifelong learning programs, including workforce-readiness programs for job seekers, and the ABC Academy.

Case Studies

Farming for Good: Why Work Is Essential for Teens to Develop and Leave Poverty

Every morning this summer, 17-year-old Jennifer travels 1 hour by public transportation from the homeless shelter where she lives to the urban farm at Philadelphia's Lutheran Settlement House. There, she earns her first paychecks as a participant in a program called Teens 4 Good.

Teens 4 Good, a program of the Federation of Neighborhood Centers, is supported by Aramark—helping young teens to rise out of poverty and learn job skills. The program is turning vacant lots into farms that support at-risk youths with meaningful jobs to help them grow. Few of these teens have strong role models in the workforce. Without help gaining employment, these teens would be left without the necessary life skills and experiences to hold a job in adulthood. For many of these young people, this is their very first paycheck.

For a teenager like Jennifer, that first job is a critical life experience. When she started with the program, she'd find ways to avoid the work: faking illness was a common ploy. By the end of the program, she learned that every morning, at 9:00 a.m. sharp, she was expected to show up ready to give this job and her coworkers her all.

The farm at Lutheran Settlement House is just one of six urban farms across Philadelphia providing more than 8,000 pounds of produce to 25 low-income neighborhoods with desperately limited access to fresh fruits and vegetables. At the end of the summer, the teens worked with Aramark employees to create an iced tea using the fruits and herbs of the garden that they can market and sell by the bottle. It's an opportunity for the teens to learn that they are more than their own muscle; they can earn their paycheck just by putting their minds to work. It's a lesson that can only be learned through employment in those critical years, to know that their ideas hold value and worth and can help them break the cycle of poverty for themselves.

Opportunities for a Vulnerable London Neighborhood

Since 2009, Aramark has partnered with Community Links in the East London borough of Newham, providing training, jobs, and other support to help revitalize this community—before, during, and after the London Summer Games.

Employees from the team working the Games volunteered to transform unused space at the center into a hub for workforce readiness for local residents looking for jobs. As Aramark assembled the staff of 3,000 to provide food service during the London 2012 Games, 40 people from Community Links were hired, giving them skills and experience for future jobs. When London 2012 concluded, several were hired back at Aramark client locations.

Workforce-Readiness Programs for Job Seekers

One of the greatest barriers for people seeking employment is a lack of basic work experience and interpersonal skills. Working with community centers, Aramark created a workforce-readiness curriculum featuring modules for both trainers and job seekers focused not only getting a job but also on keeping the job. Through the program, hundreds of individuals have benefited from career resources, including one-on-one career counseling and résumé preparation assistance.

Through classes and Aramark-sponsored career fairs with Aramark Building Community career education zones, company human resources professionals facilitate workshops, coach job seekers on skills and résumés, and assist with job placement. Hundreds of people have been placed in jobs and internships, internally and externally, as a result of this focus.

ABC Academy

The Aramark Building Community (ABC) Academy is a forum to enhance the operational and program excellence of community centers in the areas of community health and wellness and employment. The ABC Academy is managed in partnership with the Alliance for Children and Families. As part of the ABC Academy, Aramark provides workforce development grants and partners Aramark volunteers with organizations to help prepare individuals to find and keep jobs. The Academy also provides center leaders and professionals with online and in-person resources and tools, to increase their effectiveness and capacity to meet the needs of families in diverse neighborhoods.

Program Impact

The Aramark Building Community has been fully operating since 2008. In that time, more than 20,000 Aramark employees from multiple business units have donated over 50,000 hours of time. In addition, Aramark has given more than $8 million in cash grants and donations. We estimate we have reached nearly 4 million people in 52 cities. ABC has placed approximately 500 unemployed youth or adults in jobs.

Aramark Building Community has been recognized by more than 60 entities, and has also received recognition from organizations and elected officials in Houston, Kansas City, New York, Miami, Boston, Glendale (CA), and Memphis.

- In Houston, both the City of Houston and Harris County declared November 15, 2012, as Aramark Building Community Day "for its dedication to serving Houston families in need and providing them with additional resources that are great stepping stones for bettering their lives."
- Aramark was also recognized by the National Restaurant Association as the 2012 "Restaurant Neighbor of the Year" for the Aramark Building Community.
- On the local level, Aramark has been recognized by the Metropolitan Inter-Faith Association of Memphis as the "Organization of the Year," and by Don Bosco Centers in Kansas City, for "Outstanding Volunteer Service."

Conclusion

The Aramark Building Community has expanded every year since 2008, as new community center partners are added to the Aramark Building Community family, and new programs that help people prepare for and find meaningful work are launched. The needs of communities and the resources that Aramark can provide are ever-evolving, and the Aramark Building Community addresses each community's unique needs.

Reflecting on the history of Aramark Building Community, we recognize the importance of creating a thoughtful long-term plan, to help set goals, develop the program, and allow it to grow to address emerging issues in communities. Strong strategic partnerships are also essential. Relationships with other organizations with complementary initiatives that align with Aramark's goals for the program help create greater impact for the community.

Because employee volunteerism is so critical to the program's success, it is essential that a strong connection be made between employee skills and community impact. For example, at Aramark, that can mean efforts to connect human resources experts, who oversee a workforce of 270,000 people, to the workforce-readiness programs at community centers. By equipping the most engaged employees with the resources they need to execute the program, the greatest impact can be achieved.

CHAPTER 9

Boeing
Business Career Foundation Program

Rick Gross

During a March 2014 congressional hearing on the aging of the aerospace workforce in the United States, a Boeing executive told lawmakers that in some areas of the company more than half of the skilled workforce would be eligible to retire within 5 years. This statistic illustrates why Boeing is committed to investing in education and skills development in our communities from birth through college, as well as within the company throughout the stages of an employee's career. Developing a highly skilled future workforce pipeline, as well as leaders to take Boeing into its second century, is achieved through a combination of community partnership and professional development programs such as the Business Career Foundation Program (BCFP).

Supporting the company's vision to be the strongest, best, and best integrated aerospace-based company in the world, the cross-functional BCFP experience prepares participants to lead from a "One Boeing" approach. This approach encourages all employees to actively engage in and leverage the company's full capabilities and resources to achieve company goals. The various functional rotations of the BCFP, as well as cross-business unit experiences offered through the program, provide a holistic experience throughout the business functions and company. After completing the BCFP, participants are equipped to perform in various capacities as business needs arise.

Lifelong Learning at Boeing

Boeing believes one of its greatest assets is human capital. To be innovative and remain a leader within the aerospace industry, the right combination of skills and capabilities are essential. Boeing takes a strategic systems approach to how the company invests in education and skills development to reinforce the idea of lifelong learning.

Early Education

From a K-12 education perspective of strengthening education systems to adequately equip students with the skills needed to succeed in school, work, and life, Boeing is focused on preparing and inspiring students to gain fundamental, 21st-century skills through science, technology, engineering, and mathematics (STEM)-related, problem-based learning experiences. Twenty-first-century skills include the ability to think critically and solve problems, collaborate well, be creative, and communicate effectively.

Building students' abilities and interests in STEM-related skills helps to ensure that the aerospace industry and the company have access to a competitive and adaptive workforce that will lead Boeing through another century of innovation and success.

Boeing puts its education strategy in practice through investments that support high-impact, evidence-based education, nonprofit organizations and community partners, engagement by employees, and advocacy to promote strategies in education that are important to the company and communities.

Three key areas through which Boeing tactically executes its strategy are educator leadership development, support of problem-based learning experiences that build STEM-related skills, and early learning to ensure that every child has access to quality early care and education.

One example of Boeing's investment in education is the company's strategic partnership with FIRST® (For Inspiration and Recognition of Science and Technology), a not-for-profit organization dedicated to encouraging young people to become science and technology leaders. Through our work with the FIRST® Robotics Competition (FRC®), one of four programs in a progression of programs offered by FIRST, Boeing employees serve as mentors and prepare students for possible future careers by instilling an appreciation for STEM while fostering collaboration, problem solving, creativity, and effective communication skills. During the 2014–2015 FRC season, more than 500 Boeing employees will mentor FIRST Boeing teams, and hundreds of employees will provide support such as judging or volunteering at competitions.

While many of Boeing's partnerships focus on developing skills through STEM-related activities, the company also focuses on strengthening entrepreneurial and leadership skills in students through programs such as Junior Achievement, which teaches the basics of business to high school students, and events such as Washington Business Week, which hosts a week-long business simulation for high school students.

University Relations and Career Preparation

As students continue their education beyond high school, Boeing maintains a leadership role by partnering with more than 200 universities and higher education institutions around the world to ensure a workforce pipeline that can support its growing business. With these higher education relationships, Boeing's priority is to provide the very best resources and opportunities to create meaningful experiences for students who share Boeing's passion for aerospace innovation. Critical to this workforce readiness is aligning curriculum with Boeing's business priorities to directly influence the future of aerospace. Partnerships include those with technical, vocational, and training institutions; community colleges; universities; and premier research institutions.

Boeing's partnership with Green River Community College (Auburn, WA) is an example of how Boeing partners with local institutions to develop the pipeline of technical talent. Brand new in 2012, Green River Community College, in conjunction with Boeing, created three state-of-the-art training programs providing a stepping stone in the pathway to careers in the aerospace and advanced manufacturing industries. In 20 weeks, the student learns the skills required for a high-demand aerospace or advanced manufacturing job related to one of three areas: precision machining, machine maintenance, and quality assurance.

The programs are using a fresh curriculum that is industry-driven and aligns directly with job knowledge, skills, and abilities identified by the aerospace and advanced manufacturing industry. Boeing and several supply chain partners have provided their input on the curriculum and approve of its content.

In addition to influencing curriculum, partnering for research purposes and supporting student activities in key business-related areas, Boeing's student engagement includes global student-focused programs in the form of internships, fellowships, and co-ops for students so that they are prepared to enter the workforce with hands-on experience that benefits their professional development, as well as their future employers. In 2014, Boeing hosted more than 1,700 interns across the enterprise from higher educational institutions globally. In Boeing's programs, students practice high performance, ethics, and accountability; apply critical thinking and learn how to collaborate with others in a complex environment; and, most important, receive hands-on experience to last them a lifetime. These opportunities are available to both domestic and international students across the commercial and defense businesses.

One example of the internship opportunities available at Boeing is FLITE (Future Leaders in Thought and Experience). A diversity internship program, FLITE is hosted in the Puget Sound region and in St. Louis, and is a summer immersion experience for students of underrepresented backgrounds. Students are recruited from local universities in the Northwest and Midwest regions with the intention of identifying talented, diverse students to feed the Boeing Business Intern Program (BBIP). Each Friday during the summer, interns participate in the Boeing FLITE program, in which they meet to gain invaluable academic and professional skills in what is aptly named "FLITE School." On these days, students expand upon their experience through excel courses, a functional speaker series, tours, and thought leader discussions (discussing innovation around current industry/market/leadership challenges). FLITE has been a staple internship program at Boeing for the past 3 years with plans on improving and growing with each year.

Another example of how Boeing builds the talent pipeline is through the BBIP. With several hundred business interns each summer, the BBIP is Boeing's largest centralized effort to attract entry-level talent for the business functions across the enterprise. There were 215 BBIP interns eligible for full-time employment in 2014, and 67% of the interns were converted to full-time Boeing employees upon graduation from college.

Each of these programs, partnerships, and initiatives are part of a strong talent pipeline for Boeing, and helps prepare top talent transition into development programs such as the Boeing Career Foundations Program (BCFP).

Business Career Foundations Program: Accelerating Business Leadership Development

One of Boeing's most successful efforts to accelerate the development of skilled business leaders is the BCFP, a 2-year, entry-level development program designed to build participants' leadership and business acumen through a challenging, fast-paced rotation experience. The program is conducted at five major Boeing sites across the United States.

In the BCFP, participants rotate through six positions in a variety of business disciplines, including financial planning, accounting, financial operations, contracts, estimating and pricing, scheduling, supplier management, and business operations. One of these rotations can be an elective in a field such as marketing, business development, business strategy, or human resources. The program offers offsite rotations at different sites throughout the company, both domestically and internationally. Participants are allowed to join a rotation outside of their home region during the second year of the program. Participants are encouraged to rotate through multiple programs and business units to further enhance their breadth of exposure to the business. Each rotation is 4 months in duration, with a performance review at the completion of each rotation. Although the annual performance review is done by the BCFP program manager, each rotational hosting manager also does a mini, 4-month work statement set up and performance review. At the conclusion of each rotation the hosting manager provides the performance feedback to the program manager, who incorporates it into the annual review. The BCFP participants also have various training and development opportunities over the course of their time in the program. They are encouraged to engage in various networking opportunities offered to them as current program participants, as well as when they become alumni of the program.

Target Audience

As an entry-level program, the BCFP targets candidates with little or no work experience. The BCFP hiring philosophy focuses on demonstrated leadership potential rather than strict degree or grade point average (GPA) requirements. The BCFP management team works with college recruiters to identify and attract potential participants, and the effort is aligned with specific business schools. Boeing determines engagement with schools based on a number of factors, including the quality of the curriculum, the diversity of the student body, and the performance and retention of graduates at Boeing.

Recruiting for the BCFP is a multistep process. The majority of BCFP participants are selected from the BBIP. This internal application process involves an onsite interview, which includes a structured interview and group assessment. Participating in BBIP maximizes an applicant's chances of being selected, but is not the only way to enter the program. External applicants can apply online during the fall recruiting season. Strong applicants are invited to participate in first-round interviews, either over the phone or on campus. The final candidates are invited for second-round interviews at a Boeing facility, which follow the same process of a structured interview and group assessment. The external hiring process typically takes place in November.

Program Design

Typically, new BCFP participants start together as a class in late June. The program begins with a regional orientation, welcoming them to the program and giving them basic company and program knowledge, as well as opportunities to network with program supporters, alumni, and those currently in the program.

During their first rotation, the entire cohort comes together at the Boeing Leadership Center for a week of professional development and program networking. From time to time, we have BCFPs who graduate in December and start the program one rotation early in March. For these participants, a mini-regional orientation is provided, as well as the opportunity to fully participate in all of the onboarding activities with the balance of the cohort later in the summer.

Each BCFP participant is paired with an executive mentor with whom they meet on a quarterly basis. Participants are encouraged to engage with other mentors throughout the program, as new connections are made in rotating through different teams. The participants are also involved in mentoring interns as they spend the summer with Boeing. This is a great chance to experience being a mentor and to realize the skills gained in their short tenure as a working professional.

The BCFP supports business requirements and work statements through the various functions, and participants often work above normal entry-level responsibilities. These assignments are not job shadowing, that is, following another employee through the workday to learn the job, but must entail execution of a true work statement connected to the group and function. Ideally, each rotation would have a combination of typical day-to-day activities as well as big-picture projects. At the conclusion of the rotation, participants should understand what it would be like to work within that organization as well as how the organization fits in and provides value to the company.

Throughout the program, there are additional opportunities for training and development. The first day of each rotation is a full training and development day that focuses on a specific business unit of Boeing as well as a specific leadership skill. Over the course of the 2 years, each participant is given the opportunity to explore each business unit and a variety of soft skills through these formal training and development days.

During their second year, BCFP participants are required to complete a capstone project. Much like a senior thesis, the capstone project is an opportunity to provide significant value back to the company over and above the work the participants do in each rotation. There are minimal requirements of the capstone to allow for individual and company interests. The project must provide significant value to a larger organization, and the BCFP participant must be the project lead. One example of a capstone project was the creation of a dashboard that gives visibility to cost surrounding computing/telecommunications devices and travel. This serves to significantly help managers track and control cost in a more streamlined and effective manner, reducing the overall cost to the company.

Program Impact

Boeing expects the BCFP will help to attract top talent to the company, and produce employees who are more engaged and prepared to take on leadership roles at an accelerated rate. Metrics have shown that those who participated in BCFP move through the pipeline faster than the general population of employees. For example, several of our youngest executives on the selling team in the Boeing Commercial Airplanes business unit came through the BCFP.

Since the launch of the BCFP in 2000, there have been more than 500 program participants. More than 95% of these participants have successfully completed the program by receiving top scores on performance reviews and completing all program requirements, including a capstone project.

The BCFP graduates benefit from expanded career opportunities, a larger network, and ongoing leadership development for BCFP alumni. They graduate with an increased understanding of how various Boeing organizations interact, enabling them to achieve higher levels of quality and productivity early in their careers. They are promoted, on average, three to five times faster than the general population, and have increased earning potential because of their accelerated career path. They also have a solid retention rate, which is an indicator of job satisfaction.

Boeing benefits from an expanded pool of qualified leadership candidates, improving the pipeline for succession planning. Through BCFP, Boeing not only gains adaptable and strategic leaders but also reduces the time it takes to develop those leaders. We estimate that the 2-year program is equivalent to about 5 years of general experience. We are very pleased with the benefits of the BCFP both for the participants and for the company. The success of the BCFP has proven to be an internal benchmark best practice, spawning additional functional development programs in engineering, information technology, and human resources, which now each have a career development rotation program.

Ongoing Development Opportunities: Mid-Career and Leadership

As employees progress in their careers and move into leadership roles, Boeing provides development opportunities at every step of the way. Boeing employees have a myriad of opportunities to learn and grow as leaders, including formal and informal mentoring programs, daily interactions with leaders, and development programs at the Boeing Leadership Center, as follows:

- Formal and informal programs: Whether it's taking a new assignment or volunteering in our communities around the world, Boeing people never stop learning. The company offers classroom and online training, opportunities for rotational and development assignments, and a variety of collaboration tools that help people learn from one another.
- Daily interactions: Boeing leaders help employees develop the skills that will accelerate their careers within the company. Each year vice presidents mentor at least two employees who have the potential to become future leaders.
- Boeing Leadership Center: Current and aspiring Boeing leaders can attend programs at the center in St. Louis, where they team up to tackle business issues and share best practices. Boeing vice presidents teach at least two programs at the Boeing Leadership Center annually, using the "leaders teaching leaders" methodology of two-way dialogue about career experiences.

As evidenced by the aforementioned programs and partnerships, Boeing is committed to building a solid talent pipeline and encourages lifelong learning and development of talent. Each career stage is vital to Boeing's success. Investing in K-12 education fosters an interest in STEM careers and provides youths with the necessary foundation to succeed in the aerospace industry.

Partnerships with higher education prepare students for careers in aerospace, and the FLITE program and BBIP prepare business students with the training and experience to launch a successful business career and be ready for opportunities in early career development programs such as the BCFP. As employees grow, Boeing grows, and that's why lifelong career development is encouraged and supported through the variety of opportunities offered at Boeing.

Conclusion

Running a successful leadership development program like BCFP requires executive sponsors, hosting managers, and mentors who are devoted to the program's mission. Program leadership requires those who are truly engaged, and they are given time away from existing duties to develop and implement the program. Adequate funding is required at a company level to ensure consistency and success.

Internal policies and procedures need to support the cross-functional and cross–business unit movement of participants. For example, a challenge to overcome with a program of this nature is labor charging policies that hinder moving participants across business units, as this undermines the objective of providing participants with a breadth of exposure to the company. The program should be structured in such a way as to minimize tension from multiple reporting relationships, by having direct reporting and year-end performance reviews held by the program manager. Programs that span multiple locations should also try to avoid inconsistencies between sites, especially in hiring practices and budget for program activities. This can be mitigated by reporting up to one enterprise program manager.

Expansion is the logical outcome of a successful program, but should be treated with care. BCFP leaders have consciously decided to keep the program size at approximately 40 participants per year to preserve the program's integrity.

The BCFP aligns and furthers Boeing's overall commitment to learning at every career stage by offering a unique opportunity for high-potential candidates during their very first years at the company. While there are other programs further in the pipeline to continue to address top talent throughout all functions, the BCFP sets up its participants for success as future leaders from the very beginning.

CHAPTER 10

JPMorgan Chase
Business-University Partnerships Support Technology Education for Undergraduates

Jeffrey Saltz and Jennifer McDermott

t is common practice for universities to work with companies to bring real-world examples of work situations to students through guest speakers, information sessions, and internships. However, these engagements have not always led to a significant university–industry relationship that provided value to both organizations. JPMorgan Chase (JPMC) reached out to several universities in 2007 to seek a stronger, more in-depth relationship and to create an enhanced education program that would improve technology education of undergraduate students. In 2007, Syracuse University (Syracuse, NY) became the first school to collaborate with JPMC on this endeavor. University of Delaware (Newark, DE) agreed to a similar model in 2009. These two universities joined forces with JPMC to collaborate on activities in the areas of curriculum, work experience, research, and community engagement, with the following goals:

1. Transform the way technologists are trained in the classroom and on the job.
2. Drive innovation in university education and financial services technology.
3. Deliver long-term value to JPMC, to the universities, and to the broader community.
4. Create a sustainable model for world-class university–industry collaboration.

Large technology-driven enterprises, such as JPMC, need workers with technical talent and the skills required for success in today's global enterprises.

The demand for university-trained technical workers has increased significantly over the past few years, and it is evident that the problem is not a lack of jobs but rather a lack of students with the skills necessary to fill these roles. There is often a vast disconnect between how universities are educating their students and what businesses need and are looking for in their new employees. In fact, according to a December 10, 2012 article by Josh Bresin in *Forbes*, "Growing Gap Between What Business Needs and What Education Provides," 45% of United States employers say the lack of skills is the main reason for entry-level vacancies; only 42% of worldwide employers believe new graduates are adequately prepared for work, whereas 72% of educational institutions think their students are prepared. An article in *IEEE Computer Magazine* in March 2013 stated that by 2018, U.S. universities will produce only 52% of the number of graduates with computer science bachelor's degrees that will be needed to fill the 1.4 million available jobs.[1] Through unique, collaborative relationships, universities can work with corporations to develop and enhance the curriculum, and provide students with real-world working experience that can be translated back to the classroom, linking theory with practice.

In addition to students lacking the skills needed to fill technology-focused roles, there is also a shortage of diverse students attracted to or retained in science, technology, engineering, and mathematics (STEM) disciplines, making it challenging to bring unique and varied backgrounds, experiences, and viewpoints to corporations. In a report by the National Science Foundation, it is stated that women earn approximately 20% of the bachelor's degrees in computer science, even though women hold 60% of all bachelor's degrees. In 2012, the National Center for Women and Information Technology reported that the percentage of computing occupations held by women has been declining since 1991, yet the percentage of jobs held by women in almost all other sciences has increased significantly. Equally motivated to change these numbers, universities and their industry partners can work together to explore and address the key issues driving this lack of diversity.

Program Description

The collaboration model developed by JPMC, Syracuse University (SU), and the University of Delaware (UD) has demonstrated a new and unique way of establishing a relational, rather than transactional, university—industry partnership. The model focuses on having the university build a relationship with an industry partner across the interrelated areas of (1) curriculum development, (2) recruiting and work experience, (3) research, and (4) community engagement. The reasons for selecting these areas are as follows:

1. Enhancing the university curriculum helps to ensure that students are better prepared for technology careers in large, global institutions. This goal is achieved by providing interdisciplinary programs that train students in creating and running software systems for large technology-driven companies.
2. By offering students robust, innovative, experiential learning internships, students gain real-world work experience.
3. Research efforts enable university faculty and JPMC technologists to collaborate on joint projects that solve business issues while also providing interesting opportunities for students.
4. Through community-engagement initiatives, the corporation and the universities work to expand the pipeline of technology students.

To achieve the desired goals, which have been agreed upon by both industry and universities, and to ensure a successful relationship, the following steps must be taken when establishing a relationship-based collaboration:

- Set up a long-term strategic relationship.
- Focus on a full collaboration, not simply based on a sponsorship, endowment, or charitable gift.
- Integrate the curriculum across courses and programs, not just in a single course.
- Create immersive learning experiences for students, not just updates of existing course assignments.
- Generate applied research focused on areas of mutual interest, not just "directed research" or gifts to the university.
- Address all levels of each organization. Seek the involvement and support of senior executives and senior university administration officials, so that potential roadblocks that might arise within the course of the collaboration can be avoided.

From an operational perspective, the JPMC–university collaboration functions via the definition and execution of specific projects, which are linked and integrated at the program level. For example, participants are in regular communication with one another through multiple points of contact as well as regularly scheduled meetings, in order to ensure that all milestones and deliverables are met. Specifically, each research effort needs to establish a joint university-industry working team that meets on a regular basis. Similarly, each course that was developed or enhanced also needs to have a joint program team with regular updates. In terms of execution, all parties understand that they will all be held equally responsible and accountable for the outcomes.

While the focus needs to be on the structured the execution of projects, there also needs to be a spirit of openness and flexibility. This is critical for two key aspects. First, when issues arise, the team needs to feel free to brainstorm the best path forward. Second, this openness and flexibility enables the free sharing of ideas between the university and JPMC. For example, one by-product of this brainstorming was the creation of the Institute for Veterans and Military Families (IVMF) at Syracuse University. The IVMF was the first national center in higher education focused on the social, financial, education, and policy issues impacting veterans and their families after discharge from the service.

The collaboration model has created several opportunities for students. For example, as a byproduct of face-to-face meetings at the university, JPMC employees have had an opportunity to directly engage students. This engagement has ranged from classroom participation, such as a guest speaker in a class or being "pitched" a student idea (and giving feedback on that pitch), to giving university-wide talks to hundreds of students and faculty members. Beyond these informal opportunities, the collaboration has created several work opportunities for students, including 10-week summer internships, academic-year internships that enable students to work part-time while continuing to take courses, and immersion experience co-ops like internships, in which students work for 8 months but also take courses that leverage their work environment. Finally, research projects have provided yet another opportunity for student engagement, as students participate in JPMC research projects.

Program Impact

Through these relationships, JPMC has found that it is able to build a better pipeline of technology talent and to leverage university research expertise to help solve complex, strategic business issues. From a university perspective, the primary audience for this program has been college students not just in programs such as computer science, computer engineering, and management information systems, but other students who might have a desire to understand how technology is leveraged within a global enterprise. In addition, there are several initiatives within the program that are aimed at targeting younger students (kindergarten through high school) with the goal of increasing interest in STEM areas of study as well as future careers in technology.

The university collaboration effort has engaged hundreds of JPMC employees, thousands of students (often working as interns), and faculty across all schools within the universities as well as in the surrounding communities. This work has resulted in the following significant milestones that have been achieved since this program began:

- 2007: A global enterprise technology (GET) minor was established at SU.
- 2009: JPMC opened the JPMC Technology Center on SU's campus.
- 2011: JPMC opened the JPMC Innovation Center on UD's campus and established the GET minor at UD.
- 2012: The Institute for Veterans and Military Families (IVMF) was cofounded with SU. The GET Certificate of Advanced Study (CAS) was created at SU. The Institute for Financial Services Analytics was cofounded with UD.
- 2013: The systems and information sciences (SIS) major was created at SU, and the Ph.D. program in financial services analytics was developed with UD.

Benefits to Students

The benefits provided to students through this collaboration are extensive. An on-campus presence has provided students with part-time employment opportunities in a fully functioning JPMC office. The JPMC Technology Center at SU is located in an active area—the first two floors of Lyman Hall—where university classes are conducted in the rooms adjoining the JPMC space. The center has a capacity for 150 employees, with at least 50 interns working in the space. The center focuses on IT/cyber risk. Cyber functions support a range of activities, including advanced security event management and a state-of-the-art Cyber Command Center. Opened in 2011, the JPMC Innovation Center at UD is located on the first floor of Purnell Hall, with a capacity for 15 employees. Currently there are three full-time and at least 30 part-time academic interns. JPMC is also currently working with UD on an expansion of the Innovation Center, which will include a four-floor addition to Purnell Hall, nearly tripling the square footage of the current space and doubling the number of work stations available for student employees. Both campus locations have also been equipped with JPMC wireless connectivity, virtual desktop infrastructure, Cisco Telepresence capabilities, touchscreen monitors showcasing information about JPMC and the collaboration, and laboratory space for researchers to work within the JPMC infrastructure. By leveraging this infrastructure, student interns work on a variety of projects, ranging from IT/cyber risk to software quality assurance.

By incorporating the world of industry practice into the classroom, students are able to develop business skills and are given the opportunity to engage with JPMC employees (as well as employees from other companies) in a variety of ways, including guest lectures, sponsored classroom projects, and site visits to office locations and data centers. This has enabled students to better understand their area of study and see how it is applicable to the industry and to their potential careers.

The internships available to undergraduate students at SU and UD have provided long-term development through hands-on experience, mentoring, and training. Opportunities during the academic year as well as the summer have enabled students to put into practice what they have been learning and to gain a strong understanding of a real-world corporate culture. This knowledge can be used to enhance the content that the students are learning in the classroom. In addition, there is continual contact between interns, managers, and the collaboration team, to evaluate school and work performance, with strengths and opportunities discussed regularly and development plans tailored as necessary.

Through involvement in community activities such as presentations and summer camps, JPMC and the universities expose younger students to experiences and industries that they previously may not have considered as a future area of study. In addition, engaging with students at a younger age helps to better prepare them for future educational opportunities and also helps to retain interest in STEM programs.

Benefits to the Universities

To date, 80 courses and seven new academic programs have been developed at SU and UD. Each curriculum project connects university professors with JPMC employees, and these small teams work closely on program and course development, course delivery, evaluation of course deliverables, and oversight of internships. As a result of the relationship with JPMC, university faculty have also been given the opportunity to observe student internships and interact with intern managers and other employees, allowing faculty to ensure that course material is relevant and applicable to industry.

In the research space, an internal JPMC research board was established to review proposed research ideas (both internally and externally generated faculty ideas), sponsor projects, facilitate brainstorming sessions and idea generation, and, in general, help inspire large-scale research ideas. Through presentations to JPMC employees, university faculty have been better able to understand the problems that the industry is currently facing, leading to the development of research project ideas and proposals. At the University of Delaware, JPMC cofounded the Institute for Financial Services Analytics, and the first Annual Conference on Big Data was held in October 2012. JPMC has also held multiple "university research" days, inviting faculty from Syracuse University and University of Delaware to conduct joint brainstorming sessions on potential areas of applied research within a JPMC facility. Finally, faculty members at both Syracuse University and the University of Delaware have been appointed as faculty fellows, enabling them to spend 6 months, or longer, in residence at a JPMC location. Faculty fellows have been able to better understand JPMC challenges and act as a conduit for information between the university and JPMC.

Through commitments to local community organizations, JPMC and the universities have worked with middle school and high school programs to help increase the number of students, early in their education, who are interested in pursuing STEM degrees.

Benefits to the Community

This university–industry relationship has deeply impacted and benefited local and national organizations as well. One key example, as noted above, is that JPMC and SU cofounded the IVMF in June 2011, with the mission of providing higher education opportunities to veterans and their families. The institute develops education and employment-focused programs in collaboration with industry, government, nongovernmental organizations (NGOs), and the veteran community, to address the primary financial and public policy concerns of our nation's servicemen and -women, and their families.

In Syracuse, JPMC supported the "Say Yes to Education" program, with the goal of increasing high school and college graduation rates for urban students, as well as the Hillside scholarship program, which works to increase graduation rates, college attendance rates, and employability of high school students. In addition, teams of JPMC Technology Center employees, both full-time staff and interns, have volunteered over 500 hours a year to a variety of community initiatives such as Habitat for Humanity, helping employees and students build stronger connections with the surrounding community.

In addition, JPMC has participated in community-focused discussions such as the National Governors' Association panel session, "Leaders Speak: Models from the Private and Public Sectors," and SU's Future Professionals Program in May 2013. JPMC has also had meetings with government officials, such as a meeting with U.S. Senator Thomas Carper of Delaware, to discuss university collaboration issues that affect his state and the nation.

As an example of how students and full-time JPMC employees work together, during the summer of 2012 teams of full-time JPMC analysts and summer interns from the JPMC Technology Center at SU worked to deliver a diverse set of technology initiatives for a global base of nonprofit institutions. More than 40 resources contributed to six selected projects, providing nearly 1,800 hours of service at an estimated cost savings of $100,000 for the nonprofit institutions involved. In Delaware during that same summer, JPMC analysts participated on a panel in the UD pedagogical series, a 6-week program in which high school interns learn about all aspects of university life. The University of Delaware asked JPMC to give a presentation on what life is like after college in a corporate setting, preparing the students for the workplace and emphasizing why it is critical to excel in college.

In addition to working on these initiatives with SU and UD, JPMC has also worked with other universities. For example, during the summer of 2013, JPMC sponsored Rochester Institute of Technology's Tech Girlz Summer Camp. This week-long camp was for deaf and hearing-impaired girls entering 7th, 8th, and 9th grade who have an interest in STEM. During the day, the girls participated in a variety of educational activities including building a high-tech gadget, designing webpages, and a taking a behind-the-scenes tour of an amusement park, and in the evenings they engaged in social activities such as bowling, an ice cream social, and a dance party.

Benefits to JPMC

The relationships that have been fostered with these universities and communities have also proven to have substantial benefit for JPMC. The on-campus offices have provided employees with the opportunity to frequently interact with university faculty, staff, and students on various projects, events, and initiatives. The University of Delaware is located in close proximity to several JPMC offices, making the Innovation Center easily accessible to approximately 7,500 JPMC employees. The Technology Center at SU has a capacity for over 100 full-time employees. In addition, the on-campus presence improves, enhances, and builds the JPMC brand on campus and in the community, particularly as a technology firm.

Working with the universities to create and enhance curriculum has allowed JPMC to increase industry content and context in the various courses and programs, better preparing students for roles within the firm. Engaging with students in the classroom has also been beneficial when it comes to recruiting, as students can see how their coursework and degree may be applied to the industry and to their potential careers. Furthermore, the Ph.D. program in financial service analytics at UD provides JPMC with long-term and in-depth research projects as well as a supply of well-trained professionals with knowledge of theory, with the skills of modeling financial service problems, and with a firm understanding of the culture at JPMC.

Working with these academic institutions has also provided JPMC employees with education and volunteer opportunities. As a result of our relationship with these schools, employees have been offered courses at a discounted rate and have also been given the chance to apply for scholarships for graduate courses. This has added to the plethora of educational resources already available to JPMC employees, and has given them the opportunity to pursue areas of interest in both matriculated and nonmatriculated programs. As an added benefit, community engagement initiatives have allowed students to demonstrate their abilities to JPMC recruiters and technologists, who are actively involved with each event. Through engagement with programs at the middle school and high school levels, JPMC strives to assist with the retention of underrepresented STEM students in universities. These initiatives help to create a broader view of JPMC in the local communities.

A study conducted at one university by Gault, Redington, and Schlager in 2000 concluded that recent graduates who had internships during their undergraduate program were better prepared for the job market, obtained their first job more quickly, had higher starting salaries, and were more satisfied with their positions than were those who did not intern.[2] Positive internship experiences at a cutting-edge, on-campus office have also helped build JPMC's technology brand awareness on campus and have increased interest in internships from other students. The longer time frame of the GET immersion experience and extended internship has provided students with the opportunity to work on and deliver real and valuable work to the firm, while also exposing them to the company's culture. This ensures that interns who accept full-time offers at the conclusion of their internships have a meaningful understanding of what life would be like as a company employee. In addition, internships also allow JPMC to observe the results of their university curricular enhancements and help to give further insight for future areas of development.

Finally, over 20 research projects have been executed with SU and UD, with areas of focus including cyber risk and information security, analytics, improved efficiency, and large-scale database management. Results of these research projects have delivered significant value to JPMC. There have also been six nationally recognized academic publications, further promoting JPMC as a technology firm. University faculty are also invited to give presentations to JPMC employees, enabling employees to better understand emerging research trends and leading to brainstorming of additional research projects.

Sustaining the Partnerships

Several key factors enabled the success of our efforts in this university–industry collaboration. One factor was that individuals within each organization were devoted to the program's mission. While this might seem obvious, it is equally important that this support should be sought from all levels of the organizations involved, particularly senior management. On JPMCside, chief information officers, chief technology officers, senior architects, and line-of-business executives were all engaged and informed of the goals, objectives, challenges, and accomplishments of the collaboration. Within the universities, the list of active participants included the chancellor/president, provost, vice president for research, and academic deans.

Related to this engagement at all levels within all organizations, throughout this effort, there was a continuing effort to engage all the stakeholders. This was achieved through regular update meetings with executives, governance committees, recruiters and career services, and other groups within JPMC and the universities. Internal newsletters were distributed to key JPMC employees and those who expressed an interest in being involved with various collaboration initiatives. Stakeholders were invited to on-campus events, including speaking engagements, athletic games, research sessions, and networking events, which helped to create and build relationships across the firm and the universities.

In addition to engagement at all levels within each organization, communication across the organizations was equally important. We found that an open line of communication between JPMC and the universities was essential to the success of this program. For example, when issues arose, it was crucial that all parties involved were comfortable with discussing problems, concerns, and solutions in a collaborative manner. Furthermore, university faculty and JPMC staff were in continual contact with one another regarding the efforts of all parties, including deliverables expected and milestones achieved. To enable this active communication to occur, there were points of contact for each area of the collaboration, and meetings were held regularly regarding each of the four program pillars (curriculum, research, community engagement, and internships), as well as regular leadership meetings. This regular communication and face-to-face contact ensured that everything was running smoothly and as planned, despite the changing academic calendar and business demands. Equally important, these meetings enabled the rapid identification of issues, so that they could be quickly solved or mitigated, without finger pointing across the organizations.

Finally, one observed benefit that we did not anticipate, was the cross-pollination of ideas across the different areas of focus. For example, when a JPMC employee visited a campus to give a guest lecture, the connection between the JPMC employee and the faculty member often led to discussions about possible research projects. Conversely, we also had an example where a research project led to the creation of a new course. There were also many discussions on the intersection of community engagement and curriculum, such as supporting a not-for-profit organization via a class project.

Challenges

During our time working across organizations, the main challenges we encountered, and then strove to resolve, were typically caused by the cultural differences between an academic institution and a for-profit enterprise. One such cultural difference is language and the meaning of specific terms and phrases, which can vary between industry and academia. For example, a short-term university research project is typically considered a long-term effort from an industry perspective. An instance of this occurred when JPMC reached out to the faculty at one of the universities regarding the development of a new course. Ultimately, the introduction of the new course was delayed by a year in order to transition faculty into new roles more seamlessly. This timing was considered normal or even slightly accelerated from an academic perspective, but was considered to be a major delay from an industry perspective.

Another challenge is that the corporate calendar is different from the academic calendar. For example, year-end events occur in December for JPMC and in June for the universities. Also, the universities have scheduled vacations, such as winter break, that do not exist in a corporate environment. Therefore, it is important to recognize the differences in the way universities and industry operate, and timelines and schedules need to be adjusted so that they are mutually beneficial to all organizations involved.

Conclusion

All of the challenges we faced in this university–industry partnership were managed and mitigated via our focus on communication and active brainstorming. In addition, flexibility on both sides of the relationship is necessary, as changes can occur regularly within organizations and tasks may need to be reprioritized. Furthermore, we have found that a well-structured collaboration model ensures that neither side is forced into a position where it must abandon a core principle. Equally important, each side gains from a particular task. To help achieve this gain for both organizations, the parties involved should comprehend and embrace the objectives of each organization.

Note

1. Prey, J. C. & Weaver, A. C. (2013), "Fostering Gender Diversity in Computing." *IEEE Computer Society*, 46: 22–23. DOI Bookmark: http://doi.ieeecomputersociety.org/10.1109/MC.2013.97.
2. Gault, J., Redington, J. & Schlager, T. (2000), Undergraduate Business Internships and Career Success: Are They Related?," *Journal of Marketing Education*, 22(1): 48–53.

SECTION IV

COORDINATING AGENCIES

Experience and data agree: successful lifelong learning initiatives benefit from an intermediate organization that focuses on linking learning with practice. In this section, we feature both public and private agencies that coordinate lifelong learning programs. First, we share a conversation with the president of a community college system that coordinates and fosters the role of community colleges in economic development. Although we feature different types of organizations, this conversation raises the following issues that are common to coordinating agencies:

- The variety of services offered to serve different populations.
- The need to work closely with employers and education providers in order to remain relevant in a changing economy.
- The creativity in leveraging limited resources to sustain these programs.

Executive Perspective

North Carolina Community College System: Coordinating the Development of a Highly Skilled Workforce

Scott Ralls

Increasingly, community colleges serve as the bridge to more stable employment by offering industry certification programs and introductory college courses. They have the potential to play a powerful role in expanding access to high-skilled work in the knowledge economy. The North Carolina Community College system has been a cornerstone of state economic development policy since its creation over 60 years ago.

In the 1950s, with an economy dependent on farming, tobacco, and agriculture, state leaders actively planned to diversify the economy and realized they would have to provide training so that North Carolinians could work in these the new industries.

In 2014, North Carolina's economy focuses on banking, skilled manufacturing, and research. The community college system has grown to an annual enrollment of 830,000 students.

Over the past 10 years, over 40% of North Carolina's wage-earning workforce have been students at one of the 58 community colleges. The community colleges have tremendous impact on workforce development in North Carolina.

In November of 2014, we spoke with Scott Ralls, the president of the North Carolina Community College system, to discuss how the state has leveraged the community college system to strengthen the state economy through improving the education and skills of North Carolinians.

The North Carolina Community College system has been touted as a major player in the state's economic development plan. Can you describe that role? Can you provide a brief overview of how the community college system fits into North Carolina's education policies? Into workforce development policies?

North Carolina provides a guarantee for companies that are creating jobs in our state; training will be provided at state expense. (The threshold is 12 new jobs for a training class.) Training is customized to the company's needs for those new jobs. We are state and locally funded to do job-skills training. In other states, community colleges that do non-degree activities have contract relationships with employers. Here, we provide training for a subsidized registration fee.

In addition to the customized training, we offer basic adults skills, college courses that lead to degrees, and programs to learn technical and professional skills. In the last 5 years we have put a real emphasis on industry certification. We have tried to structure both our degree and non-degree programs to lead to industry credentials.

The community college system has adapted as the economy of North Carolina has shifted. Can you talk about how the system remains adaptable?

In a state system the real role is to make sure there is fertile ground so that a program can be created quickly or ended quickly. There's not a lot of bureaucracy, particularly in non-degree areas and customized training. It's almost immediate. While there are approval processes, it's all electronic and moves without formal committees. One of the things that works for us is that in North Carolina we have common curriculum standards but the determination of what is offered is a local decision. Each college has industry advisors in terms of program areas. They are very responsive to their local communities.

The state has rolled programs together to provide increased flexibility in customized programs for employers. In addition to the New and Expanding Industries Training program, we have added programs to fund training for companies making a significant investment in new technology or productivity. These programs helped us get through the recession. We could help companies with a series of plants across the United States, which was beneficial when making decisions about keeping facilities in North Carolina open or expanding after the recession.

How does the system work with organizational partners, particularly employers, to further the mission? How is that work coordinated?

It's not a state community college system but a state-coordinated system. We deliberately put the colleges front-and-center. The relationships are local, and the stronger the connection between the company and the college, the more both of them jointly benefit. The colleges and the programs grow around these companies. The partnership is more than initial startup training, but other programs grow out of the partnership. A symbiotic relationship forms. The colleges experience program growth, and gain increased resources and technology. The companies are set up to be the sources of future decisions about program development.

While we don't gain revenue from companies in terms of fees that they pay, we gain from connections and investment in our programs.

How do you measure success? What were the barriers to successfully meeting the system's mission and goals?

When we look at the degree programs, we've adopted performance-based funding for student success program metrics, primarily program completion. For job training programs, we have a significant effort with the state Department of Commerce to develop employment-based metrics. The challenge is that students who are participating in our programs are already employed, so knowing if they have a job afterward doesn't mean much. We are working toward connecting wage data to programs and determining data challenges, particularly with regard to self-employment, military employment, and data in other states. We need better occupations data. We can determine if students are employed and in what industry, but cannot determine their occupation. That has been a challenge.

What other factors did you need to address?

Community colleges have been particularly challenged. We had huge enrollment growth during the recession and simultaneous budget cuts. We had to step back and prioritize our funding structure. It used to be that everything was funded at the same amount. Could be a sociology class or a radiology class: but the costs are very different. [Radiology classes] have much smaller class sizes, more sophisticated technology. You have to spend more for instructors. You have to spend more for equipment. So we change our funding structure to prioritize science, technology, engineering, and mathematics (STEM) and applied STEM programs, and programs that lead to third-party industry certification.

We did have a payoff from the redesign of our developmental education. We made it more accelerated and more modular. We flipped the classroom environment in many cases. We were able to get about $16 million in savings.

We call it the developmental dividend, and we moved that into the highest cost technician and health care programs. We were about to increase their funding by about 15%. Over a 3-year period, we have seen an 8% shift in enrollment toward the STEM programs.

What are the next steps?

In the past, we have done training and education through the community college and had apprenticeship, employment services, and Workforce Investment Act programs within the state Department of Commerce. Recently, the secretary of commerce and I signed a memorandum of understanding. We are working toward a combined workforce effort to bring together the federally funded workforce centers with job training programs and will have a joint emphasis on apprenticeship and workforce learning. For example, in order to integrate our organizations, the community college vice president for workforce development and the assistant secretary of commerce for workforce development will now be one individual. North Carolina is working to integrate workforce development policy.

CHAPTER 11

The National Urban League
Framework to Support At-Risk Youth

Saroya Friedman-Gonzalez

ounded in 1910, the National Urban League (NUL) is a historic civil rights organization that aims to enable African Americans and other underserved communities to secure economic self-reliance, parity, power, and civil rights. NUL has local affiliates in 36 states and the District of Columbia. NUL's model utilizes a hub-and-spoke structure, in which NUL plays a central role in essential activities such as leveraging and blending funding, maintaining and enhancing funder relationships, raising awareness, providing technical assistance and training, and managing contracts. As an intermediary, NUL can strategically align partners in order to serve participants most effectively. NUL can broker relationships among government, business, and nonprofit partners, provide the infrastructure required to manage multiple partners, create systems for data collection, raise funds, manage finances, and provide quality assurance. This model frees up community-based affiliates to focus on their strengths in offering program services, which is what they do best. NUL's services are centered on five programmatic areas:

- Employment
- Housing
- Health
- Education
- Entrepreneurship

As one of the few organizations of its kind, NUL has been at the helm during the changing tides of employment programs from the turn of the 20th century until today. Whereas years ago the key to employability success was defined by perfecting a single skill set, today's successful preparation is characterized more by a participants' ability and adaptability. What it takes to prepare for today's jobs has changed significantly, and developing strategies to promote lifelong learning is ever more significant. For example, to keep costs down, employers now have the option to outsource low-skilled labor abroad. This factor, combined with the rapid growth of the technology sector, has ultimately favored a more skilled and adaptable labor force. There are increasing demands placed on middle-skills workers and proportionally decreasing demands for lower skilled labor.

Through our local affiliates, NUL provides services to many entry-level workers and must answer two vital questions:

- How can one ensure that low-skilled and entry-level workers have a fair chance of competing and advancing in today's workforce, where post-secondary training and degree attainment are the new norm?
- As a provider of services, how do we facilitate educational/training attainment when resources to promote this goal are both increasingly competitive and dwindling?

Accordingly, our programs must instill in our participants the importance of continuing education and lifelong learning processes to adapt to these changing labor markets. Given the importance of developing and refining skills over a lifetime of employment, youth employment provides an important foundation for adult success. NUL's Urban Youth Empowerment Program (UYEP™) is a signature program of NUL that provides a case study of a program targeting at-risk youths and connecting them to a cadre of services, ultimately improving their long-term educational and career prospects.

Urban Youth Empowerment Program

In 2004, NUL was awarded a $9.3 million grant by the United States Department of Labor to implement a multisite demonstration project targeted to adjudicated young adults and high school dropouts ages 18 to 24. This project became UYEP. The goal of UYEP is to deliver academic and career exploration and personal development services to young adults under the premise that early exposure to career opportunities ignites the desire for knowledge and introduces the idea of lifelong learning. Through carefully mapped out services built around work-related activities, young adults are enhancing competencies that employers want. In particular, disenfranchised youths benefit from the concept of lifelong learning, and early exposure to these services improves a young person's prospects for ongoing development and credentialing.

Program Design

The program is based on the following theory of change: For every individual who participates in UYEP, there will be increases in long-term employment (unsubsidized); participants who were in trouble with the law in the past are less likely to re-offend and return to prison; high school dropouts attain their general equivalency diploma (GED). Participants exit the program with improved literacy and numeracy (evidenced via increases in their reading and math scores on standardized tests).

To achieve the goals inherent in the theory of change, UYEP offers mentorship, career coaching, and intensive case management activities, while also providing education and training. These elements are coupled with career-oriented assignments, such as summer jobs, paid internships, and service learning projects. The UYEP model includes six common elements that are often featured as best practices in serving adjudicated youths:

- *Commitment to Rehabilitation:* focus on rehabilitation versus punishment
- *Continuum of Care:* wraparound and personalized support services
- *Integrated Education and Training:* hard skills, soft skills, and work experience
- *System Collaboration:* partnerships with outside agencies to provide services
- *Support Structures:* mentoring, as well as strong and qualified staff
- *Accountability:* use of data to ensure ongoing improvement

The demonstration program began in 2004 with 15 Urban League affiliates that were selected by a competitive request for proposal (RFP) process. After initial years of piloting and evaluating, in 2011 UYEP was refined into its current model. Again, local affiliates were selected through a competitive RFP process. Under the current model, NUL and its partnering affiliates serve about 2,000 youths living in high-poverty, high-crime urban areas across the United States.

Current UYEP Model

The current UYEP model builds on best practices documented in NUL's evaluation of the initial UYEP model. These practices include a focus on strategic partnerships with employers and public and nonprofit organizations that provide educational and workforce related opportunities; effective hiring of strong, committed youth-focused program staff; careful attention to the mental health and substance abuse service needs of participants, and linkage to effective services to address them; an emphasis on peer-based systems of outreach and support for program participants; and high-quality mentoring opportunities. These practices are based on the following four key youth development tenets that foster participant engagement and program retention:

- The opportunity for youths to build relationships with positive, caring adults
- A targeted educational and workforce curriculum that builds on youths' interests and assets
- Exposure to stipend-paying, real-world opportunities to gain workforce skills
- Linkages to comprehensive community supports and services to address barriers to success

Twenty affiliates across the country currently implement UYEP. These affiliates ensure that enrolled participants are offered the minimum services described in the following subsections.

Recruitment and Outreach. Urban League affiliates develop formalized partnerships, through memoranda of understanding, with select agencies to recruit and serve UYEP participants. Some of the organizations that affiliates must partner with include the following:

- State juvenile and adult correctional agencies, in order to receive referrals of prisoners about to be released who plan to return to the target communities being served
- Local parole offices, in order to receive referrals of released prisoners who plan to return to the target communities being served and to collaborate in serving these individuals
- Local school districts and high schools, in order to receive referrals of non-offender high school dropouts

- Local drug and alcohol abuse treatment centers, in order to provide assistance to program participants in need of such services
- Local workforce investment boards, in order to provide access to employment services provided by job centers

Additionally, NUL requires affiliates to formalize partnerships with local employers, education and training institutions, and other community-based organizations to effectively serve and place participants. Prior to enrollment in UYEP, affiliates prescreen individuals to ensure that they meet eligibility criteria, including (but not limited to) the following: age 14 to 24 at the time of enrollment; residing or planning to reside upon release from detention in a target high-poverty, high-crime community; currently incarcerated in the adult criminal justice or juvenile justice system in a state or federal prison, or in a local jail or state or local juvenile correctional facility and will be released within 90 days of being enrolled in the program; a high school dropout; and expressing a desire to complete all UYEP activities. Eligibility is determined via a comprehensive intake and assessment.

Intake and Assessment. The core of the UYEP model is the comprehensive intake and assessment and individualized service planning offered by advocate counselors (ACs). During the intake and assessment process, each participant meets with an AC who conducts a four-step assessment process to determine any barriers based on education level, skills and career interest, and level of intervention.

Affiliates use information captured from various assessments to help participants create a detailed, customized Individual Career and Education Plan (ICEP). The ICEP documents short-term and long-term education/training and employment goals. It guides decisions on job readiness and skills training activities, as well as placement and retention strategies. ACs map ICEP goals against local labor market data to enable affiliate staff to match participants with targeted training assignments that align with real opportunities for unsubsidized jobs. As participants master skills, job developers work with participants to place them into apprenticeships and unsubsidized employment.

Orientation. Affiliates utilize a presentation developed by NUL to orient every enrolled participant to the program. This presentation includes a program overview, which describes UYEP goals and objectives as well as its employment strategies and services, restorative justice and service projects, available case management services, education and training opportunities, mentorship opportunities, available supportive services, dates of workshops and special events, and participant rights and responsibilities, as well as other key program information. During orientation, participants also receive a UYEP Policies and Procedures Handbook detailing the program.

Employment Strategies and Services. Under the UYEP model, placement is provided for youths who are ages 18 to 24 and out of school at enrollment. They are placed into long-term occupational skills training, post-secondary opportunities, the military, or unsubsidized employment. Thus, affiliate employment strategies and services include strategies such as job placement, transitional jobs, on-the-job training, subsidized jobs in both the public and private sectors, participation in conservation and service corps programs, and job readiness training. The emphasis is on placing participants in high-demand, high-opportunity jobs, in the following sectors: manufacturing, technology, health care, and construction/building trades. At a minimum, affiliates are required by NUL to implement a 2-week workforce fundamentals course. As part of the course, participants write an updated résumé, a cover letter, and develop a career pathway map. Job readiness workshops are also provided on a regular basis.

Education and Training. Affiliates provide a comprehensive set of interventions to address the varying academic levels of participants. Education and training services include integrating education interventions with career and occupational development and basic skills instruction or remedial education; assessing participants for learning disabilities; providing language instruction for individuals with limited English proficiency; tutoring; providing study skills training; and conducting credit retrieval. Affiliates also counsel participants on acquiring financial aid to attend college, take them on visits to local community and 4-year colleges, and help them fill out necessary application forms for college. Depending on the participants' educational goals, they may be referred to industry-specific education, training and certificate programs that are delivered through a network of accredited community colleges and universities. By design, all 20 affiliates have strategic access to targeted vocational training and other post-secondary certification pathways. Affiliates also use ICEPs to outline prescriptive plans to help each participant improve their math and reading skills and to attain a high school degree, if applicable. Affiliates must place a high priority on helping participants obtain their high school diplomas or GEDs, and focusing on interventions to help them enroll and succeed in alternative schools, evening continuation schools, or GED programs.

Case Management. ACs serve as the participants' prime contact, and ensure that participants receive training in financial literacy; counseling regarding criminal records, civil rights, and applying for jobs; and assistance in applying for federal benefits such as Pell grants and the Supplemental Nutrition Assistance Program (SNAP) for food stamps. ACs also assist community supervision officers in serving returning young offenders and in linking them to supportive services, transportation, housing, mental health services, and other social services.

Mentoring. Affiliates solicit mentors to work with ACs to implement cultural, educational, and career-specific activities to support UYEP participants. The mentors are adult volunteers who demonstrate an ability to understand young people's perspectives and agree to support participants for a period of no less than 1 year. A minimum of 60% of participants are matched with mentors, and the assessment and matching process is incorporated into the comprehensive intake and assessment process for all young adults, including those in confinement. Affiliates offer both one-on-one and group-based mentoring, entailing no more than five mentees per mentor. Mentors must apply to be a part of UYEP, agree to participate in a 1-day training, and pass a background check screening.

Restorative Justice Projects. Affiliates must implement restorative justice projects that enable returning offenders to give something positive back to their community to make up for their criminal offenses. These projects incorporate four guiding principles: (1) provide a public good to the community, (2) provide tangible skills to the participant, (3) incorporate time for reflection, and (4) entail a public-awareness component. Restorative justice projects can include a direct service project with the community (e.g., participant interacts with elderly person); an indirect service (e.g., mixing cement that will be used to build a playground in the community); an advocacy project (e.g., participant raises awareness on an important community issue such as second chances for young adults with criminal history); or a research project (e.g., gathering data on eating habits as part of a nutrition course). Each type of project is associated with both concrete and "soft" skills, ensuring that service opportunities are effective in building specific workforce competencies as well as enhancing job readiness and appropriate workplace etiquette.

Post-Program Support and Follow-Up. Affiliates provide participants with access to follow-up services for at least 3 months after the ICEP goals are met. At a minimum, three types of post-program follow-up services are available to participants. First, the ACs schedule check-in calls with participants to reinforce the connection of the young adults to the program and its goals, express care and concern, and assess whether additional referrals are required. Second, affiliates schedule a roster of post-program workshops to facilitate the transition to less formal support. These workshops serve as "booster" sessions for some of the critical lessons of the program's life skills, financial literacy, and social/emotional learning activities. Third, affiliates establish and facilitate an alumni network for former participants to speak with current participants.

Performance Management

To measure participants' outcomes, NUL has developed the Urban League Program Data Management (PDM) Application based on CiviCRM,* which is integrated into its existing "I Am Empowered" Drupal** web platform. The program strategically aligns services and activities with pre-identified outputs and outcomes; pinpoints performance challenges in real time; and fosters best practices, learning, and peer collaboration. NUL performance monitoring activities also include monthly performance management reports on key quality and performance indicators, management meetings to critically review data and collectively solve problems, and participant satisfaction feedback solicited

---

* CiviCRM is a free and open-source, web-based constituent relationship management software distributed under the GNU General Public License. For more information, go to https://civicrm .org/.

** Drupal is a free and open-source content management framework written in PHP and distributed under the GNU General Public License. For more information, go to http://drupal.org.

through surveys and interviews. PDM facilitates the collection of participant outcomes by recording details about each participant's characteristics at the program start, including the content of barrier and skills assessments, as well as personal development and progress against goals laid out in the ICEP. By monitoring progress monthly, NUL has the ability to regularly identify areas of strength and weakness by program component, affiliate, staff member, and across participant characteristics. Monthly affiliate meetings provide an opportunity to share best practices, troubleshoot areas of weakness, and develop corrective action plans as needed. In addition to oversight by NUL programmatic staff, NUL's board of directors monitors high-level indicators on a quarterly basis to ensure that the organization is on track to meet annual goals and contractual obligations. PDM also facilitates the collection of career pathways outcomes such as number of credentials attained and wage gains achieved. These data are used to determine which career pathways NUL should prioritize and target.

Program Impact

To assess the impact of the initial UYEP model, NUL contracted a third-party evaluator over a 4-month period (September to December 2009) to objectively capture information on what worked, what did not work, and what, if any, best practices or challenges contributed to the success or difficulties of the program. The formal evaluation process revealed that there were positive correlations between completers of the program and positive outcomes.[1]

Program Participants

During the first 5 years, UYEP served 3,900 youths. Most lived at or below the poverty line (93%), were either black or Hispanic (93%), and had not completed high school (77%). A significant minority (39%) were ex-offenders (Exhibit 11-1).

Participant Outcomes

Some 2,300 participants completed the program. On average, each participant took part in three of the six program service offerings. Among participants whose predominant program activity involved workforce services, 20% en-

Exhibit 11-1. Urban Youth Empowerment Program participant demographics for the demonstration project (2004–2009).

Age	18 to 24
Race	
• White	7%
• African-American	85%
• Hispanic	4%
• Other	4%
Math and reading score below 7th grade level	30%
Ex-offenders	39%

rolled in full-time post-secondary education, and 68% attained full-time unsubsidized employment.

Although some affiliates performed better than others, the overall percentages of program completers were high (Exhibit 11-2).

The recidivism rate for all program participants (including those who were accepted but did not follow up and received no services) was 7%. This implies that there is both a selection effect (those who completed the application process were already less likely to re-offend) and a program effect, since completing the program is associated with much stronger outcomes. In both cases, this is a dramatic improvement over national averages: the U.S. Department of Justice reports that 55% of all juvenile offenders are re-arrested within 1 year of their release.

Exhibit 11-2. Urban Youth Empowerment Program participant outcomes for the demonstration project (2004–2009).

Program Completers	
• Average number of services	3 (out of 6)
Education achievement	
• High school diploma/GED	48.3%
Job placement	
• Obtained unsubsidized long-term work	58.8%
Improved academic skills	
• Improved one grade level: math	63.6%
• Improved one grade level: reading	79.5%
Recidivism	7%

Conclusion: Why the NUL's Hub-and-Spoke Model Works

The National Urban League serves as the hub of a national network focused primarily on education and employability. In the implementation of UYEP, NUL provides overall contract management, technical assistance support, fiscal oversight, and data management of the project. NUL also provides clarity and guidance on the program design, and convenes the various affiliates, serving to promote peer-to-peer communication and shared learning through sharing of best practices and lessons learned. In turn, the local affiliate organizations serve as the spokes by focusing on the provision of quality services to their participants, cultivating local partnerships to enhance program delivery, and ensuring that the goals of the program, as defined by NUL, are adequately met. Working together as hub and spokes, the Urban League has proven successful in raising the standard of living in underserved urban areas.

Effectiveness of the Hub and Spokes

Through structured program design and a standardized approach, NUL's employment programs are delivered through our network of Urban League community-based providers across the country. Both the national hub and the local spokes have clearly defined roles in program delivery. NUL, in its role as intermediary, serves in the following functions:

- Contract management
- Program design
- Technical assistance
- Fiscal oversight
- Data management
- Ongoing resource development

Urban League affiliates provide job seekers in their community with a menu of services including the following:

- Basic job readiness workshops
- Financial planning and empowerment
- Health education
- Wraparound supportive services
- Tailored educational interventions
- Paid internships, community service, and summer jobs

- Meaningful restorative justice and service learning projects
- Mentoring

One of the key benefits to the intermediary model is that community-based organizations benefit from the extra support and efficiencies created through a single convener and administrator, while the local affiliates are more aptly able to engage and holistically serve participants, affording them a robust array of supportive services offered either in-house or through strong community partnerships. Intermediaries create economies of scale and ensure that participants are provided tailored and comprehensive services by community-based organizations.

The UYEP model provides an unprecedented opportunity to address the social adjustment needs of youthful ex-offenders. The development of strategies serves to decrease participation in gang activities through the provision of full-time program activities (often dual daily activities such as education and community service) that are infused with supportive services that included group and community-wide activities and outings, and involvement with adult mentors or program staff. Partnerships with faith-based organizations, community-based organizations, and local businesses provide opportunities for participants to be exposed to business operations and behaviors while in on-site community service work assignments; for many, it is their first exposure to this kind of experience. In addition, local businesses that cannot provide worksite assignments provide trainers to participate in World of Work workshops as well as donating goods. NUL has designed the program to allow affiliates significant flexibility to address participants' varied education and work preparedness levels and local employment realities. The program is still in the process of recruiting participants, but we feel confident in our ability to achieve even greater impact, given NUL's long history and expertise in serving youths and young adults.

Note

1. Gallup-Black, A., Feldbaum, M., Johnson, M., with Palmer, A., Nevarez, N., Dailey, C.R. & Smith, K. (2009). *Turn Around Strategies for Youth At-Risk: Lessons from the Evaluation of the Urban Youth Empowerment Program. A Report to the National Urban League.* New York: Academy for Educational Development (AED). http://www.iamempowered.com/files/2010/02/Executive-Summary_Urban-Youth-Empowerment-Program-Evaluation.pdf.

CHAPTER 12

Carnegie Foundation for the Advancement of Teaching
A Networked Approach to Improving Math Education at Community Colleges

Corey Donahue and Gay Clyburn

The lack of student success in developmental mathematics is one of the most serious barriers to students' educational and economic achievement. Over 60% of all students entering community colleges in the United States are required to complete remedial/developmental courses as a first step toward earning associate's or bachelor's degrees. Then, to earn a degree, certificate, or license, students usually must complete at least one college-level math course. A staggering 80% of the students who place into developmental mathematics do not complete any college-level course within 3 years, blocking their way to higher education credentials and consequently to a wide array of technical and related careers.[1] It was this reality that prompted the Carnegie Foundation for the Advancement of Teaching to develop a program that has tripled the success rates of students placed into developmental mathematics in half the time compared with traditional programs. Carnegie has been able to maintain this level of student accomplishment, even as the initiative has grown to include new colleges, new faculty, and many more students over the past 3 years.

Carnegie has engaged a growing network of community colleges in the development of two mathematical pathways that target students who are at grave risk of failure—students who have weak K-12 preparation, who face language and special education challenges, or who fundamentally believe that they are destined not to do well in the subject. Both of these pathways—Statway® in statistics, and Quantway® in quantitative reasoning—seek to reverse a pernicious and disheartening cycle of failure for too many students by employing materials and teaching approaches that put them on a pathway of success, not just in college but in their lives and careers as well.

A Proven Success

Carnegie's aim was ambitious: to increase from 5% to 50% the number of students who achieved college mathematics credit within 1 year of enrollment. Initially, 29 colleges from across the United States, including two public universities in California, participated in this improvement network. First-year results (2011–2012) exceeded the established goals and expectations.[2] They revealed that, compared with previous developmental mathematics students from their institutions, the 1,133 students enrolled in Statway dramatically increased their success rate of passing a college-level mathematics course (with a grade of C or better) within 1 year of enrollment. Working with institutional researchers at the colleges, Carnegie established a baseline performance standard network-wide. Historically, in the colleges that make up this Statway network, only 5.9% of students who place into developmental mathematics achieved college mathematics credit within 1 year, and only 15.1% of such students achieved this goal within 2 years. In contrast, in the first year of Statway implementation, 51% achieved this milestone. In other words, Statway students tripled the historical success rate in one third of the time.

Quantway achieved comparable results. The first term of Quantway was in the spring of 2012, serving 418 students in eight colleges. Of those students, 56% earned a grade of C or better. Results for the second year of the program (2012–2013) were equally remarkable.[3] In the second year with a number of new faculty and colleges, 598 students successfully completed both terms of Statway and 445 students successfully completed the first term of Quantway, representing success rates of 52% for both. Because of these extraordinarily positive outcomes, a strong interest has emerged across the nation from both community colleges and educational researchers to join and broaden the work of Statway and Quantway. Third-year results, which are still undergoing internal reviews, show similar rates of success, with 55% of students successfully completing both terms of Statway and 57% of students successfully completing the first term of Quantway. Indeed, we have now grown the network to nearly 50 institutions in 11 states. The colleges in the Community College Pathways (CCP) Networked Improvement Community (NIC) are geographically and culturally diverse, and are distributed across the United States. These colleges are in dense urban areas, such as the City University of New York, as well as rural settings, such as South Georgia State College in Douglas, Georgia, and serve a diverse range of students in terms of language skills, mathematics preparation, and socioeconomic status.

In total, over 2,000 students have successfully completed Statway and achieved college mathematics credit, and nearly 2,000 students have successfully completed their developmental mathematics requirements via the first term of Quantway. The pathways reach the students whom community colleges need to serve well; a disproportionate number are minority students, from families whose primary language is not English, and are the first in their family to pursue a college degree.

Math Matters

We know that mathematics matters. As Anthony Carnevale, director of the Center on Education and the Workforce, notes, "If educators cannot fulfill their economic mission to help our youth and adults achieve quantitative literacy levels that will allow them to become successful workers, they also will fail in their cultural and political missions to create good neighbors and good citizens."[4] The pathways have been a draw to lifelong learners intent on gaining their associate's degree or additional skills needed for a changing workplace. About 36% of students are 25 years of age or older. In addition, 52% of those students who are 25 or older are part-time students (vs 34% for students under 25), indicating that they could be working at other jobs.

Mary Lowry was one of those students who was convinced that she would never realize her goal of earning a 4-year college degree—and that the math requirements were the reason. In her early 40s when she entered Foothill College in the Bay Area of California, this was going to be her last attempt to earn a degree. Math was standing in the way of her dream of working in social work or another field where she could "make a difference."

"I thought something was wrong with me," she said. "No matter how hard I tried—and I had really tried hard—I could not pass a math class." After testing into developmental mathematics and failing algebra for the third time, she was ready to give up. "I was embarrassed," she said.

She had been able to do well in all her classwork in high school except math; the same was proving to be true since she had enrolled in community college. "Math just wouldn't click; I just couldn't get it," she said.

Lowry is not the only student whose dreams have been deterred in this way. Community colleges are dedicated to the proposition that students can realize upward mobility through education and that learning is possible at any point in our lives. There, many students find success, but many others, like Mary Lowry, find that success eludes them.

She enrolled in Statway at the recommendation of one of her professors. Lowry recognized the uniqueness of her Statway experience from the first day. The focus on conceptual understanding applied to real-world problems was especially important for her. "I never knew what math was for; I thought I was just supposed to memorize a lot of equations and it would someday become clear to me. Working with the Statway materials and having the math embedded in real problems finally turned on that light bulb."

She also said that the pathways group work was essential. "We worked on problems together and we became like a family; I didn't want to let the others down so I probably worked harder." Creating a sense of belonging—a key predictor of student success—helped students realize that math class was not a foreign place for them to be. And the sooner they learn this, the better.

A "starting-strong" package includes a set of initial classroom routines targeted at reducing anxiety, increasing interest in the course, and forming supportive social networks. One key activity is a direct-to-student *growth mindset intervention,* a reading and writing exercise designed to challenge students' view that being a "math person" is a fixed attribute, delivered either in class or via the Internet during the first week of the course.

Lowry said that when she first was told through this intervention that research showed that she could "grow her brain," she was skeptical. However, the proof was in how well she did in the class. "After being told that I could do this over and over and then truly experiencing it, I became a believer. I had never had that kind of constant support in a class before. And now I know I can do math." Lowry's and her classmates' progress and struggle were monitored throughout the course by means of periodic short surveys intended to inform faculty about changes that needed to be made to both the lessons and the pedagogy as the term progressed. They also identified students who needed immediate interventions, so that they didn't fall behind or get lost.

Lowry's experience in Statway helped her develop her math understanding and advance her education. "I was astonished," Lowry said. "I not only began to understand math, I understood why I had not been able to figure it out before, and I knew it wasn't my fault." Lowry has now been accepted to San Jose State University and is on her way to earning a bachelor's degree.

A Gateway to Success

The pathway that helped Lowry finally find success in mathematics was not available until recently. In 2010, after a year of fund-raising and planning, Carnegie formed a network of community colleges, professional associations, and educational researchers to develop and implement the CCP initiative. The Carnegie Foundation's work has always been organized around the core problems of practice, embedded in the day-to-day work of improving teaching and learning, and occurring in the institutions where teaching and learning take place. We aim to impact high-leverage problems such as advancing community college students through developmental mathematics.

The $13 million initiative, headed by former Foothill president and current senior partner at Carnegie, Bernadine Chuck Fong, was funded by six foundations. Carnegie coordinated the work with programs such as Achieving the Dream and the California Community College system's Basic Skills Initiative, as well as reached out to national organizations such as the American Association of Community Colleges and American Mathematical Association of Two-Year Colleges.

Statway and Quantway are called pathways because they are complex instructional systems that include a common curriculum, pedagogy, and student supports. They differ from traditional developmental math courses in that they do not resemble the arithmetic and algebra classes that the students have taken before and are now repeating in community college. Both pathways use new approaches, timely topics, and relevant contexts so that students can learn to think and reason quantitatively, unencumbered by memories of past failures. Statistics and concepts of quantitative reasoning are in the foreground, with mathematics mainly as a subplot that reinforces and supports the learning of these topics. The developmental mathematics concepts required to support statistical and quantitative understanding are integrated throughout.

Rather than the traditional student struggle through a required 2-year sequence of courses leading to calculus, now students and faculty are joined in a common, intensive pursuit of a shared goal—for students to achieve college math credit in 1 year. Statway is designed as a 1-academic-year course that allows students to simultaneously complete their developmental mathematics requirements and receive college mathematics credit in statistics. Quantway is designed as two separate term courses. Quantway 1 is the first term of this program and fulfills the requirements for students' entire developmental mathematics sequence. Quantway 2 is the subsequent term course that allows students to receive college mathematics credit.

The Pieces of the Whole

To be sure, the pathways effort is not the only one to address the developmental math crisis, a problem estimated to cost the nation billions of dollars in lost earning potential. At Jackson Community College in Tennessee, for example, students enroll in a SMART (Survive, Master, Achieve, Review, and Transfer) Math sequence, a course-free curriculum of mastery-based developmental math modules designed in partnership with the National Center for Academic Transformation. At the Community College of Denver, students can enroll in a FastStart program and accelerate through two semesters of remediation in just one. Across the country, there are dozens more initiatives designed to revamp how and how quickly students complete developmental requirements.

But Carnegie's pathways are unique in several ways. They integrate developmental and college-level math using a curriculum that is deliberately designed to make explicit connections between higher math concepts and students' understanding of the world around them. They also organize math material into mastery-based modules, rather than simply breaking up a traditional course into smaller chunks.

In developing this program, Carnegie assembled nationally recognized leaders from the Mathematical Association of America, the American Mathematics Association of Two-Year Colleges (an organization that the Carnegie Foundation had tapped early on for advice), the American Statistical Association, and the National Numeracy Network to establish ambitious learning goals for CCP. Both pathways place emphasis on the core mathematics skills needed for work, personal life, and citizenship. They stress conceptual understanding and the ability to apply it in a variety of contexts and problems.

Three research-based principles vitalize the instructional design toward these learning opportunities:

1. *Productive Struggle.* As detailed in Hiebert and Grouws,[5] students are more likely to retain what they learn when they expend effort "solving

problems that are within reach and grappling with key mathematical ideas that are comprehendible but not yet well formed."[6] Consequently each new subject matter topic begins with a rich problem that engages students' thinking and stimulates this struggle to understand.

2. *Explicit Connections to Concepts.* Sometimes math is taught with a focus on procedural competence at the price of advancing real conceptual understanding.[7] Research suggests that making explicit connections between mathematical or statistical facts, ideas, and procedures can improve both conceptual and procedural understanding.[8]

3. *Deliberate Practice.* Classroom and homework tasks are designed to overcome gaps in understanding, apply what is learned, and deepen facility with key concepts.[9,10] Deliberate practice eschews rote repetition for carefully sequenced problems developed to guide students to deeper understanding of core concepts.[11]

These three learning opportunities are actualized in the specific lessons, assessments, and out-of-class resources that form the curriculum for each pathway. Three additional supports complement this instructional core of ambitious goals and aligned instructional materials.

First, integrated throughout the pathways is an evidence-based package of student activities and faculty actions, which we call "productive persistence", to increase student motivation, tenacity, and learning skills for success. Strategies focus on reducing student anxiety,[12] increasing their sense of belonging,[13] and enhancing their belief that they can learn math (i.e., countering the fixed mindset beliefs). Specific activities focus on developing the skills needed to be effective students and the flexible mindsets necessary to utilize those skills.[14,15] This is advanced through a package consisting of targeted student interventions, guidance to help faculty create more engaging classroom environments, and a lesson structure that encourages active student engagement.

Second, given students' diverse backgrounds, Carnegie also attends to the language and literacy demands in pathway materials and classroom activities, and supports are interwoven so that learning is accessible to all. A team has reviewed all instructional materials and pedagogic practices to remove possible barriers.

Third, and critical for scaling and sustaining the initiative, is the advancing quality teaching component. A robust professional development strand is key as the work moves out from early adopter college faculty and institutions to more adjunct faculty and to campuses where the pathways content, instructional organization, pedagogical practices, and data use initiatives appear more novel. The aim is to provide instructors with the knowledge, skills, and supports necessary to experience efficacy in initial use, to develop increasing expertise over time, and to engage the larger networked community in research on improving their collective practice.

Faculty involvement in the networked community began early in the project. When a first version of Statway materials was ready to be tested, a group of faculty, lessons and modules in hand, spent several intense days at Carnegie in what they termed "the cave."

After working almost around the clock, they walked away with a set of revised materials that were threaded through with needed student supports. The work continues. As the lessons went live in classrooms, other faculty joined in webinars, conference calls, and on-site, regional, and national meetings to further improve the pathways. They had one-on-one conversations with Carnegie staff. Some faculty tested particularly difficult lessons, identified specific problems, and hypothesized improvements in the materials or in their implementation. Faculty members worked together to plan instruction, observe one another's teaching, and identify the most difficult obstacles that stand in the way of student success in traversing the pathways. As all of this went live in different classrooms and colleges, Carnegie began to assemble a body of evidence about the variability in student outcomes and how the pathways work in different contexts.

A Networked Approach Using the Tools of Improvement Science

Although much of the success of Carnegie's pathways is due to the curricula and course changes, they are not what most distinguishes the program from other education reforms or research-practice partnerships. What makes these programs unique is the strategy of building a particular kind of professional network, what Carnegie refers to as a Networked Improvement Community (NIC), to organize and lead an array of continuous improvement processes with the use of improvement science. The innovation of an NIC is using a highly structured network of education professionals, in collaboration with designers and researchers, to address a practical problem. The focus on education professionals distinguishes the CCP NIC from forms of inquiry led by researchers. NICs require a coordinating hub as "an initiator of activity and an integrative force for the overall enterprise."[16] Professional leadership helps NICs tap into the innovation capacity of front-line workers and accelerate improvement. In a NIC, effective implementation means improving a process within the system with the overall goal of achieving efficacy with reliability at scale. Research knowledge is often critical for improvement, but in an NIC, knowledge demands are disciplined by specific improvement aims. To be a priority, knowledge should inform the actions or decisions of NIC members or leaders in ways that help the network achieve its aims. In this sense NICs are engaged in problem-disciplined inquiry as a feature of professional practice.

Two key tenets from improvement science guide this work. First, improvement science embraces an iterative design-development ethic. It places emphasis on learning quickly, with minimal disruptions and at low cost. By iterating over multiple cycles and multiple contexts, inferences made early in the work are continually tested over and over. It is not sufficient to know that "A can cause B." Unlike an experimental trial, the goal of improvement research is to effectively achieve B reliably in different contexts and conditions. The iterative structure of testing combined with the ongoing examination of data supports this emphasis on assuring the replicability of effects. Second, improvement research also recognizes that variability in performance is the core problem to solve. This means attending to undesirable outcomes, examining the processes generating them, and targeting change efforts toward greater efficacy for all. This requires analyses that look beyond just mean differences among groups.

Informing continuous evidence-based improvement is a rapid analytics capacity designed to focus attention on what is (and is not) working, where and for whom, and under what set of circumstances. While Carnegie values the on-average improvements already documented, the NIC goal is efficacy in every college, classroom, and for all of the diverse subgroups of students who enroll. This component provides empirical feedback informing ongoing efforts toward greater quality with greater reliability.

Improvement Science in Action

For the past 2 years, subnetworks of faculty have been working on specific improvement challenges: Productive Persistence, advancing quality teaching, furthering Quantway and Statway development, as well as pathways expansion and enrollment. Subnetwork projects cut across multiple colleges (and sometimes pathways too) and include content experts, practitioners, and researchers. Other work involves iterative tests of change (plan–do–study–act [PDSA] cycles) that might run over a full academic year. All the participants are using the tools of improvement science to do this work.

For instance, the Productive Persistence subnetwork is addressing non-academic drivers that influence whether a student remains in the classroom and is successful. The team used results from previous surveys and the research literature to identify three specific concerns that affect students' social ties in the classroom: a sense of belonging, a sense that professors care about them, and their comfort in asking questions. These drivers were selected because data from pathways students indicated that these were closely related to success (earning a grade of C or better) and persistence rates (students enrolling in the next term of Statway).

These drivers focused the work on areas that NIC members determined could be significantly improved. In the process, subnetwork members learned a new way to conduct practice research, to gather information about their students, and to look more deeply at Productive Persistence. Based on this work, subnetwork members prototyped "change ideas" related to one or more of the three drivers and then conducted iterative, short-cycle testing of the prototyped changes, the PDSA cycles, linked to those changes.

For example, subnetwork faculty have initiated improvement research on three change ideas to address students' sense of not belonging:

1. When students miss class, the instructors rarely have a systematic way of reaching out in order to understand why the students have been absent and to encourage them to attend future classes. One faculty member in the Productive Persistence subnetwork has developed routines and scripts for emailing absent students. These scripts change over the course of the semester as the relationship between the faculty member and the student evolves. Characteristics of the emails were tested through PDSAs and revisions were made. The faculty member found that attendance improved and has recommended that this script be further tested.

2. Another faculty member sought to build a sense of belonging by making students responsible for one another's presence in a *group noticing routine*, which consists of three stages. In the first stage, the faculty member groups students, who get to know each other outside of the math context. In the next stage, groups are responsible for informing the faculty member if

someone is absent. In the final stage, groups take responsibility for contacting students who are absent, encouraging them to attend future classes, and giving them any materials or information that they missed. Attendance remained strong across the semester (an 85% median attendance rate), quite different from past experiences with similar student groups.

3. In the starting-strong package, faculty members are advised to give roles (e.g., monitor, reporter, facilitator) to students in the group. Members of the Productive Persistence subnetwork developed and tested a routine for effective role functioning. During group work, students are given laminated cards that describe the expectations for their assigned roles, which rotate throughout the course. The student acting as the facilitator of the group assesses the performance of each student relative to the role he or she played on that day. The scores are then given to the faculty member and incorporated into classroom participation grades. The two faculty members who tested the strategy found that students worked together more effectively and that attendance was strong (a 92% median attendance rate).

Having demonstrated promise in this first-stage test of new classroom routines, these ideas are now candidates for further testing across the NIC. As these routines are taken up by new faculty and in different colleges, Carnegie expects further refinements will occur.

The ultimate goal is to ensure efficacy under the broadest possible conditions that confront different faculty and students. If they are successful, these innovations will subsequently take on the status of *kernel routines*—the core set of materials and practices that have demonstrated widespread efficacy and are now broadly shared and used by NIC participants.

Next Steps

After participating in something that is changing students' lives, many faculty members have become champions and promoters of the work. Carnegie staff members have also been eagerly spreading the good news. By the end of the 2014–2015 school year, 18,000 students' have benefited from Pathways and that the numbers will rapidly grow thereafter. Equally important, Carnegie will have institutionalized the practices of evidence-based quality improvement as a norm of the education workplace.

Notes

1. Bailey, T., Jeong, D.W. & Cho, S.W. (2010). Referral, enrollment, and completion in developmental education sequences in community colleges. *Economics of Education Review*, 29: 255–270.

2. Strother, S., Van Campen, J. & Grunow, A. (2012). "Community College Pathways: 2011–2012 Descriptive Report." (Report by the Carnegie Foundation for the Advancement of Teaching.) http://www.carnegiefoundation.org/sites/default/files/CCP_Descriptive_Report_Year_1.pdf.

3. Van Campen, J., Strother, S. & Sowers, N. (2013). "Community College Pathways: 2012–2013 Descriptive Report" (Report by the Carnegie Foundation for the Advancement of Teaching.) http://www.carnegiefoundation.org/sites/default/files/pathways/CCP_Descriptive_Report_Year_2.pdf.

4. Carnevale, A. P. & Desrochers, D. M. "The Democratization of Mathematics," in *Quantitative Literacy: Why Numeracy Matters for Schools and Colleges* (Princeton, NJ: National Council on Education and the Disciplines, 2003), 21–31. http://www.maa.org/ql/pgs21_31.pdf.

5. Hiebert, J. & Grouws, D. (2007). The effects of classroom mathematics teaching on students' learning. In Lester, F.K. (Ed.), *Second Handbook of Research on Mathematics Teaching and Learning*. Greenwich, CT: Information Age, pp. 371–404.

6. Schmidt, R. & Bjork, R. A. (1992). New conceptualizations of practice: common principles in three paradigms suggest new concepts for training. *Psychological Science*, 3(4): 207–217.

7. Boaler, J. (1998). Open and closed mathematics: student experiences and understandings. *Journal for Research in Mathematics Education*, 29: 41–62.

8. Hiebert & Grouws, The effects of classroom mathematics.

9. Ericcson, K., (2008). Deliberate practice and acquisition of expert performance: a general overview. *Academic Emergency Medicine*, 15: 988–994.

10. Ericcson, K., Krampe, R. & Tesche-Römer, C. (1993). The role of deliberate practice in the acquisition of expert performance. *Psychological Review*, 100: 363–406.

11. Pashler, H., Rohrer, D., Cepeda, N., & Carpenter, S. (2007). Enhancing learning and retarding forgetting: choices and consequences. *Psychonomic Bulletin and Review*, 14: 187–193.

12. Jamieson, J., Mendes, W., Blackstock, E. & Schmader, T. (2009). Turning the knots in your stomach into bows: reappraising arousal improves performance on the GRE. *Journal of Experimental Social Psychology*, 46: 208–212.

13. Walton, G. & Cohen, G. (2011). A brief social-belonging intervention improves academic and health outcomes among minority students. *Science*, 331: 1447–1451.

14. Dweck, C., Walton, G. & Cohen, G. (2011). *Academic tenacity: mindsets and skills that promote long-term learning*. Seattle, WA: White paper prepared for the Gates Foundation.

15. Yeager, D. & Walton, G. (2011). Social-psychological interventions in education: they're not magic. *Review of Educational Research*, 81(2): 267–301.

16. Bryk, A., Gomez, L. & Grunow, A. (2011). Getting ideas into action: building networked improvement communities in education. In Hallinan, M.T. (Ed.), *Frontiers in Sociology of Education*. New York: Springer, pp. 127–162.

CHAPTER 13

Africa-America Institute
Developing Leaders for Africa

Melissa Howell

Founded in 1953, the Africa-America Institute (AAI)'s mission is to strengthen human capacity and help to develop effective leaders in Africa. Alumni of AAI's programs include President Alassane Ouattara of Cote d'Ivoire; Nahas Angula, Namibia's prime minister from 2005 to 2012; Uganda's Betty Bigombe, cabinet minister and member of parliament who negotiated with the Lord's Resistance Army to bring peace to her region; and Kenya's Wangari Maathai, the 2004 winner of the Nobel Peace Prize. In the past 61 years, AAI has served over 23,000 talented men and women committed to improving conditions of life in Africa.

According to the World Bank and the African Development Bank, today's globalized economy requires a well-skilled workforce with the capacity to accumulate and transfer knowledge. Although many African countries spend a significant portion of their national budgets on education, post-secondary education continues to be a rare commodity across the continent. In South Africa, Kenya, and Nigeria, countries in which AAI's Transformational Leadership Program (TLP) currently operates, post-secondary education enrollment ranges from 3% to 15.2% of the adult population, as compared with 72.6% in the United States. These statistics shed little light on the varying cultural influences and structural barriers that promote such disparities on the continent, such as gender norms that deter the education of girls, long commuting distances from educational facilities that restrict enrollment, and inadequate teacher training to provide students access to appropriate levels of education and training. Still, these statistics present a lens through which to understand the increased opportunities and benefits of scholarships and leadership development programs supporting this population.

Initially, AAI was created by President Horace Mann Bond of Lincoln University (PA) and Professor Will Leo Hansberry of Howard University (Washington, DC) to support African students attending colleges and universities in the United States. By the 1990s, AAI's focus was providing both academic supports and professional skills training. African Nationals could attend programs in either the United States or on the African continent. In the early 2000s, AAI established itself as a thought leader, and used its platform to facilitate increased United States–Africa engagement across government, academic, nonprofit, and business sectors. These efforts laid the foundation for the TLP, designed to develop the capacity of African leaders to address the challenges faced on the African continent.

The Transformational Leadership Program

The need for advanced education and training is pronounced in African nongovernmental organizations (NGOs) that deliver some of the most fundamental services to their communities, including health care, housing, education, clean water, and sanitation, yet consistently are under-resourced. Most of the extreme conditions that developing nations face, such as high numbers of impoverished families, increased deaths caused by childbirth, repeated financial limitations that impede school completion, are seemingly inescapable experiences for many communities across the continent.

Developing and implementing best practices are not just a means to organizational success but can be the daily determinants between an individual's prolonged life or untimely death. Yet, under these same conditions, the inventive and creative solutions developed to combat these needs are restricted to small-scale production and implementation. The TLP was created to bridge the capacity gap of institutions to support NGO leaders. As a result, social sector organizations are better equipped to tackle the myriad challenges they were created to address and reach the levels of scale required to transform communities.

In 2006, AAI created the TLP to increase leadership capacity on the continent by providing training to organization leaders addressing some of the most challenging issues facing the continent. The aim of the program is to create a critical mass of leaders who can transform communities.

How is it that at certain moments and in certain orders of knowledge, there are these sudden take-offs, these hastenings of evolution, these transformations which fail to correspond to the calm, continuist image that is normally accredited?[1] — Michel Foucault

TLP in Action

Joshua R. K. Tulwo
Founder, Wei Wei Farmers Cooperative Society

To attend our program at USIU, Joshua Tulwo traveled the 8 hours from his rural, underserved community motivated by appreciation for the program that, he says, "sharpened my skills and gave me the knowledge to be a civil leader." At the outset of the EMOD program, he struggled with the requirements of his studies.

During the course of his residence at the university, he went from counting words in his papers by hand to carrying a laptop and making Powerpoints for class presentations. He now speaks of a reachable dream. As the leader of an agricultural collective serving 2,000 farmers with 15 employees, Joshua entered the EMOD program at USIU with the goal of improving the farmers' abilities to sustain themselves and their families.

He identified the following factors as contributing to problems of sustainability for the farmers' organization:

- Problems with decision making
- Overreliance on donor aid
- Poor public relations
- Underutilization of resources
- Lack of innovation
- Lack of accountability

Using his organization as the basis for his EMOD study, he concluded his thesis by writing that "there are numerous challenges that confront social enterprises in their attempts to achieve self sustainability.

"The challenges include: lack of finance, poor governance, lack of trained staff, loss of social connection, legal barriers, and political interference, amongst other factors."

On the basis of the trust his work had engendered among his neighbors, in the most recent national election Joshua was chosen as the Kilgoris Constituency Elections Coordinator for the Independent Electoral and Boundaries Commission. Responsible for a rural constituency of 50,000 people in an election process fraught with tribal politics and threats of violence, Joshua has become an advocate for his region and role model for younger people who "are aspiring to be like me. They want to further their studies and get good jobs like myself." As he wrote, "my contribution in the Kilgoris constituency has enabled the organization to achieve its core objective of being a free, fair and credible organization."

In partnerships with the Coca-Cola Africa Foundation (TCCAF) and a select group of university partners in both the United States and Africa, TLP provides training to leaders and increasingly to small and medium-sized enterprises (SMEs). With a $2.5 million investment by TCCAF, the Africa-America Institute established its inaugural partnership in 2007 at Emory University's Goizueta Business School. Later the same year, AAI partnered with the University of Pennsylvania's Wharton Business School.

At the same time, in the field of international development, participatory models of development grew more mainstream as the World Bank called for "country ownership" of poverty reduction policies. These models suggested a redistribution of power from the domestic and foreign stakeholders who normally formulate development policy in heavily indebted countries to marginalized communities traditionally excluded from the policy process.[2] AAI has aligned the TLP with these more participatory models. The communities once seen only as beneficiaries of services became key players in creating solutions, as when the Chandaria School of Business at the United States International University (USIU) in Kenya became the first partner institution to offer the TLP as a graduate degree program on the continent.

The TLP continued to broaden its scope and began to address other issues with building capacity to support not only current leaders but also the available leadership development structures within multiple communities. AAI sought more partnerships in Africa to mirror its first with USIU, where the local and familiar academic and business contexts are incorporated into training. This allowed participants the opportunity to continue contributing to their communities as opposed to displacing this much-needed city and national support, if even temporarily, from situations that were already critical and systems that were sometimes fragile and collapsible. New institutional partners, such as the Enterprise Development Centre (EDC) of the Pan-Atlantic University (2009) and the University of Stellenbosch Business School–Executive Development (USB-ED) (2011), grew more recognizable as local resources for nongovernmental and social enterprise leadership development to complement their already stellar work with small and midsized enterprises.

The result of these partnerships is a burgeoning social sector. While increasing in their ability to address capacity issues within local and international communities, they continue to struggle with overcoming the lack of reputability and respect that is traditionally afforded the private and governmental sectors.

Program Design

The effectiveness of the TLP is in its ability to train an individual to lead *for* change and impact through a balanced skill set. The integrated model of leadership theory by Ki ThoughtBridge (Indianapolis, IN) explains this effectiveness through strength in outer work, such as performance and productivity, along with inner work—self-awareness, identifying core guiding values, perceiving and interpreting a larger context, and envisioning a preferred future. Through this approach power is distributed at many levels of an organization, including to those individuals living with and working within the condition that needs to be addressed.

Common across the USIU, EDC, and USB-ED programs is a shared objective to train leaders in managing and operating sustainable enterprises that are able to deliver capacity to communities in their area of focus. These programs include (1) a 1-week extensive training program, (2) an executive education program that leads to a certificate in leadership, and (3) a traditional graduate program in business. The programs share outcomes such as demonstrating clear messaging about goals and program outcomes, rigorous and market-driven structures, and a cohort model that engineers "group make-up and dynamics . . . to reinforce the cognitive and academic aspects of the curriculum with the lived experience and dynamic aspects of instruction."[3]

Recruiting and Admissions

Many debilitating stereotypes discredit the social sector. Across Africa, some perceive the social sector as filled with disorganized businesses and led by individuals with weak technical skills, who are often young and unmotivated. However, the recruitment process for the TLP tells a very different story.

Many participants became aware of the program in its earliest stages through their affiliations with the partner institutions or through word of mouth. This speaks to the strength of the networks and organized knowledge sharing throughout the field. This trend continues to be the most influential in identifying new participants.

The TLP provides much-needed scholarship funding, essential to the inclusion of participants from low-income and marginalized groups and communities.

> I had been looking forward to and was already exploring websites and hoping that I will find funding some day to attend such course, the moment I learnt about it here in Lagos, I decided instantly to enroll. — EDC TLP alumnus

Although the different program models attract participants in different stages of their career and business development, one measure used to admit participants is the passion exhibited toward their work. There is a direct correlation between the motivation and drive of the participant and the likelihood of selection and completion of the program along with their commitment to increasing program impact over time. Participants told stories of their personal connections to the mission of their organization during their interviews that often showed how relentless they would be in increasing their leadership skills through the program.

Interviewees were asked to show their ability to work in collaborative environments. Beyond just working through a team-based approach, participants were selected based on their examples of working in community. The cohort model is a key strength of the program and facilitates the long-term success of alumni. Therefore, it is important that participants not only exhibit the ability to leverage relationships and be resourceful, but also contribute to the sharing of information and knowledge of other practitioners.

Program Models

Currently, TLP partner institutions have considerable autonomy in administering relevant leadership training with a high level of cultural adaptation within local educational markets. Supporting this "for us, by us" method of design, as management and oversight by AAI increases, the integrity of the program based within the local cultural context remains intact when the institutions are "guided by considerations of effectiveness, with slightly different emphases featured at each iteration."[4] Within this method of design, TLP includes the following programs:

- *One-Week Intensive Training.* The most recent addition to the TLP partnerships at USB-ED is a 1-week intensive certificate program training model. The program, known as "NPO Strategy and Leadership Programme," covers topics such as "stuckness," change management and theory of change, and conflict management, an area that 43% of American chief executive officers (CEOs) identified as being of their highest concern.[5] This training is followed by 10 weeks of on-the-job application and a final report submission.
- *Certificate Program.* The TLP program at EDC provides 13 modules of technical and leadership training to strengthen the abilities of participants as nonprofit CEOs in 30 days over 6 months. Also known as the Social Sector Management (SSM) program, this program follows an executive education model training and builds upon intensive engagement in day-long immersion coursework.
- *Traditional Graduate Program.* At USIU, the TLP offers a traditional university graduate model with a required master's thesis and grades tied to coursework. Sharon Ravitch and Michael Reichert noted an impressively high level of faculty and advisor interaction to support the high level of rigor and high-quality standards expected of each TLP participant. At USIU, the TLP, also referred to as the Executive Master's in Organizational Development (EMOD) program, requires 30 credit hours for completion.

Through these various models, the TLP teaches participants to define clear objectives and in turn more easily align missions and visions with strategic planning. From developing communication pathways and knowledge transfer systems, to using data to guide program improvement, to making informed decisions on creating new operational policies and procedures, the TLP impacts organizations in ways that will have a long-lasting effect on productivity and efficiency.

Program Impact

To provide an overall sense of participants' experiences with the TLP, AAI commissioned a third-party evaluation in 2013.[6] The evaluation surveyed TLP graduates and participants representing a wide variety of roles in NGOs, which included many CEOs and other top-level administrators. The survey included several quantitative questions, in which respondents were asked to rate the program on a five-point scale.

After 7 years of operation, program growth, and evolution, the TLP has reached more than 360 participants through its university programs, and an additional 650+ participants from the broader social sector through industry-relevant meetings, conventions, and symposia. The TLP programs have a 90% completion rate. From the development of a broad range of highly skilled individual leaders, improved efficiencies of the organizations, increased capacity of the community, and increased professionalism, credibility, and employability of members within the social sector, each participant organization impacts between one hundred and one million beneficiaries.

Across four dimensions (mission and goals, quality of content, quality of instruction, and value added to knowledge and skills), program completers were very happy with their experience: 99.7% to 100% of respondents rated the program as very good or great. In terms of the sustainability of the skills learned, participants also rated the program high: 98.5% good to great in terms of sustainability in the organizations, and 95.3% in the communities served by the organizations.

In addition to the surveys, the evaluators also conducted individual interviews, focus groups, and site visits to gain a more comprehensive understanding of the overall impact of the TLP. These qualitative data indicate that the major impact area for the TLP was on the organizations led by program graduates, namely changes in the structure, functioning, and capacity of each to better achieve their goals and missions. Having learned new approaches to management and increasing their overall effectiveness as leaders, participants lauded the innovation, improvement, and expansion as major breakthroughs achieved from participation in the program. Acquiring new management strategies, particularly through developing new tools and habits of self-appraisal, helped participants to focus on their individual leadership capacity, while they were able to look beyond donor dependency and fund-raising to build organizational capacity and sustainability.

Exhibit 13-1. Participant satisfaction with program.

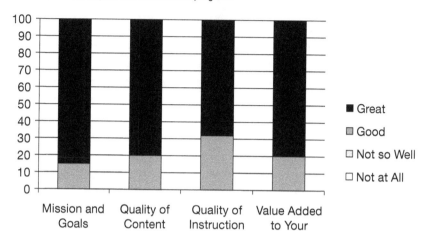

Exhibit 13-2. Participant rate of sustainability.

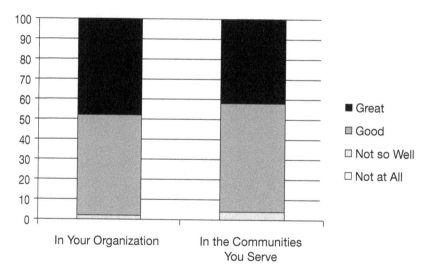

Across all three programs, participants and alumni spoke in strong terms about how they not only gained necessary leadership skills, but also developed a more wide-ranging and critical sensibility as leaders of organizations in the social sector at this moment of their country's development. Many described a broad and deep professionalization of leadership, and emphasized its impact on their approach in organizational development.

The TLP's emphasis on stakeholder and client satisfaction in the social sector dramatically changed the way participants considered the potential impact of the work their organizations do and thus how they function in relation to their clients. The need for community-based relationships was core to that teaching and in ensuring that the NGO itself is effective in serving its stakeholders' needs. The impact of the TLP on community—both the communities served by participants' organizations as well as, for some, their personal home communities—was commonly noted as a result of the program, which empowered them to expand their visions and the scope of their ambitions for their client-serving, community-based organizations. Newly confident because of the skills and approaches they learned, these leaders grew their organizations both numerically and qualitatively as their service to communities deepened and grew.

The furthest reach and impact supported by the TLP includes the social sector as a whole. As a result of the emphasis university partners placed on tailoring curriculum for this level of impact, TLP graduates have begun to re-envision the social sector itself as a site of necessary innovation and a conduit for formalized knowledge sharing. This ambition connects directly with the leaders' own goals for professionalization and for increased credibility for the sector. For example, two graduates of the TLP in Lagos currently publish new professional journals. Graduates from both the EDC and USIU have expressed their desire for the TLP's support to develop post-program institutes for professional dialogue and exchange.

Given that one of the key structures for the TLP is to encourage professional exchange, it is not surprising to find that participants seek opportunities to collaborate, and there is an almost insatiable desire to increase the frequency of these opportunities. This is a part of how the TLP training has led participants to reimagine the social sector. In fact, the thrust of the program is to expand participants' perspectives on their work and to think beyond the individuals in the sector to the collective.

After completion of the course, I was able to look at my society and think of how I, too, could transform people's lives. I established an NGO, to take care of the widows and youths generally in my state. After the course, I was also able to employ more people, as I created more business avenues. — USIU TLP Graduate

[A worker] comes from a very remote area, 400 km/8 hours away. He works for a farmer organization that had no system of operation. Through EMOD he was able to identify the organization's needs, see the lack of capacity, and have me [associate dean] come to help them plan. I helped him develop a business case for funding and to develop job description and change management plan. — USIU TLP Staff

Reimagining possibilities for the sector, including reframing organizations as social enterprises rather than not for profit, was at the core of the EDC model. This vision of sustainability through entrepreneurial thinking and cutting-edge organizational strategy was liberating to many. Adding to this, the program's emphasis on teamwork and collaboration shifted the role in which identity was understood, and a key impact of the program was that participants, alumni, faculty, and administrators no longer viewed identity (including tribal origin and gender) as a concern or potential to undermine the field/sector itself.

TLP in Action: LOTS Charity Foundation

Love On The Streets (LOTS) Charity Foundation is located in "Dustbin Estates," an area of refuse in Lagos, Nigeria, in which inhabitants build their homes with planks on top of trash dumps. LOTS has developed partnerships as a result of the LOTS participation in the TLP, without which founder Tolulope Sangosanya admits LOTS wouldn't be sustainable. LOTS, which was inspired by her grandfather who at 79 spent 2 hours a day helping Sangosanya learn to read through her dyslexia, caters to the health, social, educational, psychological, medical, and emotional needs of street kids and vulnerable children.

It has only received donations from one agency, USAID, and relies on local contributions. Developing new partnerships links directly to

the foundations' sustainability, LOTS has benefited from the TLP training that Sangosanya, who is also an Ashoka fellow, has received and the
newly developed partnerships with local organizations represented by
participants within her cohort, the board development support received
from Accenture, the supplies of Unilever's "Hygiene Pack," whose
product development she supported through its market research, and
donations of business assets like the community center where she serves
20 kids, and two cars that transport her and the local children.

The participants grew to understand the significance of the perception
and reputation of the sector as professional and systematic. They also learned
that the sector must be viewed as improving and having strong standards of
accountability.

While usually focused quite locally in their operations, participants spoke
of strategic visions that extended well beyond their immediate constituents. A
number of participants, alumni and faculty described the TLP as an incubator
for a shared vision to transform the social sector, its leadership, and the African Continent as a whole.

As leaders reimagine their communities and re-envision their roles, the
necessary training structures will also need to be reimagined to adapt to this
new, profound level of leadership.

Conclusion

The TLP's structure—systems of program development between AAI and
partner universities; the commitment of funding partners and stakeholders—
exemplifies the commitment it takes and systems needed to increase and expand
the opportunities available for NGO and SME leaders. Program graduates
include such leaders as Sophia Abdi-Noor, USIU TLP graduate, who left the
small village of Garissa in northern Kenya, where women are typically marginalized within her community, and become a sponsored participant. The
program offered skills training, which she intended to use to serve the local
needs and girls within her community. Ultimately, the program increased her
technical ability to partner WomenKind Kenya with 32 other organizations,
and propelled her career into membership of the 10th parliament of Kenya,
where she served as contributor to the Kenyan constitution.

The AAI has identified two essential elements to successfully implement effective education programs for adults: a distinct set of stakeholders and common belief systems. There are four key stakeholders whose engagement supports successful programs: (1) the local community, (2) the program management, (3) the program participants, and (4) the organizations that employ participants. These stakeholders are better partners when they share some core beliefs. In the case of TLP, the following common beliefs strengthen our programs:

- *Participation and Agency.* The program must continue to challenge and explore the relationships of power, the understanding of who is to be empowered and by whom, as well as concepts such as ownership, accountability, and agency as forms of participation. This is particularly crucial in an international development context. "Country ownership" has become the preferred poverty assistance strategy, with citizens of the developing nations asserting agency over social and economic policies in their country. However, as occurs in many cases, development activities might stem from international governmental agencies, so participants in the TLP take on "country ownership" as their responsibility as NGOs and duty as community members.

- *Models of Inclusion.* According to Rebecca Rogers, "Critical discourse analysis asserts that knowledge is socially constructed and shaped by relations of power that are both material and discursive. It rejects the premises of structuralism and instead embraces the view that certain meaning systems—or discourses—are privileged by their relationship with dominant groups in society and are, themselves, constitutive of social relations."[7] Therefore, it is important that program administrators and funders realize the critical import of including marginalized participants in the program.

- *Community as Partners and Community Leaders as the Source for Building Capacity.* As referenced earlier, the term *partnership* most often refers to external partners (international partners, trading partners, etc.) and not to communities. Within the development world, communities are often marginalized when defined as service beneficiaries and in some cases as administrators of externally or predetermined tasks in which they become empowered by other partners, including government. However, the TLP case recognizes that community-level input on how to address social capacity issues is critical to informing strategy and identifying or creating viable solutions, making community one of the best strategic partners.

- *Expansion and Replication.* In a relatively short period of time, the TLP has developed its own reputation, offering high-quality training, building credibility for the social sector, increasing institutional capacity, and creating the next generation of leaders across the continent of Africa. Yet even with this solid history, it is evident that the reach of the TLP has barely touched even just the tip of the iceberg.

As a result, AAI has paid close attention to the needs of the TLP stakeholders and set clear objectives for expanding and increasing the impact of the TLP through three new and innovative initiatives:

1. Manage the traditional TLP program model with specific focus on sustaining the strong institutional relationships and connections established between local university partners and global funding partners, like TCCAF by increasing the quantity and diversity of courses, degrees, and certifications offered. Provide opportunities for partner institutions to learn best practices from one another and for TLP alumni to further their training.
2. Expand the reach of the program by recruiting three additional partner institutions that will collectively train an average of 500 participants per year in the traditional TLP model.
3. Create more efficiency and access to the TLP trainings through an online platform, which will offer leadership, management, and entrepreneurship courses to reach thousands of new participants.

Specifically, AAI has identified six major areas for expansion that were suggested in the interviews and focus groups conducted as part of the program evaluation. It is understood that participants and alumni already see the TLP as a high-quality and valued community resource. To further address capacity issues, AAI will expand TLP services to include the following: advocate for the social sector and increase credibility in the field by positioning university partners as centers for excellence and participants as social change agents and thought leaders; build an online platform to increase access to potential participants in remote areas; offer post-training support and continuing education; increase access for specific constituencies and marginalized groups; increase and clearly define monitoring and evaluation procedures of each program site; and replicate the program in additional locations.

The value of the TLP extends beyond the design and structure of the program itself. The TLP engages and impacts multiple levels of stakeholders through many transformative qualities. It supports reviewing participants as leadership practice, re-envisioning roles and responsibilities, redefining organizations' missions, and re-envisioning the impact of the sector. Further, it encourages participants to transition from cohort to community, and commit to knowledge sharing and to creating a support system that helps to build the capacity of each organization. As a result of this collective impact, the TLP has successfully trained the leader and increased the credibility of the sector.

The TLP graduates not only are leading organizations but also are sharing best practices, informing and educating the sector, and extending their collective impact in all directions. Along with local community members, particularly those serving formally and informally as organizers and influencers, TLP graduates are creating a demand for the formalization of the social sector and demanding legitimacy and validation of their ability to organize, inform, and influence outside of a professionally structured education model. As a result of this shift, programs such as the TLP serve to address the need almost simultaneously with its being defined. The program itself is a proven contributor to local economic success, and the area of leadership development is a means to sustain it and the community at large.

TLP in Action: So-Said Charity Foundation

Having lived on the streets herself for 8 months, Concern Felicia Matins, CEO of So-Said Charity Home ("So-Said"), knows all too well that the opportunities her organization provides are life changing, and believes it can serve many more lives once members of her executive team also receive the TLP training. So-Said was founded in 2000 to rescue women and their children who are estranged from their families and living on the streets of Lagos, Nigeria. As the number of homeless steadily increase despite the city's progress, So-Said provides refuge in the form of shelter, food, and supplies to improve the health of those removed from the street, and support until they are able to find employment and reestablish their lives.

As a participant in the first TLP at EDC, Concern Felicia claims that her participation in the TLP gave her credibility. Concern Felicia learned how to enforce division of labor to get results from her team instead of doing the work for them herself. Impressively, she cites nine instrumental funding and partnership opportunities, from organizations like Dangote, Nigerian Breweries, Talent Hunt, and Heroes of Charity that result from her participation in the TLP. Some of the new funders to whom she had written hadn't responded prior to her participation in the program, but now recognized the value of her work. She attributes this shift to the visioning process she underwent of So-Said's identity and purpose, her strengthened ability to articulate this vision to her team, stakeholders and the public, and the relationships and network developed through the program.

Notes

1. Foucault, M. (1980). *Power/Knowledge: Selected Interviews and Other Writings 1972–1977*. New York: Random House.
2. Vavrus, F. & Seghers, M. (2010). "Critical discourse analysis in comparative education: a discursive study of 'partnership' in Tanzania's poverty reduction policies." *Comparative Education Review*, 54(1).
3. Ravitch, S. & Reichert, M. (2013). *The Transformational Leadership Program of the Africa-America Institute: An Evaluation of Participants' Experiences and Program Impact*. New York: The Africa-America Institute.
4. Ibid.
5. Larker, D. & Miles, S. (2013). *2013 Executive Coaching Survey*. Palo Alto: Stanford Graduate School of Business. http://www.gsb.stanford.edu/cldr/research/surveys/coaching.html.
6. Ravitch & Reichert, *The Transformational Leadership Program*.
7. Rogers, R. (2004). *Critical Discourse Analysis in Education*. Mahwah, NJ: Lawrence Erlbaum Associates.

CHAPTER 14

Northern Tier Industry and Education Consortium
A Partnership for "First Chance" Programs

Pete Butler

In late 1992, when I was the site training and development manager at Procter & Gamble's (P&G) Mehoopany, Pennsylvania, plant, I found out about a youth apprenticeship program that had been piloted in Williamsport, Pennsylvania, for the Pennsylvania Department of Education. Seeing the obvious workforce development potential, I made a business case to P&G management for applying the program to the Northern Tier region and P&G's Mehoopany plant, its largest worldwide facility with over 100 acres under one roof and over 3,000 employees.

Prior to this time, the average hiring age at the Mehoopany plant was 30 years old. Knowing that the plant invested about $100,000 per technician over their first 10 years of employment, earlier career starts (by hiring through an apprenticeship program) could add over 10 years to an employee's career, reduce turnover by up to 30%, and save up to $30,000 per employee. Coupled with lower initial training costs (training wages vs full salary and benefits), the savings potential grew to almost $50,000 per employee hired through the program. This created some excitement and strong support to move forward with the pilot.

In early 1993, a meeting was convened with six area school superintendents and representatives from several manufacturing companies to explore school-to-work (STW) funding. This group became the Northern Tier Industry and Education Consortium (NTIEC). At that first meeting, companies made the case for schools working closely with employers to meet future workforce needs. Richard Serfass, superintendent of Elk Lake Public Schools, clearly a thought leader and senior member of the superintendents' group, advocated for partnering with employers to benefit students and also help companies be more successful. The NTIEC decided to apply for a STW grant from the Commonwealth of Pennsylvania and moved forward with planning.

The goal in the first year was to place 10 youth apprentices with Northern Tier manufacturers in the fall. This was accomplished, and then 30 apprentices were placed in year 2. In year 3, the program increased to over 60 apprentices. The NTIEC Youth Apprenticeship Program (YAP) continued to grow, with well over a hundred students placed each year thereafter.

Schools districts with good business sense quickly see the value of YAP. NTIEC charges $1,000 per apprentice for the first 10 students, $500 per apprentice for the next five students, and then $250 for each additional apprentice. Thus, a district with 25 students in YAP would pay $15,000 per year. Additionally, the students benefit from work-based learning on state-of-the-art equipment with mentors in their field while addressing real-world problems. In comparison, 25 students in traditional co-op programs would cost the district about $100,000 per year for teachers' salaries and benefits. The cost for 25 vocational and technical students is even higher when you consider that districts need to provide building facilities, equipment, and instructors. In YAP, employers have stepped up to provide a paid, work-based learning experience while providing trainers, program coordinators, and mentors for each student at no cost to the districts.

Career Education Programs

The NTIEC currently provides a number of career education programs with two educational coordinators who plan and deliver joint initiatives with employers and schools. Programs serve both students and educators (Exhibits 14-1 and 14-2). Teachers and principals can earn in-service credit by spending a day in a workplace or attending a panel session at their schools. Both types of experiences allow educators to learn more about the expectations for entry into a variety of careers and what expectations are on a day-to-day basis. After completing the Educator in the Workplace program, many teachers redesign their curriculum to include more hands-on experiences that mimic activities in the workplace.

The NTIEC supports half a dozen youth programs. Although the formats vary, the common objective of the youth programs is to place students

---

Exhibit 14-1. Opportunities for educators.

Educators in the Workplace
- Teachers and administrators use an in-service day to visit one business or several.
- The formats include 1 day or a week-long program.
- Teachers are eligible for continuing education credit.

Businesses in Schools
- Teachers and administrators spend an in-service day interactive workshop with local businesses.
- Discussions center on workplace expectations and standards, education requirements, as well as the interviewing and hiring process.

---

face-to-face with employers to discuss career opportunities and educational requirements for success. One example is the Vehicular Career Day, in which about 25 people who work with vehicles bring the vehicles and equipment to the school and set up stations in the parking lot. They include linemen, drill rig operators, grader operators, state policemen, home health care workers, and many more. Small cohorts of students rotate through the stations to meet the workers. The excitement of students is palpable as they get to meet these workers face-to-face and start to consider careers of which they had no prior knowledge. Although many of the youth programs last for a day or less, NTIEC also supports a youth apprenticeship program that can last up to 2 years. In the 2012–2013 school year, NTIEC provided a variety of program opportunities for over 3,000 Northern Tier students to learn about a wide variety of local careers.

After 20 years, NTIEC is still developing new efforts. Based on recent interest by manufacturers in YAP, we are partnering with the Northeastern Pennsylvania Industrial Resource Center (NEPIRC) under contract to develop and deliver YAPs for manufacturers. We are working on manufacturing career events that are designed to inform youngsters about local career opportunities in manufacturing. We are also partnering with NEPIRC's executive director, Eric Esoda, on a grant to place experienced career coaches from the private sector in area schools. Their focus would be exclusively on careers, and on presenting a model for making informed career choices.

The tremendous progress in career education would not have been possible without the strong partnership with our Career and Technology Center (CTC). The Susquehanna County CTC's director, Dr. Alice Davis, has been a tireless supporter and a board member since NTIEC was founded in 1993. By

Exhibit 14-2. Programs for youths.

Careers in energy	• Classroom presentations for 9th-grade students by representatives from regional energy companies, including natural gas, oil, nuclear, electric, solar, and wind.
Careers in manufacturing	• Over 25 area manufacturers have face-to-face discussions with high school students who rotate through in groups of about 10 to better understand careers and education pathways for success in this key sector of the economy.
Health care career day	• Over 25 health care specialists meet with high school students for small group discussions (similar to manufacturing).
Energy career day	• Students in grades 10 to 12 meet with representatives from companies in the energy sector along with companies that support them. Usually 25 to 30 employers. Format is small group discussions.
Vehicular career day	• Middle school students participate in a 1-day event with over 25 employers that depend on vehicles in their work.
Career opportunities discussions	• One-on-one or group discussions for high school students to help them explore career options, conducted by a career specialist.
Safety City	• One-hour program by Claverack Electric for 4th graders to learn about power distribution and electrical safety issues.
Rachel's Challenge	• Program to build positive school culture in elementary, middle, and high school and to promote appreciation of diversity. • Discounts and financial assistance through NTIEC.
Health care career camp	• One-week summer camp for 6th to 12th graders with tours of health care facilities and health care staff discussions.
Youth apprenticeship	• 11th and 12th graders can participate in a 1- or 2-year internship, under the supervision of worksite mentor. • Students are eligible for course credit. • Businesses are eligible for a tax credit.

capitalizing on busing from the eight sending schools, the CTC has partnered with NTIEC on four or more career events per year.

Finally, professional credentials and integrated school and workplace learning plans are long-term goals for the program, but we currently do not have resources to adequately address these opportunities. One promising effort currently underway with leadership from Bill desRosiers, community affairs coordinator for Cabot Oil and Gas, will provide a seamless pathway for youngsters into the natural gas industry, which is booming in the Marcellus shale regions of Pennsylvania. It begins with early career awareness, job shadowing, college credits in high school, an associate's degree program at Lackawanna College, and employment with Cabot or its affiliates. NTIEC and Cabot hope to see this model replicated for other sectors in the future.

Youth Apprenticeship Program

As noted earlier, the NTIEC was created to support the YAP, which remains the consortium's flagship program. Apprentices are placed with employers for 1 or 2 days per week. In most cases, one of the days is a normally scheduled school day and the second day may be on the weekend. Some students also participate in a summer YAP on a full-time basis. Apprenticeships can last up to 2 years in high school.

Typically, potential apprentices are identified by their high school's guidance counselors. The counselors send student information to the NTIEC's educational coordinators. The NTIEC staff visits the schools to discuss opportunities with interested students. The coordinators work with employers to match students with available positions. YAP participants are high school juniors and seniors and even some college students who have been in the program since high school. The program has participants from the entire academic spectrum: top-of-the-class college-bound students as well as students who plan to enter the workplace after high school. All seem to benefit from the work-based learning experience and find that their academic work has new relevance.

Apprentices are hired through each company's normal hiring process, which can include interviews, employment tests, and drug tests. Students are helped with résumé writing and interviewing skills, and are schooled in workplace ethics and norms prior to starting. At the beginning of the apprenticeship, NTIEC staff members work with employers to develop a training plan and periodically visit apprentices in the workplace to ensure a quality experience.

Students want to participate in the YAP for a variety of reasons. It is not just great exposure to a career and possibly a direct pipeline to a full-time job; it is also a paying job. Students are paid at normal entry-level rates* per em-

---

* The one exception has been hospital internships, which are normally unpaid.

ployer norms. In addition, most high schools allow students to earn one credit for participation, and employers grade the students' workplace performance. NTIEC and employers provide framed certificates for successful completion of the YAP program. Exemplary performers are selected for added recognition, including certificates and monetary awards of $100. These student awards are presented during award ceremonies at the end of the school year. Still, the students seem to recognize that the greatest value is the opportunity to gain meaningful work experience in their field of interest, which will make their résumé stand out when they apply for jobs after graduation.

Impact of NTIEC Programs

Since 1993, NTIEC has served nearly 29,000 youths. This includes 2,000 youth apprentices, 12,000 students through the career education programs, and 15,000 through the Rachel's Challenge program. The NTIEC's business–education partnership remains successful because of the benefits for youths, for businesses, and the community.

Benefits for YAP Participants

Marleen Butler, an NTIEC educational coordinator for 14 years, reports that YAP transforms high school students into mature young adults. There are many examples of students who were doing poorly in school, perhaps due to boredom, difficult family situations, peer pressure, and other personal challenges. The YAP's combination of strong adult workplace mentoring, new and interesting situations, and a clear challenge allow students to take that first step toward a career. Butler believes that the transformation and growth in students is largely due to "total immersion" in the adult world. Students are challenged to accept responsibility and add value to the company, and most rise to the occasion. The change is obvious. It is heartwarming to hear parents' comments after students have been in the program for a few months. They are astounded by the rapid growth and maturity of their sons and daughters.

Parents also win as their children can start post-secondary education with a career focus. This translates into fewer false starts—and hopefully fewer tuition bills—as compared with students who enter college without a focus and take additional courses as they try to decide on a major. Students who go directly into the workforce after high school are able to become self-supporting faster, and parents again benefit as their children avoid the "homing pigeon" trap.

Benefits for Employers

Why do employers continue to participate in the NTIEC career education programs, particularly making the investment in apprentices? For starters, companies get the pick of the crop for future employees. The youth apprenticeship creates a tremendous loyalty that, if students are hired into full-time positions, translates into reduced turnover. Employers save on initial training costs, and, when hiring for full-time positions, have a skilled individual from the outset. Reductions in costly quality or production losses can be a huge payoff for employers as well. While the NTIEC has no formal monitoring system in place, employers continue to participate and are eager to hire youths as apprentices and hire apprentices as full-time employees.

Experiences of Individual Employers

Although many employers participate in the NTIEC, a few have made a deep investment in the YAP program. Two of these are Procter & Gamble and Tyler Memorial Hospital.

Procter & Gamble's Mehoopany Plant. Melissa Mapes, the YAP leader at the P&G Mehoopany, Pennsylvania, plant, reports that the YAP is their preferred method of hiring, and they continue to host 10 and 20 apprentices per year. Prior to YAP, this P&G plant never hired 18- to 20-year-olds. The average age of a new employee was 30. To date, the Mehoopany plant employs over 80 alumni of YAP, with career training and development savings of $4 million. Savings from higher starting skills are likely much higher (reduced equipment downtime, fewer quality control incidents, etc.).

Given these benefits, P&G's Mehoopany plant manager has challenged the plant's human resources staff to grow the program to accommodate more than 30 apprentices per year. The employees hired through YAP have proven to be the best new hires in the plant's history, and have enjoyed accelerated skill development and promotions when compared to their non-YAP peers.

Tyler Memorial Hospital. Tyler Memorial Hospital in Wyoming County, Pennsylvania, also found YAP is a great pipeline for registered nursing staff. After years of challenging recruiting efforts, Gayle Gipson, training and development manager, concluded that skilled youths from the rural community of Wyoming County would be more inclined to live and work there than would potential employees from outside the area. The hospital worked with

NTIEC to place high school apprentices at the hospital. Many of these students went on to earn degrees at local colleges, to earn their registered nurse licenses, and to return to work for Tyler. Tyler also supports the regional Health Care Career Day, with eight to ten professionals from a variety of specialties. Tyler Memorial Hospital's revised recruiting strategy is a great example of sustained partnering between educators and employers to solving a critical community employment need.

Benefits to the Community

Prior to the NTIEC's career education programs, most of the best and brightest students left the Northern Tier after high school. It was hard for them to see any local opportunities. Since 1992, the perception of career opportunities within the region has improved. More and more young people are opting to stay. In addition to many fine smaller companies, global enterprises such as P&G, Cargill, Siemens, Chesapeake Energy, Cabot Oil and Gas, and Williams Pipeline are now better able to meet their workforce needs. After many years of poor economic prospects after the collapse of the coal industry, YAP has become a key contributor to an upward spiral of success for northeastern Pennsylvania. The NTIEC most recently has partnered with the rapidly developing natural gas industry in the region to help develop their future workforce. Bill desRosiers, Cabot Oil and Gas Company's community affairs manager, worked with NTIEC to develop and deliver a "Careers In Energy" program that has been successfully piloted with hundreds of area students. We are currently rolling out this program to several school districts. The program gives students first-hand exposure to professionals in the nuclear, electric utilities, solar, wind, and oil sectors, in addition to the natural gas sector.

Sustaining the NTIEC's Career Education Programs

The NTIEC has been around for 20 years. What makes the consortium successful? What resources sustain the workforce development initiative?

Factors That Contribute to Success

Determined, passionate, visionary leadership is needed to sustain local progress over time in spite of serious shortfalls in state and federal funding. There is little constancy of purpose at the state or federal level. Programs like school-to-work just start to get some traction and then are abandoned for the next new program. When state administrations change, so do priorities, and promising initiatives are dropped. Without perseverance by local leaders, most school-to-work transition programs are abandoned. NTIEC has been able to piece together modest local support from schools, employers, and foundations over the years, with budgets that range from $150,000 to $200,000 per year to serve five Northern Tier counties with one full-time and three part-time employees. NTIEC is extremely fortunate to have Don Abplanalp, a 30-year veteran small business owner, who brings employers and schools together in our western counties, and Marleen Butler, a workforce development specialist, with over 25 years' experience in work-based learning, who brings employers and schools together in our eastern counties.

Over the years, NTIEC's staff has come from all sectors and has included retired school superintendents, retired business executives, workforce development specialists, and retired vocational educators. The staff members have a passion for the work and, because many of them are retired or near retirement, they are not driven by financial needs. The critical abilities are driving results; connecting the dots for educators, business leaders, students, and parents; building a positive image for the programs; and celebrating success at every opportunity.

Staff members bring their experience and passion to coordinating joint efforts between schools and employers in the NTIEC. This is not unique to the Northern Tier; wherever we see success with youth apprenticeships in Pennsylvania, there is an intermediary agency such as NTIEC coordinating the work of the partnership. NTIEC and other coordinating agencies can manage the logistics involved in recruiting youths into career education programs, matching student interests with employer needs, and monitoring the quality of the experience for apprentices and the quality of their effort. These partnerships are essential. Federal and state funders for schools should consider incentives to encourage stronger partnering with employers. Employer investments in career education programs help youths develop into responsible adults and reduce the financial burdens on public schools by leveraging community resources to help develop the skills of the next generation of workers. Career awareness and developing key workplace skills in a school setting is limited in effectiveness and costly. Work-based experiences not only work better, they can provide experience on state-of-the-art equipment without the need for schools to invest in vocational training centers.

Challenges

School participation is most often supported by administrators who have experience in the private sector, in the military, in vocational education, or in agricultural programs. Educators who have spent their entire lives in schools, focused entirely on academic achievement, seldom see the value of work-based learning. NTIEC has had success winning over educators to the work-based learning approach through the Educator in the Workplace Program. Another valuable experience for educators is to get a tour of the workplace by their youth apprentices. Most are impressed by the depth of learning, the scope of job responsibilities, and the increased confidence displayed by the YAP participants.

Unfortunately, raising awareness and developing support for the program is an ongoing process. Turnover makes it important to continue career awareness programs for educators. When school districts change superintendents, administrators, guidance staff, or other key supporters of an apprenticeship program, the programs are too often discontinued. The same is true when administrations change at the state or federal level. Organizational partnerships must expand relationships beyond individual leaders.

Raising awareness is a constant objective. One effective approach at P&G is the year end YAP celebration. Educators and parents attend the event and students share highlightsfrom their YAP experience and tour visitors through their work areas. Both students and mentors are recognized with framed certificates of appreciation from NTIEC.

Resources to Sustain Programs

Financial needs have been the biggest challenge to sustainability. Over the years, work-based learning has become a key priority of the Pennsylvania Workforce Investment Board. This priority has resulted in regional career education partnerships (RCEPs) that were funded for several years with Workforce Investment Act (WIA) discretionary funds. Due to recent reductions in discretionary fund percentages, the WIA funds have dried up. Private companies such as P&G, Cargill, Cabot Oil and Gas, Chesapeake, People's Bank, and Frontier Communications have been very generous with donations ranging from $5,000 to $100,000. Local foundations such as the Taylor Family Foundation, Wyoming County Community Health Foundation, and others have also helped with grants ranging up to $15,000. A strong and engaged board has been essential to NTIEC's sustained success, with many of the members serving for 20 years.

Having a board that understands the value of career education and actively supports it is key. A good example is Fred Robinson, who after retirement from Osram Sylvania, volunteers to emcee the NTIEC's Career Day events. Donna Porter, Mountain View High School's guidance counselor, has placed 15 students in YAP, and Brian Zeidner of Claverack Electric has frequently taught student workshops on careers in the electric utilities. Minturn Smith of P&G stepped in to fill the executive director role at NTIEC when an unexpected vacancy occurred. We were especially pleased when Mark Carpenter, one of NTIEC's first youth apprentices, joined the board and more recently accepted the role of board chair. He is living proof that the YAP experience changes lives in a positive way. After his successful YAP stint at P&G, Carpenter went on to earn an MBA and is the chief financial officer of Sire Power Select, an international company based in northeast Pennsylvania. He acknowledges that YAP was key to his fulfilling his true potential and making solid career choices.

Conclusion: The Need for "First Chance" Policies

Why do we need youth apprenticeships? There are many wrong turns that today's youngsters can take, resulting in dropping out of school, drug abuse, incarceration, or just wasting several years before finding a career path. After working with YAP for 20 years, I am persuaded that responsible adult mentors in the workplace and the pride that honest work instills are an important way to reverse these trends. We need "first chance" programs like YAP to replace the costly "second chance" programs like remedial education, drug rehab, welfare, and incarceration.

Unfortunately, neither Pennsylvania nor the nation has effective "first chance" workforce development policies. WIA funds (some $170 million per year for Pennsylvania) are restricted to programs for people with barriers to employment. While providing second chances is a noble cause, we may get a much better return on our tax dollars by leveraging effective career awareness and workplace skill development programs to counter the apathy and lukewarm attitudes that many students have toward public education as it is currently delivered. It makes sense to help the vast middle group of students (our future workforce) who have not thought about possible careers or about how to prepare for them. Should we choose to invest in this effort, the return on investment will far outstrip the cost.

The estimated cost for nationwide investment in "first chance" workforce development programs like Pennsylvania's RCEP model is $250 million/year, or about $5 million per state per year. First- and second-year funding of $100 million and $150 million would support a reasonable ramping up to full capacity. If new money is not available, policy changes could allow more flexibility for current WIA funds by elimination of restrictions. For example, although Pennsylvania receives about $170 million in WIA funding, currently only 5% of that funding is not promised to specific "second-chance" programs. If even 10% to 20% of the funding was unrestricted, it would enable the Commonwealth to serve thousands of students with youth apprenticeship programs and millions with enhanced career education programs. I would also recommend that federal and state funding for education partially depend on schools partnering with employers to implement these programs.

Based on my 20 years of experience with work-based learning, I am persuaded that every dollar invested in intermediaries brings an additional 10 dollars or more to the table from employers. This includes wages for workplace mentors and trainers, student wages, equipment and supplies, and cash donations. In a resource-starved education system, this brings new resources to help educate our next generation.

"First chance" programs would eventually reduce the need for "second chance" programs, which are very costly. Savings accrue to both society and individuals by preventing false starts in college, reducing unemployment, reducing juvenile justice costs, as well as preventing youths from dropping out of school or otherwise losing their way. I know from first-hand experience that NTIEC youth apprentices, with the help of their workplace mentors, are quickly transformed into responsible, focused young adults with goals for career success and the knowledge to get there. They grow up to become contributing members of society. Developing such programs nationwide is critical to our future. It will require joint leadership from government, education, and the private sector. Most important, success will depend on local intermediaries with funding not just for a single year but secure, multi-year support to provide the "boots on the ground" needed to get the job done. The effort is akin to gardening; it requires constant, sustained focus over time to get the desired results. Historically, gaps in funding have hurt students and raised skepticism from both employers and educators.

We know how to establish youth apprenticeships, we know they benefit students, and we know they meet employers needs for a skilled workforce. We know it is less costly to do it right the first time. We simply need the will to do it!

CHAPTER 15

Jobs for the Future
Adapting European Vocational Education Models for American Youth

Nancy Hoffman

The best European vocational education systems have a set of character-istics that, taken together, are not matched anywhere in the United States. The systems have special youth policies; they see the younger generations as important to support, protect, and engage with as an invest-ment in future prosperity. And in partnership with employers and unions, they educate 40% to 75% of their young people in vocational education and training (VET) systems that link education and labor market needs and in-clude substantial learning in the workplace.

The following key factors make a VET system strong:

- The system is formed through public/private partnerships with the state, local education authorities, schools, employers, and labor unions.
- Employers have a major role, usually codified in a legal framework, in defining the qualifications required for clusters of occupations in their sectors of the economy.
- With support from organizations representing their occupational sector, employers take responsibility for building the curriculum and developing and carrying out assessments.
- With employer participation, a government education agency, usually at the national level, is responsible for standardization of the system and for quality control and improvement.

With this system in place, employers open their enterprises to young people, usually starting at around age 16.

Among European systems, the most familiar to Americans are what are called "dual" or "apprenticeship" systems, the classic structure in which students spend 3 days a week at work or in a training organization and 2 days in school. ("Dual" refers to learning at school and at a workplace.) In such systems, the workplace, not the school, is the center of the students' learning environment. They progress from full-time school through about age 15, to a mix of work and school in the vocational system in the course of attaining a qualification through about age 19, to full-time work in the labor market. These "alternance" arrangements generally last 3 to 4 years as the young person attains skills, knowledge, competencies, and, in some cases, training as a manager in the chosen field. In a number of systems, a vocational qualification also makes a student eligible to enter a technical higher education institution or, with some extra preparation, a university.

The Need for Multiple Postsecondary Routes

There is much to admire in these systems. In 2011, the Harvard Graduate School of Education released *Pathways to Prosperity: Meeting the Challenge of Preparing Young Americans for the 21st Century.*[1] The report argued that our current education system was too narrowly focused on the goal of preparing all young people to pursue a 4-year college or university degree, whereas other postsecondary routes to careers might far better suit significant numbers of students.

As only one young person in three obtained a 4-year degree by age 25, and roughly 30% of the job openings projected over the next decade required some education beyond high school but not necessarily a 4-year degree, the report's authors called for much more attention to building career pathways in high-growth, high-demand occupational fields that spanned high school and community or technical college preparation and could provide young people with skills and credentials valued in the labor market. The vision the report laid out was influenced in specific ways by the best European VET systems. This chapter briefly explores elements of the European VET systems that might be adapted for the United States, as well as those are too incongruous with U.S. education policy to be workable here. But first an update on the response to the Pathways report.

Given the high costs of college, and the attention given to the mismatch between the skills employers seek and those that job applicants have, the report struck a cord with policymakers and with those who are concerned about the future of young people. Consequently, in 2012 the Harvard Graduate School of Education and Jobs for the Future, a Boston-based nonprofit group focused on creating educational and economic opportunity for low-income youths and adults, decided to invite eight states—California, Georgia, Illinois, Massachusetts, Missouri, New York, Ohio, and Tennessee—to join them in creating the Pathways to Prosperity Network.

The Pathways to Prosperity Network

The Pathways to Prosperity Network creates career pathways for students in what is known as grades 9 to 14 (discussed below). Two more states, Arizona and Delaware, joined the network in June 2014.

We are attempting to build a stronger career education system in the United States, one that is more responsive to the needs of the labor market. Along with the states in the Pathways Network, the federal government, some philanthropies and corporate foundations, and nonprofit organizations and states beyond the network are engaged in this work. In fact, it may not be premature to say that a movement is in the making to rethink the role of career preparation in the high school curriculum. (For an update on the work thus far, see "The Pathways to Prosperity State Network: A Progress Report, 2012–2014."[2])

But, most readers would say, the United States has career and technical education (CTE) in every state. Doesn't the Perkins Act support it, and don't states put their own dollars into high school and postsecondary programs to prepare young people for careers? Don't we have vocational schools and programs? The answer, is "Yes, but. . . ." Most CTE programs have the following shortcomings: For most of its history, CTE was seen as the option for weaker students who either did not want, or did not have the preparation, to go on to postsecondary education, rather than as an opportunity for a wide range of students to choose an applied learning approach. For this reason, the reputation of vocational education suffered.

In addition, vocational education became a target of the civil rights community because many students of color and low-income students were tracked into vocational schools and programs. The message to these students from counselors and teachers was, "You're not college material," which removed students' freedom to choose to attend a 2- or 4-year college.

Finally, the data showing that the United States has middling achievement results for 15-year-olds in the international comparison known as PISA (Programme for International Student Assessment[3]) have served to focus education policymakers, teachers, and school leaders on raising academic achievement levels to the exclusion of career preparation. Thus, many comprehensive high schools ended their career preparation curriculum and stopped integrating CTE and academics. Ironically, by focusing so heavily on mathematics and literacy to the neglect of their application in the real world of careers, educators have failed to demonstrate to the majority of students the utility of what they are learning in school.

The Pathways to Prosperity Network is organized around a simple framework, the foundation of which is a grades 9 to 14 career pathway—a career academy or comprehensive program of study that spans high school and 2 years of community college and includes all requirements for completion of a high school diploma and a post-secondary credential with currency in the regional labor market. Other levers in the framework include the following:

- *Career Guidance*: an early and sustained career-information and advising system to help students and families make informed choices about educational career paths
- *Employer Engagement:* employers committed to providing learning opportunities at the workplace and supporting the transition of young people into the labor market
- *Intermediaries:* local or regional intermediary organizations to provide the infrastructure, coordination, and support for the development of such pathways
- *State Leadership and Policy:* to support, scale, and sustain career pathways

Behind these levers and in the approach we are taking to implementation are lessons adapted from European vocational education. The attitude toward European vocational education adopted in the Pathways Network is best expressed by a thoughtfully worded few sentences from Henry Levin of Teachers College, Columbia University: "Careful comparative work raises new possibilities for any country to think about and also allows us to see our own taken-for-granted practices with new eyes. It tells us that there are other ways to get to a goal and broadens our thinking about what these might be." Nonetheless, at every turn, when we note that VET works well abroad, and that the United States would do well to consider it, we have had to counter the standard U.S. responses to the program: "They track 12-year-olds," and "U.S. employers would never engage in such a program." The first of these statements was true a decade ago, but not today. The second is the major challenge of the Pathways Network.

The most persuasive arguments that VET "works" outside of the United States is in the finding that VET produces very high rates of upper secondary completion (schooling to around age 19), and that almost all participants make smooth transitions into the labor market after completing upper secondary school. Countries with strong VET systems have upper secondary completion rates that top 90%.[4] (Upper secondary is actually a benchmark closer to the completion of a high school diploma and a career certification or a CTE degree from a community college.) The rate of U.S. high school completion—a lesser standard—is about 80%, depending on how and over what length of time statistics are compiled. Serving the majority of 16- to 19-year-olds, VET also results in very low youth unemployment rates—below 10% in strong VET countries, and even below 5% in Switzerland and the Netherlands.[5] These low rates rose only slightly during the economic crisis of 2008, while in the United States teens face the most challenging labor market since World War II, with youth unemployment hovering around 20%. It is the lowest income teens who have the greatest difficulty in attaining strong career education, opportunities for internships and apprenticeships, and access to well-paying jobs with career ladders.

Adapting Aspects of the European System

The Pathways design has been influenced by and has attempted to adapt for the United States such aspects of the European system as governance, credentialing, work experience for young people, intermediaries, and employer engagement. In part, we cannot aspire to do what strong European VET systems do because the United States is, at the same time, both one country and 50 separate states that have considerable leeway because of the weak federal role in education. We can, however, work in individual states to adapt the laws, regulations, and ways of doing business to better serve the needs of young people. But today, while some states are making progress, there isn't a state in the union that has the makings of a scaled dual system, and one is not likely to emerge. A model of career education that utilizes some elements of the dual system but that is suited to the United States is very much a work in progress.

The key aspects of the strong European VET systems that are least likely to be adapted in the United States are the multipartite governance systems that encode in legal agreements among governments, employers, unions, and other social partners the joint responsibilities required to educate young people for careers and civic life, and the systems of standardized qualifications that specify the competencies (skills, knowledge, and behaviors) that are required for almost all occupations.

In regard to governance arrangements, VET systems have legal cooperative agreements that spell out the roles and responsibilities for each partner, including how the curriculum is designed, how assessments are carried out, how various aspects of the system are funded, what the requirements are for training vocational teachers and trainers (those who work inside companies), and, very important, what mechanisms exist for keeping up with labor market trends so as to manage apprenticeship openings and opportunities. Under these legal arrangements, a critical role of the public sector is to ensure that the education provided is broad enough to produce well-rounded citizens and workers who can move between companies and roles within broadly defined occupations. While the United States has many public–private partnerships that address specific workforce needs and serve in advisory capacities, such as workforce investment boards, P-16 (preschool through college) councils, chambers of commerce, and nonprofits, they are not formally engaged in designing and running the education and training system.

Qualifications are a different matter. The international Organisation for Economic Co-operation and Development (OECD), based in Paris, defines a qualification system as "all aspects of a country's activity resulting in the recognition of learning." Most European countries and the European Union itself proceed under the assumption that almost all occupations are regulated, and that the key knowledge, skills, and competencies required to attain a specific qualification are codified. Qualifications are multidimensional, marrying systematic and contingent knowledge about a broad field of endeavor with the social and personal qualities that are entailed in performing a specific occupation. Depending on the country, qualifications vary in specificity and emphasis, covering a spectrum from specific skills, to work processes, to habits of mind suited to an occupation. For example, attitudes are an official element in the Netherlands' qualifications systems, while Australian qualifications are more focused on the content of a work role as broken down into component parts.

In countries with qualifications systems, students know from the outset that if they attain a qualification for doing web design or early childhood education or landscaping, potential employers know exactly what learning experiences they bring to the job. For example, in the Netherlands, 700 occupations have standardized qualifications. In France, there is no standardized qualification for becoming a music therapist, so the occupation does not exist. Such systems structure the outcomes of vocational education and are also the underpinnings of countries' policies to promote a lifelong learning credential for those learning "anytime/anywhere." The European Union is harmonizing member country vocational qualification systems under a framework that will make credentials more easily transferable within the Union, and will align vocational qualifications with those of "academic" higher education in accordance with the Bologna Process, the work accomplished over the last several years to make divergent systems of higher education comparable.

Anyone familiar with the dizzying array of certificates, certifications, licenses, and other kinds of credentials awarded in the United States will know that even among occupations that do have standardized credentials, in many cases, chaos reigns. Some credentials are transferable, portable, and highly respected, while others mean almost nothing except to the holder and perhaps to the institution that got paid for awarding it. And while standardized credentials exist in fields such as information technology (e.g., Cisco and CompTIA [Computing Technology Industry Association] certifications), nursing, and dental hygiene (licensure), some states regulate hair braiding and nail polishing while others leave credentialing to private groups, and large swaths of the economy in most states have no qualifications other than those an employer lists in a job vacancy posting. While there are organizations working to simplify and extend the credentialing system, this is not a task Pathways can handle.

So what is Pathways able to adapt? There are two key characteristics of European VET systems that deeply influence our work—the provision of a mix of school and work for 16- to 19-year-olds that initiates them into the adult world and challenges them to take on real-world responsibilities; and the support for intermediary organizations to link employers and educational institutions.

The Netherlands, for example, offers young people the choice between two attractive VET options—school-based and company-based—that both provide substantial work-based learning (up to 60% in school-based programs and 80% in an apprenticeship). VET schools, which resemble community colleges in size and atmosphere, host their own enterprises, and young people can be seen in these institutions carrying out normal functions of the enterprises in which they have selected to train. Apprentices' wages are negotiated in collective agreements and are at least equivalent to the minimum wage, so that young people are essentially recompensed during their later teenage years.

A second attractive characteristic of the Dutch VET is that programs have varying lengths, with a popular vocational training option taking 4 years. This pathway prepares young people for middle management positions in their specific occupation or career area. The predominant company-based programs train in technology fields, while VET schools have a wider variety of options. Both approaches come under the same administrative framework, and, in both cases, schools are responsible for linking the curriculum with practical training in workplaces. Those with qualifications obtained via the dual pathway find work sooner because they have more practical experience and because most already have jobs since they generally stay on in their host companies.[6]

Seeing young people at work in a variety of settings—factories, banks, insurance agencies, automotive shops, and bakeries—convinced the Pathways framework designers that choosing a first career area at age 15 is a positive step, not a limiting one. Trainers and teachers in Europe have the attitude that people change careers, of course, and that once a plumber or a web designer does not mean always a plumber or a web designer. The goal is to give each young person enough work experience to launch them into productive adulthood, to open the door to post-secondary education, and to ensure that they become lifelong learners. Given the dearth of opportunities youths have in the United States today to get any work experience at all, and the great toll this takes on our lowest income youths, we are convinced that schools and employers must work together to provide employment opportunities, and that early career advising is an urgent need in most school systems. In Austria, Germany, the Netherlands, Switzerland, and several of the Nordic countries, VET is the main supplier of well-trained workers for the labor market. Called the "foundation" or "backbone" of the economy and society, vocational training is provided in the Netherlands for about 40% of all workers at least through the upper secondary level, and currently about 68% of young people choose vocational education over the academic route.[7] One can hardly call this a tracking system when it is the mainstream choice that offers an array of post-VET options for attaining further degrees and credentials; students compete for sought-after placements. While VET still does not have the status and prestige of the academic pathway to university in even the highest performing systems, one comes away from visiting VET schools and workplaces convinced that we are asking far too little of many teenagers who would thrive and produce if given adult work responsibilities, adult guidance, and a paycheck.

The Role of Intermediary Organizations

Intermediary organizations are a much more complicated matter. They are the hidden engines of European VET systems. Whether organized by sector association (construction, communications, commercial banking, transportation, social services) or by region, intermediaries work between educational institutions and employers to make it possible for employers to induct young people into the world of work and to ensure that training is sufficiently broad. Supported by a mix of public and private funds, intermediaries represent employer groups in creating qualifications, assessments, and curricula in partnership with education authorities. Many carry out aspects of training, such as providing orientation for apprentices or running short courses of interest to multiple employers in a sector. In some systems, they may execute contracts with trainees or apprentices and even hire them and send them out to companies. Such organizations are also part of a tiered governance or steering system sending representatives of their sector to sit on national skills councils or to negotiate with labor unions.

The Pathways framework requires the establishment of intermediary organizations to link employers and educational institutions with the primary purpose of aggregating and making available work experience opportunities for students. Intermediaries are needed in a variety of forms, since schools and community colleges cannot be expected to aggregate work-based learning experiences at the scale needed, nor can single employers, especially small and medium-sized companies, do the legwork and provide the training needed to set up productive internships and apprenticeships. And while schools and community colleges generally embrace and call for more work-based learning opportunities for their students, little information is available about the employer supply side of work-based learning opportunities. Intermediaries can collect such data and provide the match between supply and demand. Among the regions in the eight states in the current Pathways State Network, several are developing intermediaries building on the model used at the Boston Private Industry Council (PIC), which for over three decades has been connecting young people with employers in large numbers. The City of Boston places around 9,000 young people in summer jobs, with the PIC handling all the private employer placements. But such organizations are rare in the United States. The PIC is a workforce investment board, but chambers of commerce, community foundations, and new built-for-purpose organizations are performing intermediary functions, and interest in these organizations is growing.

Finally, while the Pathways work can move forward in states lacking a qualifications system and tripartite governance, the value proposition and design of the Pathways to Prosperity Network rest on engaging employers in taking young people into their workplaces in substantive and sustainable ways. This is the sine qua non of the Pathways design, and the jury is out about whether private companies in the United States along with public and nonprofit employers can be convinced that commitment to creating a youth talent pipeline is in their best interest and critical to mending the fraying social fabric in the United States today. At this writing, we can name a few bright spots on the horizon, but nothing that would convince us that employers are yet willing to engage in partnerships like those between European companies and the education ministries. Too many regions lack the intermediary organizations that play an important role in engaging employers.

Bright Spots in the United States

Among the bright spots are career academies, early college high schools that integrate career credentials, and modernized vocational schools. Many of these have business partners and advisors who provide some work-based learning, but nothing of the scale or as systemic as the European VET. In 2012, IBM took the initiative to establish Pathways in Technology Early College High School, a grades 9 to 14 school set up in partnership with the City University of New York and the New York City Department of Education. Similar models sponsored by companies or with substantial employer engagement are springing up in other settings. SAP, the German business solutions company, is opening several schools, as are other companies in New York City. New York State has funded 16 regions to adapt the pathways in technology (PTECH) model. And both the U.S. Department of Labor and the State of California have made substantial investments ($100 million for Youth Career

Connect and $500 million for California Pathways Trust, respectively) to build regional career pathways.

Also promising is the growing visibility in the United States of European companies seeking workers for their enterprises in the United States. Since a good number come from countries with strong VET systems to set up production in the United States, they search for and are surprised not to find the pipeline of well-trained workers familiar to them from their home countries. Thus, a number of these companies are working with community colleges to adapt apprenticeship models suited to the United States. Georgia, North and South Carolina, Tennessee, and Wisconsin all have growing youth apprenticeship opportunities, and other states have long had small-scale programs as well. Finally, if there is any silver lining to the fiscal crisis that has brought hardship to so many American families, it is that a much wider segment of the population now understands the need to promote technical skills development among youths, and with that, the opportunity for applied learning. Hence, we are hopeful that new models will emerge and that some of the stigma of vocational education will evaporate as young people graduate from 21st century pathways with work experience and a smooth transition into the labor market.

Conclusion

The Pathways to Prosperity State Network is influenced by the following factors:

- The clarity of choices for 15-year-olds: either the applied or the theoretical pathway or what the United States would call either CTE or academic high school
- The salutary impact of providing teenagers with a mix of school and work
- The absolute requirement that CTE or VET systems cannot be successful without strong intermediaries to link employers and education institutions
- The necessity for employers to build a "talent pipeline" of young professionals (as apprentices are called in Switzerland)

While many educators still believe that European systems track 12- to 14-year-olds into jobs from which they cannot escape, the reality is far different. First, in a number of countries, VET is the option for the majority. Second, and very important, good systems keep skills development broad enough so that students don't end up "owned" by the enterprise that trains them. Third, employers are deeply proud of the young people they train, and are pleased with their contributions. And most important, in the best systems, what we see is that 16- to 19-year-olds flourish and mature in vocational education with the support of teachers, trainers, and their company coworkers.

Notes

1. Symonds, W., Schwartz, R. & Ferguson, R. (2011). *Pathways to Prosperity: Meeting the Challenge of Preparing Young Americans for the 21st Century*. Cambridge: Harvard Graduate School of Education.
2. http://www.jff.org/publications/pathways-prosperity-network-state-progress-report -2012-2014.
3. PISA results, 2012. http://nces.ed.gov/surveys/pisa/pisa2012/pisa2012highlights_1.asp.
4. Organisation for Economic Co-operation and Development (OECD). (2013). Education at a Glance. http://www.oecd.org/edu/eag2013%20(eng)--FINAL%2020%20June%202013 .pdf; and OECD. (2010). Learning for Jobs and Jobs for Youth. Paris: OECD Publishing. See also Bishop, J. (2010). "Which Secondary Education Systems Work Best? The United States or Northern Europe" Working papers 2010, paper 105. Ithaca, NY: Cornell University. http://digitalcommons.ilr.cornell.edu/workingpapers/105.
5. http://www.oecd-ilibrary.org/employment/youth-unemployment-rate_20752342-table2. Each country compiles its data differently, and the OECD data have a large margin of error. For April 2014, see La Situation sur la Marche du Travail, Department Federale de L'Economie, de la Formation, et de la Recherché, SECO, which shows youth unemployment in the 3% range. http://www.news.admin.ch/NSBSubscriber/message/attachments/35156.pdf.
6. See Apprenticeship supply in the Member States of the European Union, 2012.
7. See Overview of the Dutch vocational education and training system, Country Report 8, 2012, CEDEFOP, REFERNET, Netherlands. http://voieproeurope.onisep.fr/en/initial -vocational-education-and-training-in-europe/dutch-system/ and http://www.government .nl/issues/education/secondary-vocational-education-mbo.

CHAPTER 16

Swiss Federal Office for Professional Education and Technology
Advanced Diploma Examinations for Professional Credentialing

Ursula Renold

ifelong learning is one of the most important challenges of the 21st century due to several societal and economic changes, such as an aging population, ongoing globalization, and rapid technological changes. It is no longer possible to enter into the labor market and to stay there without regularly continuing one's education. However, simultaneously continuing or furthering one's education while earning a livelihood is not easy for most of the population to do. At different ages, learners have different needs for educational content and form. Moreover, the education system should take better account prior learning. Improving education and workforce development across the life span requires a flexible program that is closely linked to the needs of the labor market.

Background

The professional education and training (PET) program presented in this chapter has a long standing tradition in Switzerland. It started in 1933, with the federal advanced PET diploma and was expanded in 1963 to include the federal PET diploma. Until 2004, these diplomas were considered industry-driven credentials and not tertiary (post-secondary) education programs. PET is an example of how the responsibilities of lifelong learning and training can be shared among the learners, the organizations that provide the education and training, and the businesses or governmental bodies, as stated in the preface to this book.

The federal PET examinations are an integral component of the Swiss education system, leading to the two diplomas cited above. The federal PET diploma is normally a prerequisite and admission condition to enter into the upper levels of education. The advanced PET diploma is considered the highest degree in the occupational field. In some programs, a Ph.D. may be considered an admission prerequisite.

When the federal advanced PET diploma was enacted in the first Vocational Education and Training Act in 1933, it was considered to be a purely professional developmental program and not a formal degree of tertiary education. The second type of program, the federal PET diploma, was enacted in the second federal Vocational Education and Training (VET) Act in 1963. Systemically, both educational levels were upgraded with the fourth Vocational and Professional Education (VPET) Act in 2004 by integrating these programs into the tertiary education level. They included not only commercial and industrial work and educational areas but also the employment fields of health, social work, art, agriculture, and forestry.[1] The structure of the Swiss education system and the embedded national PET exams discussed in this chapter is shown in Exhibit 16-1.

Program Description

The national PET examinations are the core of the career preparation system in Switzerland. They assess the competencies required in the labor market because they are closely linked with the professional organizations of an occupational field. Switzerland currently has approximately 800 such programs, which are implemented nationwide. These programs cover the entire spectrum of occupational functions in the Swiss economy, including corporate auditor, information technology specialist, master electrician, sales manager, financial analyst, police officer, head of production, human resources specialist, site manager (structural engineer), and marketing manager.

The program is open to a variety of target audiences and uses different training forms depending on the prerequisites and time constraints of the learner. These features make this program very attractive to a broad target audience of different age groups during the entire working life. The average age of candidates is 32 years at the federal PET diploma level and 35.2 years at

Exhibit 16-1. The Swiss education system.

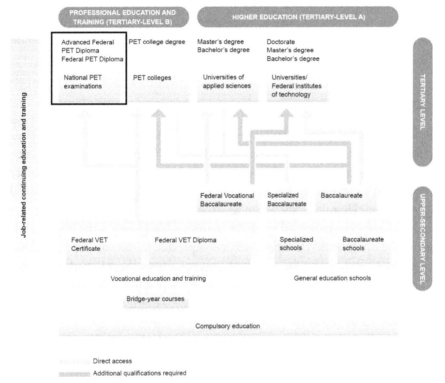

Source: Swiss Federal Office for Professional Education and Technology, 2012, p. 6.

the advanced federal PET diploma level.[2] All of the candidates must have several years of professional experience. A study has found that, on average, 8 to 9 years have passed since the acquisition of the candidates' previous educational qualification or degree.[3] Most candidates aspire to earn a PET diploma in order to be promoted in their company.

The professional organizations take the lead in determining the guiding the principles and content of the exams. They determine the competency requirements, draft the examination rules, and administer the yearly examinations. Other partners involved include the federal administration, which approves and supervises the examinations. The federal administration also acts if the examination results are contested. Public and private education institutions offer individual preparation courses according to the specific needs of the candidates. However, these courses are not regulated. The vast majority of candidates who prepare for and take the examinations are already employed either part-time or full-time. In most cases, their company covers part of the cost of the preparation courses,[4] because most companies want their employees to develop the necessary professional skills and to meet the qualification standards of the professional association.

Program Design

Formally, the program entails a federally regulated examination with clear qualification standards, exam criteria, and detailed regulatory admission conditions. The guiding principle, objectives, and examination requirements are established by the professional association and are approved by the federal government. Uniquely, the exam assesses the tasks that professionals are called on to perform typical working situations. This ensures the employability of the candidates. The approach is comparable to the so-called problem-based learning method, where the problems come from the real world of work.[5] This ensures the learning transfer from theory to practice. The exam is written by representatives of the companies who have expertise in the professional field assessed by the exam.

One of the main advantages of this program is the individualized educational path that each candidate takes to prepare for the examination. Although the tests for all candidates are the same nationwide, the preparatory courses can vary greatly, depending on the candidate's prior learning. Attendance in the preparatory courses is voluntary.

Four pathways to the federal PET diploma are shown in Exhibit 16-2. This exhibit shows the permeability of the Swiss education system. Higher education, continuing education, retraining, the upgrading of skills, and qualification throughout one's entire life are possible. For example, workers can start by taking two or three courses to retool their skills. Then they realize they can earn a formal degree if they take more courses in areas in which they lack knowledge, and thus they decide to prepare for one of the regulated examinations. Because of the individualized education paths, the length and method of training is highly variable, depending on how many preparatory courses candidates need and on how much time they have available to prepare. The education system is flexible to meet the different needs of the workforce. This program enables permeability between the academic and vocational or professional education pathways.

Exhibit 16-2. Different pathways (A–D) to the advanced federal PET diploma in human resources management.

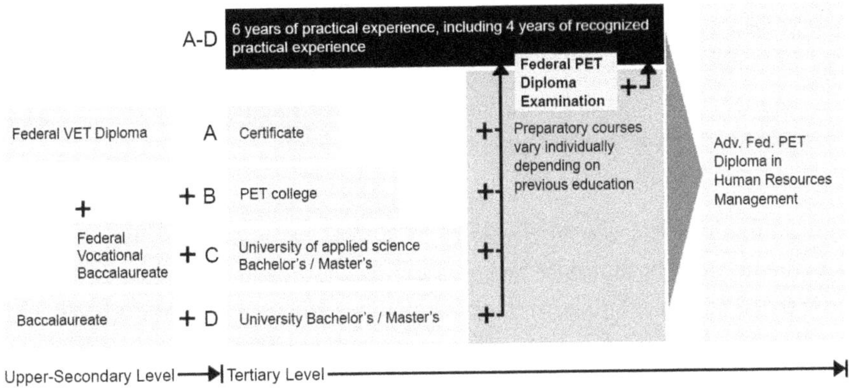

A, B, C, D = Education and training background of candidates: entry to the PET sector can occur from all levels, even from higher education institutions

Practical experience means how much years people have worked in different jobs before they take the federal examination. For example, they may have worked 2 years in business administration as an allrounder or 4 years in an HR department. Recognized practical experience means how many years a person has in the occupational field in which he or she would like to complete the federal examinations. The latter is an admission requirement for review. The professional organization that carried out the examination decides if that work experience is counted for admission to the examination. For example, if a person does an Adv. Fed. Diploma in HR Management, he or she has to prove (e.g. submitting employment references) that he or she has worked in HR departments of companies for at least 4 years as a deputy manager or in an equivalent leading position.

Source: Swiss Federal Office for Professional Education and Technology, 2012, p. 11.

Program Outcomes and Effects

Expectations for program outcomes and effects are diverse. Employers expect that the program will provide well-qualified professionals to improve the productivity and innovation performance of their company in the new economy. Candidates wish to develop their career, to pursue their passions, to take on more responsibility at work, and perhaps to earn a higher salary. The program fulfills these expectations.

Number of Individuals Served

It is difficult to determine how many people are currently enrolled in the preparatory courses, because enrollment is voluntary. But there are a large number

Exhibit 16-3. Number of diplomas awarded in the federal PET program.

	2000	2005	2009	2010	2011	2012
Advanced federal PET diploma	3,232	3,195	2,656	3,160	2,969	2,815
Federal PET diploma	8,082	11,368	12,196	13,144	13,141	13,582
Total	11,314	14,563	14,852	16,304	16,110	16,397

Source: Swiss Federal Statistical Office, 2013.

of examinations that the professional organizations administer. Exhibit 16-3 lists the number of diplomas awarded each year, which raises the question of how these numbers compare to other qualifications at the tertiary level. The number of educational degrees at tertiary level B is comparable. In addition to the federal examinations, the degrees are quantified at the tertiary level as bachelor's, master's, and Ph.D.s at universities; bachelor's and master's at the University of Applied Sciences and at teachers' universities; and the PET college degree. The total number of degrees at the tertiary level was 69,968 in the 2012 cohort.[6] Approximately one of every four candidates took the national PET examination.

There are about 800 different federal examinations. Exhibit 16-4 lists the 20 most frequently completed PET exams in 2012; a total of 7,901 exams were taken. These 20 professions covered approximately 59% of all of the federal PET diploma examinations. On the advanced federal PET diploma level, among the top 20 professions, 1,937 exams were taken (Exhibit 16-5). The 20 most common professions covered approximately 69% of all degrees.[7]

Enrollment/Completion Ratio

The individualized preparation process for this program make it difficult to obtain detailed information about the candidates. But a nonrepresentative research study in 2009 provided the average exam rates of the two programs for 2006–2007 (Exhibit 16-6).

Thus, the average graduation rate from the preparatory programs was 85%, the success rate on the exam was 87%, and the registration rate was 96%. This means that 96 out of 100 students on average registered for the exam. Of these 96 students, 87% were successful, which results in an overall completion rate of 85%. Conversely, 13% of the candidates failed. The reasons for failure were diverse. In 25% of all cases, the lack of skills of the candidates was re-

Exhibit 16-4. The 20 most common professions in the federal PET diploma examinations in 2012.

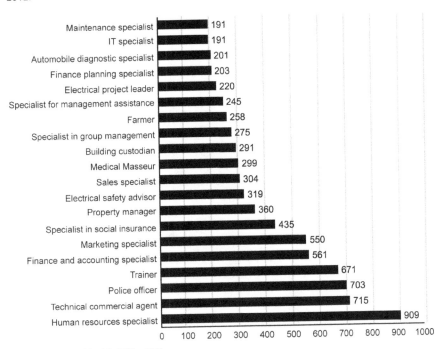

Source: Swiss Federal Statistical Office, 2013.

sponsible for the failure. In other cases, excessive time demands at work interfered with preparing for the exams, or the preparation courses did not sufficiently match the design of the exam.[8] These candidates needed either more preparation time or better preparation guidance.

Return on Investment Metrics

Because the program is well established, there are several metrics and newly gathered research results available. One study focused on two metrics: impact on salary and return on education. According to the study, the average gross monthly income of the successful candidates considerably increased, and the candidates were given more responsibility.[9] The program helps candidates fulfill their aspirations and find the next step on their career path.

Exhibit 16-5. The 20 most common professions in the advanced federal PET diploma examinations in 2012.

Source: Swiss Federal Statistical Office, 2013.

Exhibit 16-6. Average exam rates of the federal PET diploma, 2006–2007.

Degree	Career Goal	Exam Rates		
		Graduation Rate	Success Rate	Registration Rate
Federal PET diploma	Economy	74%	78%	95%
	Technology	80%	84%	90%
	Education	98%	99%	100%
Federal and advanced federal PET diploma	Agriculture	71%	85%	82%
Advanced federal PET diploma	Economy, technology, education	74%	76%	98%
Total		85%	87%	96%

Source: Büro für arbeits-und sozialpolitische Studien (BASS) (Centre for Labor and Social Policy Studies. This is private research institution. The study was made on behalf of the Swiss Federal Office for Professional Education and Technology.), 2009, p. 80 (most recent data is shown).

Exhibit 16-7. Prevalence of mixed education pathways.

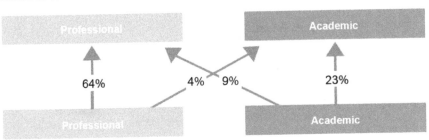

Source: Swiss Federal Office for Professional Education and Technology, 2012, p. 12.

Another study found that "the labor market rewards the additional qualifications that individual gathers while switching between the two sides [vocational or academic] of the educational system."[10] In the so-called mixed education paths, when students first chose a vocational or professional pathway and later sought an academic education, or vice versa, wages were on average 10% to 30% higher compared with workers who chose a traditional academic or professional pathway (Exhibit 16-7). The program may become an incentive for employees to plan their careers, independent of their educational background. It is a very efficient instrument to retool their skills for the new economy.

Important outcome and impact indicators are described in the Swiss Education Report.[11] The return on education for the formal degrees for males in the Swiss education system is shown in Exhibit 16-8.

Although these statistics cannot provide detailed information regarding the specific returns on the education of the program discussed in this chapter, the high returns on education, which can be achieved in the tertiary B area is shown in Exhibit 16-8. The high fiscal return, in particular, is striking, and may be due to the fact that the participants receive very little subsidy from the state but earn high wages after training. Thus, the state receives high tax revenues from these participants but paid them low subsidies, which explains the high fiscal returns on education.

Benefits to Employers

From the employer's perspective, the program is a necessity for gaining qualified employees, especially since approximately 98% of all companies in

Exhibit 16-8. Private, fiscal, and social returns on education for males.

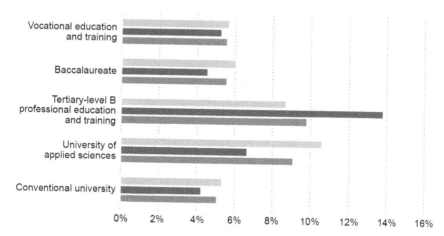

- Private benefits of education
- Fiscal return on education
- Social benefits of education

Source: Schweizerische Koordinationsstelle für Bildungsforschung (Swiss Coordination Centre for Research in Education SCCRE. This is an institution under the auspices of the Swiss federal government and the Swiss Conference of Cantonal Ministers of Education (EDK).) (Swiss Education Report), 2010.

Switzerland are small to medium-sized enterprises that could not afford to train their own workers. Thus, the program is also a necessity for the Swiss economy, as it is it appears to increase the productivity and innovation of employees. The Swiss Economic Institute (ETHZ) is currently researching this issue, and analyzing whether and to what extent the degree mix of employees has an effect on productivity and innovation.

Lessons Learned

The long tradition of this program shows that employers and employees support its ongoing development, and candidates are devoted to its mission. The cooperation between the involved partners has worked well over time. Nevertheless, it is important that the program is continually evaluated, so that weaknesses can be identified and corrected and to ensure the program's continued success.

Despite the high fiscal return on education on the tertiary level, questions remain about whether there is sufficient financial equity among the candidates and the employers, and whether some candidates experience problems in financing their preparation and in finding time to study.[12] These issues have been addressed in a research study that provided important insights, even though the participants in the study did not form a representative sample.[13]

The most important element for the functioning of the program is the commitment of the employers. Employers also must continue to support their professional associations. Employers must be prepared to motivate their employees for training and to support them during the educational process. Due to an increasing school dropout rate, Switzerland faces a problem with the recruitment of well-qualified professionals. Identifying and retaining employees should be the companies' goal, and thus this type of training program will play a large role in attracting young professionals.

Challenges to Implementation

Although the Swiss professional examinations program has very good outcomes, it is difficult to determine what value such a program would have worldwide. Outside of Switzerland, only Germany and Austria are aware of these s types of programs. One of the major challenges in the future will be to generate international awareness of this excellent program, which may be worth emulating in other countries. The European Qualifications Framework, which is an organization guided by the European Union (Copenhagen process), could help disseminate this program worldwide.

The Swiss government is currently working on a national qualifications framework to compare qualifications in the Swiss education system with validated qualification standards and outcomes, so that some of these training programs may be recognized as being equivalent to a master's degree.

Expansion and Replication

The program has great potential to be replicated, especially as Switzerland's fourth Vocational and Professional Education Training Act[14] also covers health, social, and artistic professions. The aging of society in Switzerland, as well as in other countries, requires more skilled professionals in the future and specifically more lifelong learning possibilities to retool skills. Thus, new national programs will be launched in these professional fields, including programs in fields that have been established in recent years, such as the advanced federal PET diploma in anesthesia, intensive care, and emergency care.

Conclusion

The Swiss federal and advanced federal PET diploma examinations program is a success for all partners involved. It is an example of how to improve workers' lifelong learning. It is a great advantage to tailor this program to an individual's needs. Tailored learning pathways also take into account prior learning outcomes and make education more efficient. Switzerland's program offers adults who are already on the job the possibility to retool their skills for the new economy.

The international recognition of the Swiss diplomas is a challenge. The European Qualifications Framework could provide a means for more transparency in qualifications and degrees. This study can help to launch a broader discussion on the transferability of such an approach to other countries, so that the program may be recognized worldwide in the near future.

Notes

1. Swiss Confederation, Vocational and Professional Education and Training Act of 2004, Article 2: object and scope. "This Act applies to all occupational fields except those covered by the higher education sector (ISCED 5A)...."
2. Econcept, *Befragung der Kandidatinnen und Kandidaten der eidgenössischen Prüfungen im Bereich der höheren Berufsbildung.* Bern: OPET, 2011, p. 22.
3. Ibid., p. 26.
4. Office for Labor and Policy Studies (BASS). *Finanzflüsse in der höheren Berufsbildung—Eine Analyse aus der Sicht der Studierenden.* Bern: OPET, 2009.
5. Renold, U. (2000). Mit Problem-Based Learning Sozialkompetenz fördern. *Trainingsansatz für die Erwachsenenbildung: Grundlagen der Weiterbildung-Praxishilfen. Ausgabe Februar.*
6. Swiss Federal Statistical Office (2012). *Swiss Training System, Training Indicators, Diplomas and Competences, Trainings Competed for Tertiary Education.* Bern: Swiss Federal Statistical Office.
7. Ibid. Author's calculations.
8. Bass, p. 79.
9. Econcept, Ibid., p. 33f.
10. Tuor, S.N. & Backes-Gellner, U. (2010.) "Risk-return trade-offs to different educational paths: vocational, academic and mixed." *International Journal of Manpower*, 31(5): 495–519.
11. Swiss Coordination Centre for Research in Education (SKBF) (2010). *Swiss Education Report, 2010.* Aarau, Switzerland: SKBF.
12. Econcept.
13. Ibid., p. 79. Most recent data are referenced.
14. Swiss Confederation, Vocational and Professional Education and Training Act of 2004.

SECTION V

THE PATH FORWARD

n the preceding chapters, we have discussed the relationship between the evolving global market economy and the relative contribution of a lack of sufficient job skills preparation. In addition, we have highlighted exemplary individual programs and initiatives that have proven successful nationally and internationally.

This section explores key attributes for success and recommendations for the next steps. Specifically, we will address the following:

- Key elements and attributes of successful lifelong learning programs
- Lessons learned from exemplary regional, national, and international models
- A framework approach for developing effective models

CHAPTER 17

What Do We Know About Programs to Support Lifelong Learning?

Michelle LaPointe and Jason Wingard

here is a constant refrain in all the lifelong learning programs profiled in this book: learning is dynamic and important at all stages of life and career. Within this refrain, there are myriad variations. There are both "first chance" programs intended to get young people off on a solid path in education or career, and "second chance" programs to support those who have had challenges meeting their education and training goals. Other programs target working adults to help them deepen their skills and progress on their career path.

Organizations invest in lifelong learning with a variety of goals: mentoring and leadership training for young men so they can successfully finish high school and college; employers creating programs to develop their employees' careers; businesses supporting workforce development in their communities; as well as more traditional professional and graduate education. Across the programs, there are a few attributes that stand out as possible predictors of success. These include partnering between organizations; designating an organization to coordinate the learning program; fostering "soft" skills such as communication and collaboration; and creating learner-centric opportunities, often leveraging new technologies to individualize education.

Partnerships Strengthen Lifelong Learning

With few exceptions, these exemplary programs partner with another organization to provide a high-quality learning experience. Three very different examples come from the National Football League (NFL) Player Engagement

Program, Middlesex Community College, and JP Morgan Chase's partnership with both Syracuse University and the University of Delaware. The NFL works with universities on such projects such as leadership training at the University of Pennsylvania's Wharton School of Business, and secures workplace internships for players through partnerships with Microsoft, Merrill Lynch, and Cisco. Middlesex Community College partners with local universities to provide a pathway from an associate's degree to a bachelor's degree, and works closely with local employers to ensure that graduates with career credentials are trained to meet today's work demands. JP Morgan Chase approached several universities to address a need for new hires with the ability to apply their technical computer skills in a large financial institution. The partnership is relational, rather than transactional, and the company, the universities, and the students have benefited from the collaboration.

These multi-sector collaborations are necessary to provide universal education and training aligned with the dynamic pace of life and work in the 21st century. Employer-provided on-the-job training can come too late or lack the depth needed to master the skills and to adapt them in new settings. Employers rely on a strong formal education system to provide employees with problem-solving skills, content knowledge, and communication skills that provide a foundation for a career. To develop those skills, education providers must offer authentic, hands-on experiences where students can apply knowledge, but these experiences can be difficult to simulate within the confines of a classroom. Educational organizations need the participation of business and community organizations that can provide real-world settings for applied learning opportunities. At all stages of life and career, organizational collaborations foster the context for dynamic, adaptive learning.

Role of Coordinating Agencies

For adult learners seeking to upgrade their job skills, it is essential that education providers work with employers to determine what skills, scenarios, and traits are critical in today's work environment. These partnerships address complex needs, and they benefit from an additional partner to help coordinate and align programs between schools and employers. Coordinating agencies maximize the benefit to the partners by serving as a bridge in the process from formal development, to on-the-job readiness, to redevelopment. Together, the

Exhibit 17-1. Four C's.

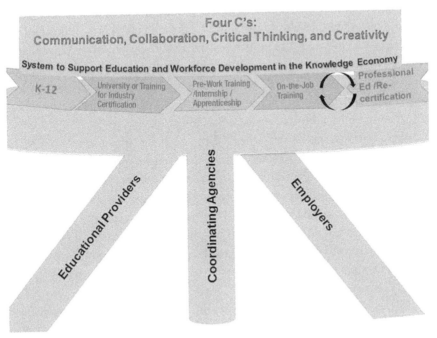

three types of organizations provide stability in a system of lifelong learning that we described in the Preface (Exhibit 17-1).

The Northern Tier Industry and Education Consortium (NTIEC), discussed in Chapter 14, is a strong example of how an intermediate organization can coordinate lifelong learning in a local economic region. The industry and education leaders who created the consortium realized that they did not have the time to devote to establishing a high-quality school-to-career program. They incorporated a separate organization, largely staffed with retirees from both the industry and the education sectors, to coordinate programing. The consortium works with employers to create opportunities for youths living in the region to learn skills that are aligned with careers available locally, and coordinates with schools to connect both students and teachers with these opportunities.

At the state level, the North Carolina Community College System, discussed in Section IV's Executive Perspective, was created to support the state's economic development policy. North Carolina provides job training at no cost to employers who are creating at least 12 new jobs or are upgrading facilities within the state. Local colleges find that this initial investment by the community college system develops into partnerships with employers. The employers realize they have an ally in maintaining a skilled workforce. The colleges often receive donations from their business partners, for example to upgrade training equipment. The North Carolina Community College System is a strong intermediate organization that fosters close partnerships between individual community colleges and local businesses.

On a national level, the Carnegie Center for the Advancement of Teaching, discussed in Chapter 12, recognized the need for a coordinating organization to foster collaboration and to share best practices among community colleges. As this work was well aligned with the organization's existing mission, the center assumed the role of an intermediary organization. The Carnegie Community College Pathways program created a national network to enhance the remedial education programs available at community colleges to help learners access both post-secondary education degree programs and industry credentials.

In the United States federal investments in career development have been limited, but there notable examples from other countries. In Switzerland, a federal agency plays the coordinating role between industry and education institutions as they work together to educate and train citizens. The Swiss example that was discussed in Chapter 16 focuses on tertiary (post-secondary) education, but the highlighted programs and policies are part of an aligned system that provides work-based learning for students beginning in secondary schools and continuing through graduate professional education programs. Within a free-market economy and a federal republic, the Swiss Professional and Vocational Education and Training system facilitates the participating of federal and state-level governments with myriad employers to combine classroom and practical learning opportunities for students at every stage of life.[1] In the United States, Jobs for the Future, discussed in Chapter 15, serves as a coordinating agency as it helps high schools and districts in the United States adapt career development partnership models that are common in Europe.

These coordinating agencies represent a range of organizations, focusing on different stages of life and levels of governance. Coordinating agencies are also important within an organization: Boeing created a separate office to coordinate the Business Career Foundation Program, discussed in Chapter 9.

In contrast, an external agency like NTIEC is important in focusing several employers and education providers on regional efforts within a state. Nonprofit organizations can develop a national network to develop a community of practice or provide technical assistance to support local school–employer partnerships. Governmental organizations can accredit and monitor university-based credentialing systems that are aligned with professional standards. They may target "first-chance" programs for youths, remedial education, or professional credentialing. The point is that these intermediate coordinating agencies serve the goals of the lifelong learning partnership and take a variety of forms based on the needs of the system of learning.

Focus on "Soft" Skills

While some programs prioritize cutting-edge technical skills, it is increasingly common that programs seek to instill "soft" skills such as collaboration, communication, and leadership. This is highlighted in very different leadership development programs. In New York City, the JP Morgan Chase Foundation, as discussed in Chapter 3, provides mentoring and academic support for high school boys and monitors their social-emotional development. In Britain, the University of Liverpool, as discussed in Chapter 6, offers an online master's in business administration program that instills not just an understanding of different leadership styles but when each may be appropriate. The Africa-America Institute's Transformative Leadership Program, as discussed in Chapter 13, fosters collaborative leadership skills to enhance participants' ability to work within their communities.

The World Economic Forum's fellowship program, as discussed in Chapter 4, develops each Fellow's self-awareness and systemic awareness. Boeing's Business Career Foundation Program (BCFP), as discussed in Chapter 9, develops leadership and a leadership pipeline by fostering relationships in which program participants can both learn from their mentors, who are leaders within the company, and develop leadership skills by serving as mentors to summer interns. In addition, the Urban League's Urban Youth Empowerment Program, as discussed in Chapter 11, helps young adults gain the interpersonal skills and formative work experiences that shape attitudes toward work and personal development. The knowledge economy, ironically, places less emphasis on content knowledge alone and more on the ability to apply and communicate knowledge.

Technology Expands Access to Lifelong Learning

Finally, we presented programs that leverage technology to allow participants to individualize their learning experience. This is particularly true for online programs, such as the MBA at the University of Liverpool, as discussed in Chapter 6, which provide the freedom to fit coursework into a busy life. A more hybrid example is the Joint Council on Thoracic Surgery Education's online course to support residents learning thoracic surgery, as discussed in Section II's Executive Perspective. In the past, resident education depended heavily on memorization and lectures.

While content knowledge is still vital—surgeons don't have the luxury of stopping an operation to look up information—this new model expects residents to cover the material on their own time and at their own pace. Face-to-face sessions with faculty are devoted to applying knowledge or targeting support to better understand a complicated topic or procedure, rather than the lectures and PowerPoint presentations that have been a staple of resident education.

Factors for Success

In addition to these organizational factors, we observed several external factors that influence success. These include industry standards that define professional qualifications, creative ways to resource programs, and the importance of tailoring programs to community context. These external factors play out in different ways in each of the programs profiled.

In Switzerland (indeed, across Europe) there are professional credentials for most industries, created by employers in conjunction with education and training institutions. This model is echoed in the new model for a thoracic surgery residency: medical schools are working closely not only with the professional associations of surgeons but also with anesthesiologists and the medical device industry to ensure that resident education includes the latest techniques and information about medication technology. In Massachusetts, Middlesex Community College, as discussed in Chapter 5, has a long history of working with employers to remain relevant in the local economy. These partnerships help their students complete industry certifications while they earn college credit.

Sustainable programs find creative ways to finance their work. The programs presented in this book are funded in a variety of ways: some rely on grant writing, others are developed and directly funded by the sponsoring employer, and still others receive funding from all the partners participating in the program. Boeing's BCFP, as an internal company program, is fully funded by Boeing. The Fellowship Initiative, fully funded by JPMorgan Chase, is an outlier. Program leaders acknowledge that without that support, they would not be able to maintain all aspects of the high-quality youth development program. In most cases, program funding is short-term and requires combining several sources of support. For example, the Joint Council on Thoracic Surgery Education is funded primarily by thoracic surgery associations but also receives in-kind contributions from the participating medical schools and raises additional money from industry. In North Carolina, the state legislature has made it easier for the community college system to combine grant funding both within the higher education system and with the state's Department of Commerce to share resources and to better align workforce development initiatives. The NTIEC also has multiple sources of funding. The consortium receives contributions from members, and employers provide pay for participating youth apprentices. In addition, NTIEC relies heavily on fluctuating state and federal grants. But cobbling together funding can be a tenuous way to support programming.

Finally, each lifelong learning and workforce development program is shaped by its community context. NTIEC is the most obvious—the consortium was designed to develop the workforce in a rural part of northeastern Pennsylvania. Aramark, discussed in Chapter 8, also designed its workforce development program to meet the needs of various communities where it does business. Several JPMorgan Chase offices are near the University of Delaware. This proximity has increased the number of Chase employees volunteering at the university and increased collaboration and cross-pollination of ideas between the organizations and across disciplines at the university. Conversely, the Joint Council for Thoracic Surgery Education is shaped by its professional community, working closely with medical schools, professional medical societies, and cardiac device makers.

Lessons Learned from Effective Lifelong Learning Programs

Each of the programs described in this book is a complex endeavor that enhances benefits including the participation of multiple partner organizations, engaged stakeholders, and a deep understanding of the needs of stakeholders.

Given the length of the development continuum and the complexity of skill needs, a multi-partner approach is important for providing high-quality, universal, lifelong education and training. In addition, as discussed in the chapter about the JPMorgan Chase university partnership, it is important for an effective partnership to develop a "relational, rather than transactional . . . partnership." Partnerships should focus on common goals and seek to make each task a win-win. Partnerships must be structured and transparent. They should also establish collaborative relationships early on so that when issues arise everyone is comfortable with discussing problems and concerns, and developing collaborative solutions. Finally, it is important to invest early to provide a foundation that provides opportunities and allows both individuals and employers to plan and implement strategies for success.

Support of Stakeholders

Partners need the support of internal and external stakeholders. Sustainable programs have allies at all levels of each partner organization as well as in the community. Engaging stakeholders is part of the ongoing work to continue to leverage resources from multiple sources. The Joint Council on Thoracic Surgery Education, for example, has designated both program leaders and subcommittees to engage faculty at other medical schools. Businesses must also be aware of the need to engage internal and external stakeholders and be willing to use their brand to further the lifelong learning initiative. For example, United Technologies Corporation (UTC), discussed in Section III's Executive Perspective, has created a culture that supports education at all levels. Without this organization-wide commitment, it would be difficult for individual employees to take advantage of paid time off to study or attend classes. In another example, staff at the Fellowship Initiative is thankful that JPMorgan Chase is willing to use the reputation of the organization to garner and solidify support for the youth leadership development program.

Learner-Centric Education

Education and training must become more learner-centric, which, with today's technological advances and online programs, is easier to achieve than in the past. For example, educational providers have a variety of instructional methodologies from which to choose. With today's diverse populations of learners and varied learning styles, there is a need to tailor programs both in content and instructional approaches. UTC is aware of this need, and allows employees to select their own degree program, even if it does not appear connected to their job. The company understands that pursuing an education will generally expand skills and develop competency. For example, some learners are likely to benefit from on-the-job training or classroom training, while others find online learning more feasible. In addition, given the importance of "soft" skills, educators should be careful to look beyond grade point average (GPA) or academic achievement; it is equally important to pay attention to leadership skills, the ability to collaborate, and the ability to adapt to dynamic situations. Mentors and advisors should monitor the holistic needs of the learner and not just progress through the program, especially with youths who may be negotiating this type of educational experience for the first time or those seeking a second chance at education or job training.

Understanding the Needs of Learners and the Community

Another lesson from these successful programs is the importance of developing a deep understanding of the target population or community. It is important to undertake a comprehensive needs assessment before developing a program to support lifelong learning and workforce development in a particular community. The community might include the population of the local region or, in the thoracic surgery example, the professional community. It is equally important to evaluate the program regularly, to identify and resolve challenges. In addition, the program partners should periodically reassess community needs in order to ensure that the program is still relevant.

Invest Early

Finally, while it is important to have "second chance" programs available, "first chance" programs can make a difference and shape an individual's entire career. These programs, targeted to youths beginning their working life, are often less expensive, because the return on investment is high, and they mitigate the need for additional services, such as remedial education and case management for individuals who may be under the jurisdiction of the courts, and reduce the need for public assistance since people are likely to have more stable employment at an earlier life stage. The United States has limited investment in "first chance" workforce development programs; most federal initiatives are targeted to the unemployed, rather than to helping people develop skills relevant in the economy and connecting youths with early work opportunities.

This book highlighted several "first chance" programs: NTIEC's youth apprenticeship, Jobs for the Future's Vocation Education and Training programs, JP Morgan Chase's partnership with universities, and Boeing's Business Career Foundation Program. Each of these programs recruits youths finishing school (whether high school or college) and gives them authentic experiences designed to prepare them for a career with the sponsoring employer. The return on investment for these employers has been high, and participant satisfaction is reflected in the early productivity and long tenures of program participants with these companies.

Note

1. For more information, see European Commission's Advisory Council for Vocational Training, 2013. *Best Practices in Vocational Education and Training: Switzerland* http://ec.europa.eu/education/opportunities/vocational/documents/swiss_en.pdf.

CHAPTER 18

What Might an Effective System of Lifelong Learning Look Like?

Jason Wingard and Michelle LaPointe

The lifelong learning programs described in this book suggest components of a system of lifelong learning. The goal is to move beyond disconnected programs to integrate a seamless system to support the education and training of all. A system would require a comprehensive understanding of the local context and target population, well-defined economic and community goals, and identification of the resources needed to develop and sustain such a system.

Six Steps for Developing a System of Lifelong Learning

1. Engage employers and community in an audit of education and workforce development needs/skills needs/available resources.
2. Identify and engage necessary partners and supporting sponsorship and investment.
3. Select or create a coordinating agency to facilitate the system.
4. Determine the goals and program design.
5. Pilot, evaluate, and refine the program.
6. Take the initiative to scale.

An Approach to System Development

In a country as vast and diverse as the United States, regional factors and have impact on lifelong learning requirements. For example, the economy and population of Southern California face an entirely different context than in

New England. Thus, any national policy regarding lifelong learning and workforce development must take into account these regional differences in both industry and the population base as well foster local economic and societal "ecosystems."

Understanding Community Context

The Northern Tier Industry and Education Consortium (NTIEC) is an example of a local micro-ecosystem with a common population base, common community context, and local employers that provide common types of jobs (manufacturing, health care, etc.). Middlesex Community College recognizes that biotech provides a considerable percentage of employment opportunities employer in the greater Boston metropolitan area and thus has focused on programs that foster the development of skills appropriate to that sector. While a first and crucial step in developing a system of lifelong learning is identifying the regional ecosystem, there is likely a defined context and organizations that have focused on regional economic development, such as the Workforce Investment Board or the local chamber of commerce.

Defining the ecosystem is only the first phase of a needs assessment. Next, it is important to collect and analyze data: economic statistics, interviews with local leaders for all sectors, and focus groups with residents. What is the economic base? Are there any natural synergies or complementary sectors that could expand the economic base? What jobs are available in those sectors? What skills are needed to fill those positions?

Creating Partnerships

With a deep understanding of the community context, it is essential to identify partners from the three sectors: education providers, employers, and coordinating agencies. Each type of organization has a distinct role, and together these organizations provide stability and foster sustainability. In addition to identifying lead partners, it is essential to recognize and engage community stakeholders. (Ideally, there is overlap between the people consulted in the needs assessment phase and the important partners and stakeholders.) What resources can these partners invest in a system of lifelong learning and workforce development?

When partners are identified, it is important to delineate their roles and designate an organization to coordinate the work. In some places, there may be an existing organization that can operate as the coordinating agency. In others, it may be better to incorporate a new organization that is solely focused on this work. There are pros and cons to both approaches; the important piece is hiring people who are passionate about the work and can move it forward.

Partners need to clarify common and measurable goals for lifelong learning in the ecosystem. Common goals guide the development of programs and policies that will shape the system of lifelong learning. Once the programs are fully designed, it is prudent to start with a small-scale pilot program.

Implementation

Careful implementation of the program includes collecting formative data on the quality of the program and to guide ongoing course corrections. After a period of 2 or 3 years, data collection should expand to include outcome data. Together, formative and outcome data facilitate evaluating the effectiveness of the program. It is important to incorporate evaluation and continuous improvement into the design of the program and the implementation plan rather than layering on improvement efforts after the program is implemented.

Finally, after making any necessary course corrections, the programs and policies are ready to go to scale. This often requires identifying additional supporters and additional resources. Sustainable programs pay constant attention to stakeholder engagement and fund-raising. Data collection is also an ongoing task. As in the pilot phase, full implementation should also be conducted carefully and include data collection from the beginning. Evaluation and continuous improvement are essential to ensure that the system of lifelong learning is meeting its goals.

Conclusion: A Crossroads

The United States currently lacks a system for high-quality education and workforce readiness. Without a coherent learning system in place to prepare people to participate in society and the economy, employers will be ill-prepared to conduct business. The talent pipeline is weak, and coordinated resources for development are not uniformly available at any level. Ignoring the current dearth of appropriately prepared and high-value human capital is a mistake that renders organizations not only ineffective but also obsolete. We can either choose to invest in our people and maintain the dynamic economy and high quality of living in the United States, or we can slide into a stagnant economy and increasing disparities in the quality of life in this country.

Employers may dismiss this crisis if they are able to identify qualified candidates to fill their existing needs, but investing in the continuous professional development of those employees is critical for maintaining the necessary skills in a dynamic economic environment. Employees who were highly skilled when hired require ongoing support to keep pace with rapidly changing expectations. To remain competitive, businesses must invest in their most expensive and most valuable asset—skilled employees. Even in cases where the cost of training is higher than it has ever been, the relative cost of *not* doing it is even greater. Staff turnover and recruitment are unnecessary expenses, and they cost more than investing in employees. Further, the return on investment for people development is now higher than it has ever been, given the increasingly rapid advancements in technology and innovation.

The reality is bleak, but the organizations presented in this book have demonstrated that it is possible to create programs and policies to support learning at every stage of life. The range of programs underscores the idea that many types of organizations can take on this work. Successful businesses invest in their own workforce. Community-minded organizations develop the talent in their local area. Nonprofit organizations provide direct services to support learning in their communities. Institutions of higher education offers education and training to people at many stages of life: "first chance" supports for young adults, remedial education, and graduate education for experienced adults. A variety of organizations coordinate partnerships to reinforce these programs and policies. This book has demonstrated that all types of organizationscan fostered access to lifelong learning and have reaped a high return on their investment.

We included a wide range of organization in the hopes that you will recognize your organization and will begin to think about how you could support lifelong learning. When reflecting on options for developing your own program, consider the following questions:

- Assessment:
  - What are the needs in your community? What strategies described in the book might address them?
  - What skills and knowledge does your organization prioritize? Content knowledge? Technical skills? Collaboration? Creativity?

- o What resources does your organization have to support lifelong learning?
  - o What resources exist in your community to support lifelong learning?
  - o What state or federal resources can support the program?
- Planning:
  - o Thinking about the strategies described in the case studies, what strategies could enhance your companies' workforce?
  - o What barriers in your region have limited the education and training programs?
  - o How will you identify partners within your community?
  - o How can you access external resources to support the program? Share costs with other organizations? Solicit support from foundations or professional associations? Apply for state or federal grants?
  - o How will you know if the program is successful? What goals and metrics will provide the information you need?
- Execution:
  - o How will you develop and maintain strong partnerships to support lifelong learning in your community.
  - o How will you tap into potential resources to implement and sustain the program?
  - o Reviewing the examples presented in this book, what factors are linked to successful implementation?
  - o How will you measure progress toward goals and adjust execution to align with goals?

These questions can prompt conversations within your sector or community about identifying both common needs and common goals. Ideally, these discussions will help reveal opportunities to collaborate in support of both the employers' need for a skilled workforce and to removed the regional barriers that hinder workers' abilities to develop those skills. Ultimately, we all lose—employers, employees, and society—if we do not address these issues. Despite the up-front costs, the return on investment in education and training is high. Lifelong learning benefits all of us.

CONTRIBUTING AUTHORS

Peter Butler, retired Engineering Manager at Proctor & Gamble in Mehoopany, PA, is the Executive Director of the Northern Tier Industry and Education Consortium.

Gay Clyburn is the Associate Vice President for Public Affairs at the Carnegie Foundation for the Advancement of Teaching.

Carole Cowan, Ed.D., served Middlesex Community College for nearly 40 years, initially as a professor and ultimately spending 24 years as president of the college.

Murray M. Dalziel, Ph.D., former Director of the University of Liverpool Management School, is the Dean of the Merrick School of Business at the University of Baltimore.

Corey Donahue is a Special Assistant to the President of the Carnegie Foundation for the Advancement of Teaching.

Bev Dribin, M.B.A., is Aramark's Vice President for Corporate Affairs.

John Fallon is Chief Executive Officer of Pearson PLC, one of the largest education and publishing companies in the world.

Saroya Friedman-Gonzalez, M.P.A./M.S.W., is the Vice President of Workforce Development for the National Urban League.

Rick Gross, M.B.A., is the Vice President of Finance for Airplane Programs of the Boeing Company.

Calvin Hadley, M.P.A., former Program Manager of the Fellowship Initiative, is currently a Senior Adviser to the president of Howard University.

Nancy Hoffman, Ph.D., is a Vice President at Jobs For the Future where she directs work on youth Career pathways systems.

Melissa Howell, M.B.A., Chief Design Officer of Social Impact Design Studios, manages the Africa-America Institute's Transformational Leadership Program.

Jennifer McDermott is the Executive Director of Technology for Social Good & University Collaborations at JPMorganChase.

Twinkle Morgan, M.B.A., is the Founding Director of The Fellowship Initiative.

Gilbert J. B. Probst, Ph.D., is Managing Director at the World Economic Forum and Dean of the Global Leadership Fellows Program (World Economic Forum).

Ursula Renold, Ph.D., formerly Director of the Swiss Federal Office for Professional Education and Technology, is the Head of the Education Division at the KOF Swiss Economic Institute at ETH Zurich.

Mark Rigdon, Ph.D., is the Executive Director of the Global Philanthropy Group at JPMorgan Chase.

Eric S. Roland, M.A.L.D., former Associate Director of the Forum of Young Global Leaders at the World Economic Forum, is the Director of Partnerships at Phillips Academy's Tang Institute.

Jeffrey Salz, Ph.D., former Technology Director for JPMorgan Chase, is Professor of Practice at Syracuse University with a joint appointment at the School of Information Studies and the College of Engineering and Computer Science.

Andreas Schleischer is Director for Education and Skills at the Organization for Economic Cooperation and Development (OECD).

Troy Vincent is the Executive Vice President of Football Operations for the National Football League.

INDEX

CPSIA information can be obtained
at www.ICGtesting.com
Printed in the USA
LVHW082032101218
599938LV00025B/1065/P